Life as Activism

June Jordan's Writings from the Progressive

Life as Activism

June Jordan's Writings from the Progressive

Edited by Stacy Russo

Litwin Books
Sacramento, CA

Litwin Books
PO Box 188784
Sacramento, CA 95818

http://litwinbooks.com

This book is printed on acid-free, sustainably-sourced paper.

Library of Congress Cataloging-in-Publication Data

Jordan, June, 1936-2002.
   Life as activism : June Jordan's writings from the Progressive / edited by
   Stacy Russo ; foreword by Angela Davis ; preface by Matthew Rothschild.
      pages cm
   Includes bibliographical references and index.
   Summary: "A complete collection of June Jordan's columns for The
   Progressive, published between 1989 and 2001"-- Provided by publisher.
      ISBN 978-1-936117-90-1 (alk. paper)
1. United States--Civilization--1970- 2. United States--Politics and
government--1989- 3. United States--Social conditions--1980- 4. African
Americans--Politics and government. 5. Jordan, June, 1936-2002. I.
Progressive. II. Title.
   E169.12.J6567 2014
   320.97309'04--dc23
                        2013050956

Table of Contents

Foreword

Published during the last decade of the twentieth century, these columns remind me just how much June Jordan's formidable voice is missed today. She was a poet, but also equally a journalist, and no ordinary journalist, for her illuminating accounts of ongoing events were always infused with her unique poetic vision. She was absolutely serious about her role as a member of the press. "I am a working journalist," she said in an interview with Peter Erikson,

> I have a press card. I don't think I'm a whole lot prouder of anything in my life than that press card I have with the San Francisco Police stamp on it… I knew everybody in Harlem, all the politicians, I knew Malcolm X, I knew all these people because I was a journalist, because I went around asking questions with my pen and my pad. As a result of functioning as a journalist, I got very addicted to facts, and listening to the way people say things, and what they actually say and don't say, and to seeing things for myself rather than waiting to hear second- and third-hand what supposedly happened some place.[1]

The value of this press card was sometimes symbolic, for it urged her to comment on virtually all of the important issues of the time. But at other times it gave her access that she could not have otherwise obtained—she witnessed the devastation of the 1989 Loma Prieta Earthquake up close, for example—and therefore allowed us, her readers, to benefit from her addiction to facts.

Reading these articles, one is inevitably struck by June Jordan's inveterate optimism, the hope she expresses even under the most hopeless conditions. She always discovered a path, no matter how narrow, that led toward justice and equality. This hope was complemented by a determination so vast that it could urge her into battle even when the odds seemed utterly insurmountable. And it was always fueled by her righteous rage: "I do not believe that we can restore and expand the freedoms that our lives require unless and until we embrace the justice of our rage."[2] Never one to equivocate, June's words were always direct and exuded the kind of honesty required not only to acknowledge the emperor's obvious nudity but the complexity of the cover-up as well.

At a time when we are much too quick to describe our political emotions in terms of disenchantment with the powerful—as if we were justified in depositing our grand hopes there in the first place—June Jordan's voice reminds us that promise resides in our collective resistance, even when we choose a single individual to represent what we hope to achieve in the world. June chose Nelson Mandela to represent the indomitable character of freedom struggles. Mandela was such a powerful representative because, by himself, he did not appear to be an exceptional individual so far removed from ordinary people and circumstances that he could be perceived as the heroic figure ushering the masses to freedom. She was impressed by "his practical, pragmatic vocabulary which does not accommodate delusion or despair," and by the fact that "his summoning of a 'democratic and free society in which all persons live together in harmony and with equal opportunities' resonated as common sense."[3] It was his commonsensical representation of justice and equality that June found seductive. And in describing why Mandela's freedom was such "big news," she reveals an important secret about her own way of viewing the world. Freedom was not some specter in the distance—it was not the mountain top. Rather it was a calculable set of conditions that would provide housing and healthcare and education and happiness to an ever-increasing number of people.

Just as June identified with the South African struggle, she also held the cause of Palestinian freedom close to her heart. Both the South African people and the Palestinian people possess, she repeatedly insisted, "a human right to sanctuary on this planet."[4] If at the time she wrote these columns, the South African people seemed to be moving along a trajectory that would guarantee them that right, and were increasingly supported around the world, the same could not be said for the Palestinians. Because of the global influence of the state of Israel, even people who felt drawn to the Palestinian cause were often fearful of the possible consequences of standing with Palestine. But June was as fearless as she was principled and, as these columns demonstrate, never hesitated to speak out against the occupation.

What is remarkable about these articles is their resonance on our contemporary political landscape. Many of the issues confronting us are inheritances from the time evoked in these pieces, unwanted legacies of those who failed to resolve our most pressing social problems. Conditions demanding affirmative action, the pandemic of violence against women, corporate destruction of the environment and the persistence of war—are no less important today than they were then. But we are also reminded how quickly political propaganda becomes naturalized within our everyday vocabularies. June writes about the emergence of what she called the "bizarre notion"[5] of illegal aliens. How quickly this idea has ceased to seem strange and has come to be cavalierly used as a simple descriptor for vast numbers of people who often have no other alternative than to attempt to rebuild their lives in the U.S. Her defense of immigrant rights foreshadows what has become one of the most important contemporary struggles for democracy.

Many of June Jordan's columns reflect her penetrating consciousness of her own positionality and the moral conscience that always accompanied this self-awareness. As a professor of African American Studies at UC Berkeley, she founded a project that would cultivate similar sensibilities in her students—Poetry for the People. As she brought poetry to her students, and as she and her university students took poetry to high schools, to juvenile halls, and to jails, she helped to spread the compassion and dedication to change that was at the heart of her work. She also taught them about ways of seeing, so evident in these columns, that combined the immensities of our challenges with the intimacies of our experiences. This program continues to explore new terrain. And these essays further reveal the instructive alchemies of her work: the global and the home-grown, the political and the personal, the poetic and the journalistic, posited in productive tension, that will help us discover new pathways toward freedom.

Angela Davis

Preface

I miss June Jordan. And after you read these breathtaking essays and poems, you'll miss her, too, and you'll want her back, as I do.

No one wrote like June Jordan, packing her lines with beauty and love and righteous anger.

No one fought harder with her words than June Jordan.

No one, with the possible exception of James Baldwin, used the essay form so powerfully to indict racism in America.

She hated bullies, whether they were white supremacists or Israelis inflicting daily indignities on Palestinians.

She savored freedom: to struggle, to travel, to be with a lover.

And her poet's ear and care bestowed grace upon everything she wrote.

I first met June Jordan when she was giving a reading at the University of Wisconsin on a hot evening in Madison in the summer of 1988. My wife had shown me the notice in the paper that this poet (whom, I'm embarrassed to say, I'd never heard of) was in town.

I didn't know what to expect. Then she knocked me out.

She struck me with her art and her defiance.

I remember she read her 1978 "Poem for South African Women," where she writes about mothers hurling an irreversible force of protest against apartheid, and where she challenges others to join them, even unto death. That poem ends with the iconic line (later borrowed by Barack Obama): "We are the ones we have been waiting for."

I was sold. I was the associate editor of *The Progressive* then, and I knew at that moment that I wanted to invite her into our pages.

I was so bowled over that I stayed after the reading and bought copies of all the books of hers that were on sale in the hallway.

Early the next morning, I started to read her 1985 collection called *On Call: Political Essays*. She slapped me on the very first page.

"In a sense," she wrote, "this book must compensate for the absence of a cheaper and more immediate print outlet for my two cents. If political writing by a Black woman did not strike so many editors as presumptuous or simply bizarre, then, perhaps, this book would not be needed. Instead, I might regularly appear, on a weekly or monthly schedule, as a national columnist."

That day, in the office, I proposed to rectify this situation by taking June Jordan up on her offer. And soon she was writing for us.

For many years, she would send her columns in by fax. They were written in her distinctive, though barely legible, handwriting. Part of the fun was merely deciphering the words. But the gasping thrill was to see the art unfold line by line and to feel the power of the prose.

If you read, for instance, the essay on Mike Tyson, "Requiem for a Champ," you'll know what I mean. The essay astonished me the first time I read it, and it astonishes me today, fifty times later. When she told me she was going to do her column on Tyson's rape conviction, I was expecting her to write him out of the book of life. But her heart was much bigger than that, and her vision much deeper. Read it!

In her final piece for us, "Do You Do Well to Be Angry?" she is writing just after 9/11, and she's warning us about the arrogance of George W. Bush and Dick Cheney, and the havoc they are about to wreak. But she doesn't stop there. She gets to the core: the fallacy of American exceptionalism. And she urges us to make a clean break with it, and replace it with "a slow kiss dedication to equality and justice."

This was who June Jordan was: defiant yet tender; direct yet artful. She did not confine her affections to the borders of this country; she didn't believe in borders of any kind. I know of no writer who was more fully engaged in the historic moments and burning issues of her day.

She wasn't above the fray; she was in the fray. And she was forever urging us to enjoy that slow kiss.

Matthew Rothschild
Publisher and Senior Editor of *The Progressive*

Editor's Acknowledgements

Several people made this book possible. I am grateful for the support of June Jordan's Literary Trust, particularly Christoph Keller, who encouraged me in the pursuit of this project from the beginning and remained consistently positive, kind, and helpful. I would like to thank my mom, Rena Shotsberger, for many conversations regarding June and this project. Sadly, my mom passed away before seeing the idea become a reality, but her spirit is here. Much gratitude is also due to Theresa Paulsrud and Julie Artman for talking with me about this project when I was in the proposal stage. I would like to especially acknowledge Annie Knight for reading my proposal and offering her advice. Much appreciation is due to Matthew Rothschild and Angela Davis for their generous and beautiful contributions. I am also forever thankful for Rory Litwin and his willingness to take on this project. Without his support, this project may have never found a home. Thank you, Rory.

Editor's Note

The story of how this book came to be begins in 1993 when I enrolled in a course at UC Berkeley: Women's Studies 12: Coming into the World Female. The professor was June Jordan. I was twenty-two. The semester I spent in June's classroom was an influential period in my life. June showed me how to live life to the fullest. Activism was at the center of this vision of life. Even as an activist working in the midst of great horror and injustice, June's spirit was full of joy and beauty. In her classroom, we discussed difficult issues and real-life situations, but we spent an equal amount of time reading poetry. The poems illustrated how the personal was political, yet they also demonstrated how a profound statement, one of resistance and protest, could be crystallized into something of beauty. This would be enough, but what I learned in her class was much more.

During that semester, *Mothers Jones* published an article targeting the discipline of women's studies.[6] This article outraged June and many of us. She organized a protest at the *Mother Jones* offices in San Francisco that many students in the class attended. Her classroom was not isolated to the Berkeley campus—it extended far into the local community and beyond.

There was another day that semester when June was absent. The teaching assistant informed us she was going to be interviewed on the radio at the time of our class related to a political issue. We listened to the interview that day. Due to the passage of time, my memory fails me on the content of the interview, but the impression it left on me remains to this day.

June missing class that day to speak to the community through the radio and her organization of the *Mother Jones* protest provided examples of what I have come to call a living activism. There was nothing pedestrian about June's life. Truly, each day seemed to be another opportunity to do something.

Beyond June's practice of a daily, living activism, she provided an unwavering example of inclusiveness. As her writings in *The Progressive* illustrate, June was concerned with all oppressed people and acts of injustice. One of the essays that provides an unwavering example of this is "The Hunters and the Hunted" from October 1999. It is one I have returned to over the years and something I recommend to people I encounter who are not familiar with June.

At the time of this writing, it is exactly twenty years since I was in June's classroom. I'm now a librarian at Santa Ana College. In both my professional and personal life, I'm concerned about the access to information and the preservation of important cultural and historical documents. While conducting some research into June's works several years ago, I discovered the fragmented nature of her *Progressive* essays. Some of them appear in anthologies; others are in out-of-print books; and some, especially later ones, are in subscription databases, yet many are only available in print in the original magazines, which are not readily accessible.

The power of June's writing and the need to preserve her work and introduce her to new readers led to this book you are reading. Here we see an individual absolutely engaged with her community and her world. We see a brilliant example of a living activism. You are about to experience an extraordinary thing. May you be inspired!

Stacy Russo
Santa Ana College
November 2013

Finding the Way Home

February 1989

On a cold night, more than twenty years ago, Bucky Fuller[7] was explaining why he always wore three watches, simultaneously, on his left wrist. I remember two things that he said, "Man is not a tree," he told me, and "All of America moves out of town every five years."

Because I had been living in nearby Brooklyn for most of my life, and also because, by then, I had sipped my way through more than one glass of wine, I readily accepted the first assertion, but I balked at the second; my mind could not assimilate any information more subtle than the difference between a man and a sycamore. Subsequently, of course, I realized Fuller had been completely serious. In fact, nowadays, it happens faster than that: Every three years, "all of America" moves out of town.

As this new year begins, I find myself inside that privileged mainstream of nomadic Americans. I am looking for a better place to live. I am choosing between climates, predictable colors of the sky, racial and ethnic mixtures among possible colleagues or neighbors, artistic or intellectual communities in place, available political camaraderie, and the financial and physical costs of housing in relationship to work. I am trying to find my way home.

Two-and-a-half years ago, I forever abandoned the homogeneous, street-deserted, house-bound, heterosexist desperation of the Long Island suburbs and returned to my beloved Brooklyn where, I knew, my eyes and ears would never be lonely for diversified, loud craziness and surprise. But tonight I am exhausted by routine danger and the price-tag attached to my single lifestyle. I am no longer amused by the six-block walk between the garage where I must park my car and the building where I must climb three flights of (carpeted) stairs before I can enter my own living room. But, mostly, I am seeking an escape from answering-machine ellipses and the need to take an exorbitant taxi before you can sit beside a lover or a friend. I want a surrounding of lovers and friends. I want that safety. I want safety that I do not have to purchase at the expense of a healthy personal life.

And so, following the average American clock to the minute, I think I will probably move somewhere new by the middle of 1989. In the meantime, in my wondering, wandering heart, in my fearful and hungry state of acute disequilibrium, I am homeless. But I am overloaded with privilege. I am wracked by real-life options that transmit the same amazing message: You can choose where you will live. You can cut and run or fly and stop and land in a happier spot than the one that you now occupy.

Having settled my own intimate objectives for the new year, it is not difficult to identify related political issues that I must engage. This is my short list: For 1989 I dedicate myself to the memory of Lisa Steinberg[8] and to the future of the Palestinian people.

Six-year-old Lisa really is dead. Did anyone ever show her an old-fashioned storybook of fireside evenings on the hearth with Mom and Dad and Brother and Sleeping Dog practically comatose with tender contentment? Or how about a television series showing cops and teachers and other kids from down the hall and rabbis and social workers and rock stars and poets and doctors and lawyers and mayors and governors berserk with outrage and speeding with determination and setting up benefits and tearing down doors and holding a solitary beaten child very very close to their hearts? Did she ever see that? She did not.

There was nowhere for her to go. There was no one worthy of her inevitable trust. She could neither invent nor discover her own safety, her own benign environment. The bottom-line translation of child abuse means that Lisa Steinberg lived and died homeless in America.

I refuse coexistence with the unspeakable indictment of that fact. And whatever it takes, telegrams to legislators/hammer and nails/bodily intervention/money through the mail/regular bouts of "baby-sitting" at-large or, yes, adoption, per se, I am resolved to save at least one child from the violence of our insanity and neglect. To this end, I will be searching for relevant comrades and group initiatives to support.

In the meantime, on the eve of Yasir Arafat's courageous "We want peace. We want peace. We are committed to peace. We are committed to peace. We want to live in our Palestinian state, and let live" statement in Geneva, the Israeli government "confined" 650,000 Palestinians to their "homes" and cut off the electricity. The bottom line for six million Palestinian men, women, and children is that they are living and they are dying, homeless, in full view of the whole world. I refuse coexistence with the unspeakable indictment of that fact.

But where is the outcry against the murder of more than 300 Palestinians subjected to the fatal caprice of military occupation? Where is the evidence of horror and moral and political mobilization when any single Palestinian is shot and killed "by accident," or otherwise? Who among us would accommodate to an absence of civil liberties or no control over the light switch in our house?

Who would accept military proscription of the funeral services for any member of our family?

I believe that the issue of a home for Lisa Steinberg and the issue of a home for the Palestinian people is one and the same: The question is whether non-Europeans, and whether children, everywhere, possess a human right to sanctuary on this planet.

And so, no matter where and when I move again, I will be working with everything I've got to change the apparent answer that obtains today. As Bucky said, "Man is not a tree." We have no excuse. We are neither ignorant nor fundamentally inert, except, of course, by choice.

No Chocolates for Breakfast

April 1989

Valentine's Day, 1989: Actually, any Valentine's Day of any year is something of a sore point for black women in white America. Flowers and wine by candlelight have always been pretty scarce items in the housing projects and tenements or raggedy shacks where most of us live, if we have someplace, indoors, to sleep and keep a hard-won semblance of a family alive. They've been scarce, as, oh—let's say—scarce as sweet-talking lovers who stick around, hands-on, to mitigate the Monday-morning blues.

But, meanwhile, we've been managing, you know, entirely without chocolates for breakfast.

For example, I can't think of a single black woman who has a wife. And I could easily fill the Manhattan yellow pages with a list of woeful, specific disadvantages summarized by that fact. And yet we work in greater numbers than our white counterparts. We head more households. By ourselves, we're raising the great majority of black children. We earn less than white men, white women, and black men, period.

And, none of us has a wife. Not one of us has somebody devoted and programmed to say amazing things like, "That's all right, honey, I'll take care of the laundry—and the garbage," or "Don't worry about it; I'll stay home with Kamali," or "I'll get dinner together," or "I'll clean up," or, most importantly, "Why don't you just sit down."

But let me not exaggerate the debit side of things! We do have "experts." I bet anybody ten cents: If Black women disappeared tomorrow, a huge retinue of self-appointed and *New York Times*-appointed "experts" would have to hit the streets looking for new jobs.

It seems we can't be beat for blame. I mean, whenever these experts find two or three black women, why, the next thing you know, there is a pathogenic This or a pathological That. Seems we're generally not doing good enough or else we're doing altogether too good. Either way, me and my sistren, we apparently function as the hopeless carriers, if not the causative agents, of bad news.

Anyway, Valentine's Day, 1989, and I begin by calling an extremely successful black woman writer who is the sole support of two sons and who happens to be somebody I love. We do not talk long even though neither of us has to excuse herself and run to the door where Western Union's staggering under a load of passionate telegrams addressed to the one-and-only-dearest-treasure-in-the-world, meaning me, or my friend. Immediately afterwards I go into the local stationers and I choose the prettiest, the most delicate and obviously hand-made birthday card to send to my friend, whose name-day's coming up fast. As I wait to pay the (white) man my $2.50, I spot a Decorative Magnet ("fine porcelain enamel") featuring an absolutely leprous Aunt Jemima. I can feel this homicidal rush of blood to my face. But I'm cool.

"How much," I ask the (white) man behind the counter, "how much is that particular little obscenity over there?"

He eyes me carefully. "Four dollars," he says, but then deciding, I guess, that I'm real keen to remove this lurid affront from the public realm, he tells me, "Five."

Silent, we assess each other. I'm serious. But so is he. I throw five dollars on top of the birthday card and slam back into the street.

No telegram is one thing, but Aunt Jemima on my Valentine's Day?

That's about as gratuitous, as malevolent, and as bedeviling as *The New York Times*. Two Sundays ago, front page, they laid out this pseudoscientific headline with all their usual pomp: EXPERTS FORESEE A SOCIAL GAP BETWEEN SEXES AMONG BLACKS.[9] According to the information the experts selected for evaluation, 60 per cent of black students in colleges and universities are women: i.e., fewer black men currently attend institutions of higher learning than do black women. "This imbalance among blacks," the experts proceed to explain, "will have broad, harmful consequences not only on campuses but throughout American society." What a crock of patriarchal malarkey.

Is it God-given that men of whatever description "should" know more, earn more, wield more power than women? I have never heard anybody say that the virtual monopoly of black men in the realm of public elected office, up to and including the U. S. Congress—this "imbalance," this de facto minority state of affairs of black women—implies "broad, harmful consequences" to anything. Have you? I have never heard anybody bemoan the fact that Jesse Jackson is not female. Have you?

And besides, there's a whole lot of catching up that's got to happen. I know of a prestigious West Coast university feverishly trying to hire not one but three black women on its faculty, all at once: Imbalanced? Black men constitute 1.9 per cent of that total faculty while black women amount to a pitiful 0.3 per cent.

I'll tell you about "harmful": Harmful is the manipulation of 0.3 per cent and 1.9 per cent so that, instead of uniting to demand a more than ludicrous degree of representation as a people, we descend into internecine gender wars at our collective expense.

The point is not about black boys versus black girls: The point is that, as of 1988, 49 per cent of black children, six-years-old or younger, "live" below the poverty line.

Can anyone doubt that this is a calamity? This will have "broad, harmful consequences not only on campuses, but throughout American society." That black women are falling behind somewhat more slowly in a single arena of our national life is not disastrous. There is a disaster, yes, and I have every reason to hope that whoever can turn it around will get started, very soon, on the straightaway, lucidly antiracist track that will take us, as a people, where we need to go.

In the meantime, looking ahead to Valentine's Day, 1990: Can't you guys violate your own traditions and, just once, just for one teeny-weeny year, can't you tighten your belts, so to speak, and leave us the hell alone? Or, to paraphrase an Aretha Franklin classic: Don't Send Me No Experts: I Need a Man Name Dr. Feelgood—and I could also use me a wife.

Waiting for a Taxi

June 1989

We weren't doing anything. We hadn't hurt anybody, and we didn't want to. We were on holiday. We had studied maps of the city and taken hundreds of photographs. We had walked ourselves dizzy and stared at the other visitors and stammered out our barely Berlitz versions of a beautiful language. We had marveled at the convenient frequency of the Metro and devoured vegetarian crepes from a sidewalk concession. Among ourselves, we extolled the seductive intelligence and sensual style of this Paris, this magical place to celebrate the 200th anniversary of the French Revolution, this obvious place to sit back with a good glass of wine and think about a world lit by longings for Liberte, Egalite, Fraternite.

It was raining. It was dark. It was late. We hurried along, punch-drunk with happiness and fatigue. Behind us, the Cathedral of the Sacred Heart glowed ivory and gorgeous in a flattering wash of artificial, mellow light.

These last hours of our last full day in Paris seemed to roll and slide into pleasure and surprise. I was happy. I was thinking that, as a matter of fact, the more things change, the more things change.

I was thinking that if we all, all of us black, all of us women, all of us deriving from connected varieties of peasant/immigrant/persecuted histories of struggle and significant triumph, if we could find and trust each other enough to travel together into a land where none of us belonged, nothing on Earth was impossible any more.

But then we tried to get a cab to stop for us, and we failed. We tried again, and then again. One driver actually stopped and then, suddenly, he sped away almost taking with him the arm of one of my companions who had been about to open the door to his taxi.

This was a miserable conclusion to a day of so much tourist privilege and delight, a day of feeling powerful because to be a sightseer is to be completely welcome among strangers. And that's the trick of it: No one will say "no" to freely given admiration and respect. But now we had asked for something in return—a taxi. And with that single, ordinary request, the problems of our identity, our problems of power, reappeared and trashed our holiday confidence and joy.

I am looking for a way to catch a taxi. I am looking for an umbrella big enough to overcome the tactical and moral limitations of "identity politics"—politics based on gender, class, or race. I am searching for the language of a new political consciousness of identity.

Many of us function on the basis of habits of thought that automatically concede paramount importance to race or class. These habits may, for example, correlate race with class in monolithic, absolute ways: i.e., white people have, black people have not, or poor people equals black people. Although understandable, these dominating habits of thought tend to deny the full functions of race and class, both.

If we defer mainly to race, then what about realities of class that point to huge numbers of poor white people or severe differences of many kinds among various, sometimes conflicting classes of black people?

Or, if we attend primarily to factors of class, then we may mislead ourselves significantly by ignoring privileges inherent to white identity, per se, or the socially contemptible status of minority-group members regardless of class.

Both forms of analysis encourage exaggerated—or plainly mistaken—suppositions about racial or class grounds for political solidarity. Equally important, any exclusive mode of analysis will overlook, or obviate, the genuine potential for political unity across class and race boundaries.

Habits of racial and class analyses also deny universal functions of gender which determine at least as much, if not more, about any citizen's psychological, economic, and physical life-force and well-being. Focusing on racial or class or gender attributes will yield only distorted and deeply inadequate images of ourselves.

Traditional calls to "unity" on the basis of only one of these factors—race or class or gender—will fail, finally, and again and again, I believe, because no simple one of these components provides for a valid fathoming of the complete individual.

And yet, many of us persist in our race/class habits of thought. And why is that? We know the negative, the evil origins, the evil circumstances that have demanded our development of race and class analyses. For those of us born into a historically scorned and jeopardized status, our bodily survival testifies to the defensively positive meanings of race and class identity because we have created these positive implications as a source of self-defense.

We have wrested, we have invented positive consequences from facts of unequal conflict, facts of oppression. Facts such as I am black, or I do not have much money, or I am Lithuanian, or I am Senegalese, or I am a girl, or my father mends shoes, become necessary and crucial facts of race and class and gender inside the negative contexts of unequal conflict and the oppression of one group by another, the oppression of somebody weak by somebody more powerful.

Race and class, then, are not the same kinds of words as grass and stars. Gender is not the same kind of noun as sunlight. Grass, stars, and sunlight all enjoy self-evident, positive connotations, everywhere on the planet. They are physical phenomena unencumbered by our knowledge of our experience of slavery, discrimination, rape, and murder. They do not presuppose an evil any one of us must seek to extirpate.

I am wondering if those of us who began our lives in difficult conditions defined by our race or our class or our gender identities, I am wondering if we can become more carefully aware of the limitations of race and class and gender analyses, for these yield only distorted and deeply inadequate images of ourselves.

There is another realm of possibility: political unity and human community based upon concepts that underlie or supersede relatively immutable factors of race, class, and gender: the concept of justice, the concept of equality, the concept of tenderness.

I rejoice to see that last year, more than eight million American voters—black and white and Latino and Asian and Native American and straight and gay and lesbian and working-class and Ivy League—voted for Jesse Jackson.

I rejoice to see that 300,000 people demonstrated for pro-choice rights in Washington, D. C., on April 9, 1989.[10] Of that 300,000, an estimated 100,000 who stood up for women's rights were men.

I rejoice at this good news, this happy evidence of moral and tactical outreach and response beyond identity politics. This is getting us where all of us need to go.

On the other hand, the hideous despoiling of Prince William Sound in Alaska, the Exxon spill of ten million gallons of oil contaminating 3,000 square miles of those previously clear and lovely waters, makes plain the total irrelevance—the dismal inadequacy—of identity politics, or even national politics. From the torn sky of Antarctica to the Port of Valdez in Alaska, we need vigilant, international agencies empowered to assure the survival of our life-supporting environments.

But we are creatures of habit. I consider myself fortunate, therefore, to keep coming upon immediate, personal events that challenge my inclinations toward a politics as preoccupied with the known old enemies as it is alert to the potential for new allies.

Less than a month ago, I traveled to Liverpool, England, for the first time. I brought with me a selection of my poetry that includes poems written during the 1960s, during the Civil Rights Revolution. I had heard about the poverty characteristic of much of Liverpool, but I was not ready for what I encountered face to face.

One of my hosts was Ruth Grosvenor, a young black woman who described herself, at lunch, as a half-caste Irish-Caribbean. I asked her for more detail about her family background, and she told me about her mother, who had grown up in Ireland so poor she regularly used to dig in the pig bins, searching for scraps of edible garbage. And for additional pennies, her mother was given soiled sanity napkins to launder by hand.

Ruth's mother, of course, is white. I had lost my appetite, by now, completely, and I could not comprehend the evident cheeriness of Ruth, who had moved on in conversation to describe the building success of the Africa Art Collective in Liverpool that she co-directs.

"But," I interrupted, "what about your mother? What has happened to her?"

"Oh," Ruth told me, instantly switching subjects but not altering her bright and proselytizing tone, "my mother is very happy. She remarried, and she has her own little flat, at last. And she has a telephone!"

I felt mortified by the contrast between what would allow me, a black woman from America, to feel happy and the late and minimal amenities that could ease the daily experience of a white woman living in England. To speak with Ruth's mother, to speak for Ruth's mother, I would certainly have to eschew facile notions of race and class correlation. On the basis of class alone, Ruth's mother might very well distrust or resent me. On the basis of race alone, I might very well be inclined to distrust or resent Ruth's mother.

And yet, identity politics aside, we both had infinitely more to gain as possible comrades joined against socioeconomic inequities than we could conceivably benefit from hostilities exchanged in serious ignorance of each other.

After our lunch, we drove to the Liverpool public library, where I was scheduled to read. By then, we were forty-five minutes late, and on arrival we saw five middle-aged white women heading away towards an old car across the street. When they recognized me, the women came over and apologized: They were really sorry, they said, but they had to leave or they'd get in trouble on the job. I looked at them. Every one of them was wearing an inexpensive, faded housedress and, over that, a cheap and shapeless cardigan sweater. I felt honored by their open-mindedness in having wanted to come and listen to my poetry. I thought and I said that it was I should apologize: I was late. It was I who felt, moreover, unprepared: What in my work, to date, deserves the open-minded attention of blue-collar white women terrified by the prospect of over-staying a union-guaranteed hour for lunch?

Two and a half weeks after Liverpool, I sat sorting through my messages and mail at the university where I teach. One message kept recurring: A young black man—the son, in fact, of a colleague—had been accused of raping a young white woman. The message, as delivered by my secretary, was this: Call so and so at once about the young black man who supposedly raped some white woman.

I was appalled by the accusation leveled against the son of my colleague. I was stunned to learn that yet another female student, of whatever color, had been raped. I felt a kind of nausea overtaking me as I reread the phone messages. They seemed to assume I would commit myself to one side or the other, automatically. The sides, apparently, were Young Black Man versus Young White Woman.

I got up from my desk and snatched the nearest newspaper I could find. I needed to know more. As best I could tell, the young black student could not have raped anybody; he has several witnesses who establish him off campus throughout the evening of the alleged assault. As far as I can tell, the young white woman had been raped and she was certain, if mistaken, about the face and the voice of her assailant.

I declined to make any public comment: I do not yet know what the truth of this terrible matter may be. I believe there is a likelihood of mistaken identification on the part of the victim. And I believe that such a mistake, if that is the case, will have created a second victim, the wrongly accused black student. But these are my opinions merely. And I cannot comprehend why or how anyone would expect me to choose between my gender and racial identities.

I do not agree that rape is less serious than any other heinous felony. I do not agree that the skin color of a female victim shall alienate me from a gender sense of unity and peril. I do not agree that the mistaken accusation of a black man is less than a very serious crime. I do not agree that the genuine gender concerns that I embody shall alienate me from a racial sense of unity and peril.

But there is a route out of the paralysis of identity politics, even here, in this ugly, heartbreaking crisis. There is available to me a moral attachment to a concept beyond gender and race. I am referring to the concept of justice, which I am prepared to embrace and monitor so that justice shall equally serve the young black man and the young white woman. It is that concept and it is on behalf of both the primary and the possible second victim of yet another on-campus rape that I am willing to commit my energies and my trust.

Returning to the recent rainy evening in Paris, I am still looking for an umbrella big enough to overcome the tactical and moral limitations of identity politics.

Yes, I am exhilarated by the holiday I enjoyed with friends, and I am proud of the intimate camaraderie we shared. But somebody, pretty soon, needs to be talking, sisterly and brotherly, with the taxi drivers of the world, as well.

The following poem by June Jordan appears as an inset in the preceding column, "Waiting for a Taxi" from the June 1989 issue.

Solidarity
for Angela

Even then
in the attenuated light
of the Church of Le Sacré Coeur
(early evening and folk songs
on the mausoleum steps)
and armed
only with 2 Instamatic cameras
(not a terrorist among us)
even there
in that Parisian downpour
four
Black women (2 of Asian 2
of African descent)
could not catch a taxi
and
I wondered what umbrella
would be big enough to stop
the shivering
of our collective impotence
up
against such negligent
assault

And I wondered
who would build that shelter
who will build and lift it
high and wide
above
such loneliness.

The Dance of Revolution

August 1989

> "As a favor to me
> Let's not talk any more about old dances.
> I have an entire world on the tip
> of my tongue."
>
> *-Victims of the Latest Dance Craze*
> *By Cornelius Eady*

Every once in a while, it happens. You can't even predict or block this ugly, overwhelming kind of thing. Suddenly, you're writhing flat at the absolute bottom of your morale. Nothing important or good seems possible. And the enemies strike again.

Perhaps they will kill the waters of Prince William Sound.[11] You cannot visualize this horror but you can feel the hideous choke, the gagging agony: ten million gallons of oil spilling into one helpless throat of the Earth. And what is to be done?

Or, yet another woman falls victim to male violence. Is it a white woman jogging in the park? Is it a black woman, as she approaches the building where she lives? Is it a Latino woman who finds obscene and threatening notes stuffed under the windshield wipers of her car? Was one of these women well-educated or working class or well-to-do or ambitious or friendly or pregnant or Republican or busy or tired or the newly wed wife of the man who beat her to death?

Like the pristine waters of Alaska, the human female of the species cannot escape an apparently American continuum of gratuitous and savage hostility or neglect. Whether it's a multinational corporation destroying irrecoverable and lovely parts of our world or suburban teen-agers choosing to gang-rape and sodomize a high-school classmate ("Anyway, she was sort of retarded, so what's the big deal?"), the ruinous legacy of violence neither shrinks nor fades in the light of another day. And you know it, you accept that you may formulate political protest or privately comfort a friend, but you can neither cure nor overcome the consequences of defilement and contempt.

Everything appears familiar and doomed. Nothing looks clear or tractable or positively guaranteed. And so, even if you come upon a city reservoir standing full and sweet and open to the skies above Baltimore, for example, your unavoidable second thoughts will emanate from automatic fears for its safety, and your own. The commonplace face of your mother/your sister/your daughters/your wife/your girlfriend will trigger concern: What are their day-by-day chances up against an omnipresent, statistical countdown to terror and attack beyond recovery?

And so you capitulate to all the bad news: You retreat. "What is to be done?" slurs into "What difference does it make?" Horror and rage capsize into bitterness and self-pity, and the screaming of your soul confirms the wisdom of a miserable inertia. Reaching backwards, you embrace perspectives quite inimical to hope. As Keats wrote, these times lead you to the valleys of the spirit "where but to think is to be full of sorrow/And leaden-eyed despairs."

And, because there is no such thing as a politics of futility, questions of courage or cowardice do not arise. Issues of right and wrong fail to bestir any response. You push along, slowly, from one terrible loss to the next. For sure, you cannot save anything or anybody from the destruction that now preoccupies your mind. Evil is old. Evil is long and powerful and everywhere. You unplug the telephone and call it a night.

Repeatedly, this happens. And so you stick it out. You put your money on surprise, and you wait.

Two months ago, I was waiting for a really big surprise. I needed one. And, sure enough, the world, entirely outside my control, astounded and aroused my sleeping heart.

First, I happened upon a poem by the young black poet, Cornelius Eady, whose lines appear at the beginning of this column. Cornelius was not born to silver spoons or crystal stairs. Cornelius is not stupid or unconscious. But his poetry just flies along with generosity, wit, sexy good sense, and joy. And I thought, "If Cornelius can hang in here, happily, then who am I to moan and groan around the house?"

Second, some friends of mine were visiting from England and, because I knew they were "over the moon" fans of Madonna, I checked the papers to see what might be happening. On May 24, 1989, at the Brooklyn Academy of Music, we found a benefit concert, "Don't Bungle the Jungle!," hosted by Madonna and Kenny Scharf. Starring the B52's, Rob Wasserman and Bob Weir, and the Del Fuegos, among others, the concert raised money and consciousness for the rain forest in Brazil.

My friends and I attended this event. Impatiently we sat through various performances, waiting for Madonna. At the conclusion of the concert, comedian-singer Sandra Bernhard walked on stage looking gorgeous and wrapped in an American flag while she carried lit incense pushed into the end of an extremely bizarre cigarette holder. After delivering an alternately hilarious and impassioned jeremiad that rallied the crowd against AIDS/homophobia/homelessness/racism and official indifference, she invited the audience to welcome "somebody."

Madonna appeared, dressed in an outfit identical to Bernard's and following a final recitation of facts about the jungle (every second an area of tropical forest the size of a football field is lost forever), launched into a fabulous, jump-rendition of the venerable Sonny and Cher classic, "I've Got You Babe." Well, to the complete amazement of everyone present, Madonna and Sandra Bernhard then clasped hands and, in each other's arms, sang Sonny Bono's song again, this time as a duet:

...I got you to hold my hand
I got you to understand
I got you to kiss goodnight
I got you to hold me tight

As the London *Daily Sun* reported, May 26, 1989, front page, "The Love Birds...stunned an audience with their lesbian romp." As a matter of fact, I never before in my whole life saw anything like it. I could hardly breathe. And when they finished the song, I was on my feet, along with the rest of that packed Brooklyn throng, cheering for them. Talk about guts! Talk about news! Talk about exhilaration of the soul!

Eleven days later, I stared at that lone Chinese man who stood in front of the advancing line of tanks at Tiananmen Square in Beijing. Inside the tank, another man had to stop or run over—and crush—his courageous compatriot. The man inside the tank drove to the right, trying to avoid his challenger. The man in the street moved to the right. The tank swerved to the left. The man in the street moved to the left. They were dancing. The tank resumed its front-and-center position. The man in the street jumped on the tank, and threw his body on top of it. Talk about guts! Talk about news! Talk about exhilaration of the soul! In one week, I had seen the dance and the love that genuine revolution delivers into the world. The courage and the passion of Madonna and Sandra Bernhard in Brooklyn, and then the lone Chinese challenger of Tank Number One on Tiananmen Square have snatched me out of the failings of my own faith.

I am back on the block, looking for trouble and expecting good news, with nothing less than "an entire world on the tip of my tongue."

Where Is the Rage?

October 1989

Even among people who still use the "L word" to describe themselves, trashing the 1960s as some kind of huge, juvenile mistake has become quite commonplace. Or we encounter the perversities of history denied (*e.g., Mississippi Burning*) or we flinch from the well-meant but certainly jejune manipulation of "Martin," "Malcolm," and Birmingham, Alabama, 1963, in the brave new world according to Spike Lee (*e.g., Do the Right Thing*).

But maybe that's okay. Superficiality, distortion, and denial constitute neither wonderful nor heinous events, per se. But nowhere, so far, in this commercial retrospective on a decade as radical and as consequential as that great American afterthought, the Bill of Rights, nowhere can we find properly respectful efforts to identify the distinctive mass attributes that led to a revolution in civil rights at home and a callback of the troops from abroad.

I think it's about that time.

I think none of us—hindsight wizards that we are—none of us has proven ourselves nearly as wise, as effective, as persevering as the myriad and mostly anonymous Americans who fought to desegregate the privileges of freedom and who stopped a war.

Since "The Sixties," what have we accomplished, exactly? If we had anything going for us, anything remotely commensurate to the depth and the force of those now almost unimaginable ten years, we, consequently, would also have universal health care, or a Federal megahousing program, or children in totally nonabusive child-care situations, or all of the above, at the least. We need these conditions of being alive every bit as much as we need not to be shot through the head by a sheriff determined to block black voter registration.

But we possess none of these necessities. And, instead, basic supports for our rightful autonomy as individual citizens, basic guarantees, and bitterly contested entitlements have been taken away from us.

The United States Supreme Court, once a reliable if ultimate recourse for progressive and even revolutionary grievances, has become a retrograde wellspring for enormous economic and social distress. At the end of its 1989 deliberations, the Court could point to no fewer than seven successful attacks against affirmative-action policies and guidelines. That's a lot of damage. Three of the worst rulings are these:

- *Ward's Cove v. Atonio*, which pretty much immunizes the concept of "business necessity" from fair-play scrutiny and assessment.
- *Warren v. AT&T Technologies*, which protects the principle of "seniority" from antidiscrimination challenges to undue work-force homogeneity.
- And, most remarkably, *Martin v. Wilks*, which allows for "reverse discrimination" suits brought by white men, for instance, who might, otherwise discover themselves a little bit penalized for laziness or inattention. Such plaintiffs can now make their lamentations any number of years after the allegedly objectionable "affirmative action" has taken place. In other words, no statute of limitations controls such shameless claims to injury.

Taken together, these particular Court findings dispute or disregard the separate and altogether unequal histories of women and minorities. They ridicule the grief that underlies the call for reparations or redress. They constitute a racist and sexist assault upon millions of Americans even as they try to deny the reality and meaning of such social disease. And, blithely, they overturn humane functions of the law as it relates to the weak who cannot procure alternatives to state protection of their interests.

In addition, the conservative five-justice majority has jeopardized reproductive choice earlier secured for women in *Roe v. Wade*. And they have extended the death penalty, and they have further curtailed the legal prerogatives of prisoners.

Given the coming consequences of these decisions, public response has been mild. Purporting to reflect our general response, the media have characterized these brutal decrees as "tragic." But "affirmative action" is not an academic subject for comfortable debate. Reproductive choice is not some trendy item to toss or keep around the house. If you cannot get an education or a job, if you cannot choose what will or will not happen with your own body, then what freedom do you have?

I remember the 1960s as first and last enflamed by mass demands for freedom. And I know that the extraordinary tumult of that time produced more freedom in our daily and collective lives than ever imagined by most of us standing shoulder to shoulder and holding hands and singing those songs that seem embarrassing today.

The Sixties worked because we knew that the absence of civil rights did not amount to "tragic" circumstances. Depriving me of my freedom or murdering Vietnamese families in my name was neither unkind nor ineluctable. It was wrong. We used a different language back then. We stood, immovable, because we believed we were right. An upfront moral formulation of the issues did not hurl us into quandaries of rhetoric: The American Left was right, and the rest of America was wrong.

Today, it is the American Right that stands, immovable, because Jesse Helms really believes in the moral rectitude of his perspectives and his vision. He does not equivocate. He does not mourn the loss of any battle; he and his kinsmen become enraged. They beat up black students, they burn abortion clinics, they hound television stations, art galleries, legislators in a fearsome fervor. And they get what they want, more and more frequently.

I can remember the rage that convulsed my body and my mind and my imagination when I learned about the racist bombing of the Sixteenth Street Baptist Church in Birmingham and the murder of those black children. I do not recall any equivocal emotion in my heart. I was livid. That was evil. That was wrong. And, along with a decisive number of other Americans, I was ready for whatever it took to exorcise the hideous power of that hideous hatred from my life.

The neglected legacy of the Sixties is just this: unabashed moral certitude, and the purity—the incredibly outgoing energy—of righteous rage.

I do not believe that we can restore and expand the freedoms that our lives require unless and until we embrace the justice of our rage. And, if we do not change the language of current political discourse, if we do not reintroduce a Right and Wrong, a Good or Evil measurement of doers and deeds, then how shall we, finally, argue our cause?

Now that the Supreme Court has removed itself from humane and democratic functions of the law, shall we persist in beggarly petitions to that agency? Should we surrender our grievances and wither away in civil silence? Have we lost heart? Have the streets and the highways and the bridges of America closed down? Can we not take to them in anger and in expectation of relief? Is it better to scream or to die?

If we are afraid to insist we are right, then what?

Unrecorded Agonies

December 1989

The long-neglected animal rose up, jerked free from regular control, and shook itself alert and furious. The long-neglected animal began to growl and shake and howl and shake and, shuddering, became a beast incapable of slow or soft or satiate and, suddenly, in rabid revolution rising with jaws wide and ears flat to the risen hair, the long-neglected animal howls at the silence of too many years abused and hungry; too many years of cowering in arrangements with patterns of contempt; too many years of too much burden carelessly laid upon its back.

5:05 P.M., Berkeley, California, October 17, 1989

I am returning from an upright idyll in the Berkeley hills, a solitary four-mile walk among flowers and under trees so fragrant I can feel myself intoxicated as I dream about a young black woman, nineteen years old, who never moved among such commonplace and public smells and colors thriving easily. She lived in Brooklyn and she died there, gang-raped on a Brooklyn roof and thrown off, thrown down, screaming but inaudible. Her unrecorded, unremembered murder joined her to the legions of black women whose demise, whose violated bodies never lead to rallies/marching/vigilante vendettas/legislation/loudspeaker-scale memorial services/determined prosecution and community revenge.

I had been dreaming about her, this "unidentified victim" of my own neglect. I would, I thought, compose an unforgivably belated tribute, "Requiem for What's-Her-Name," supposing I could rouse myself from such environmental languor as the California hills at sunset frequently induce.

My feet could not find the ground. I had been stepping off the curb to cross the street and then my right foot hovered in a terrifying new infinity of space. There was no ground below me. The earth titled violent and absolute. I thought, "This is it, this is the end of all of it." I stretched out my arms struggling for balance, for flight. Under me, nothing held together. In front of my eyes, the world slipped to a dizzying diagonal. And then a shuddering convulsed my body and the neighborhood around me, and I felt a roaring, and I sensed the madness of apocalypse. And with the shuddering, the one word *earthquake*[12] finally occurred to me: This was that flash quivering of catastrophe to which all difference must submit; this was the possibility of death in universal brief.

It stopped. Perhaps fifteen seconds had elapsed. The inside of my head was reeling and ringing. I wanted to throw up. Now the plentiful and thriving trees changed characters and menaced my own safety: Would they fall on me as I passed underneath them, inching my way home? Against my racing heart, I slowly picked my steps toward the front door of my home. Inside, pictures hung askew or had fallen to the floor. Tapes, CDs, and books lay scattered. Two candleholders on the dining-room table tremble out loud, incessantly. But I was still alive. I could see and hear everything. I turned on the TV.

Game three of the World Series had been preempted by God. Power was out. Phones were out. The TV stations ran on batteries or generator equipment. A photo of the Bay Bridge kept taking over the screen. A fifty-foot span on the bridge had fallen.[13] Cars had fallen. Water was leaking. Gas was leaking. Houses were falling. Houses and other buildings crumbled and fell. Fires started up. Fire spread. A mile-long section of the 880 freeway in Oakland collapsed. Hundreds of motorists had been trapped and crushed and killed.[14] There was no electricity.

This was a 6.5 earthquake. No, a 6.7. No, a 7.0. This was a 7.0 earthquake. This was major. This was huge. Nothing since 1906 had seized and consumed and deranged and terrorized and endangered and incinerated and maimed and wrecked what is called "The San Francisco Bay Area."

A million calls a minute reached for the voices of the survivors. Circuits jammed. The heart of the living beat hard and very fast as aftershocks and secondary tremors passed through the terrain, rumbling and swaying to destabilize the earth. Nowhere felt steady.

I groped outside and, hand over hand against the outside wall of the house, I attempted to find the gas valve: "Turn off the gas! Do not smoke or light any fire! Turn off the gas!"

In San Francisco, somebody on the twenty-eighth floor of an office building thought she had died, already, as the structure rocked back and forth. And a young mother picking up her infant daughter from a day-care center literally picked her up and clasped her to her chest as glass broke and glass flew everywhere. From Candlestick Park Stadium, police evacuated 62,000 baseball fans. And now the Marina section of the city, a posh water-front settlement of older homes, caught fire and blazed into oblivion and there was no obvious, no regular means to escape: The Bay Bridge was down and the Bay Bridge was closed and it was hours before anyone figured out alternative routes out of the stricken city.

The sun was gone. Below, the usual night-blossom of Berkeley lights had disappeared. The lights that remained gave the appearance of airport runways: geometric strings around vast patchworks of darkness. Across the Bay was nothing whatsoever. There was no light in that dark envelope of horror and tragic surprise.

And because the network TV studios are clustered in San Francisco, and despite the fact that the epicenter of the earthquake lay some fifty miles to the south of San Francisco, and although, in fact, the overwhelming great loss of human life befell the city of Oakland, and because there were no phones and mobility routes for cars and trucks, and because everyone concentrated on what he or she could see or hear for himself or herself, the world was learning about the fallen Bay Bridge and the colossal fires of San Francisco and the ungovernable destruction of property and the old and the new homeless, and none of this was wrong or less than stupefying, less than awesomely chaotic. But, also, and really, from the first minutes forward we knew—even if no one remembered and even if no one mobilized about what we knew—we knew, we heard, we even saw by dint of aerial photography, we saw the smashed mile tombstone of the 880 Cypress Street Freeway in Oakland where, we were told, at least 274 human beings perished within fifteen seconds, they perished in a paroxysm of unrecorded agony.

It was 10:30 p.m. before I realized I did not have to sit by myself, inert. I am not a paramedic, but I have a press card. And even though city officials were begging everybody to stay off the streets and roads, that didn't necessarily mean "me": I could get up and get out and make some kind of eyewitness, or try.

Berkeley was silent. The streets were silent. Here and there a streetlamp had crashed to the ground and policemen in police cars gathered behind fuchsia pink flares gushing up pitiful bits of smoke. God, it was dark. Well-kept single-family houses sat quietly to the side and the car sped into the night. I kept thinking as I glanced at the block after block of thoughtful shelter and mowed lawns, I kept thinking how easily there could be no human life; how small the gestures of lovers and the living must seem inside the galaxies of our complete burning universe; how slight a hand is love; how heavy is the deathblow to a life.

And there we were, my friend and I, outside the Emporium Capwell, a square-block department store in downtown Oakland. Private security guards stood about, whispering to each other, or not saying anything anymore. It looked as though the structure had sustained hours of artillery attacks. Every one of the street-level display windows lay pulverized and glinting bright on the sidewalks. Nude mannequins landed upside down in the darkness. A young Latino man in service uniform was sweeping the glass, his back to the torn-out section of the building where ordinarily he would not be able to afford to shop.

"How long have you been here?" I asked.

He shrugged and gave me a smile as sweet as Nicaragua.

"How long will you work tonight?"

"I don't know," he answered me, "I work until they tell me I can go."

The security guards were black. The workers sweeping up the mess appeared to be Latinos. The man inside the ruined store, the man taking inventory and ordering people about in the desolate rubble was white.

We left the Emporium Capwell and sped toward 880. Police barricaded access to the site. Behind the barricades, card tables with emergency first-aid supplies wobbled under their load but stood ready. Stretchers waited, side by side. Ambulance sirens sounded the burst of sorrow, and the ambulances and the rescue trucks and the tractors and the fire engines and the police on motorcycles and the TV and print media people in their passenger cars circled and parked and circled and looked and halted and waited and circled, and there were no sightseers anywhere, and there was no eating or apples or playing a boombox or smoking a cigarette, but couples held hands and people spoke in hushed fashion and stepped, gingerly, closer and closer, and you felt the commanding commonly somber response of teen-agers and black construction workers and black and white policemen and the mixed paramedic rescue squads, and it was all the same quiet because we were all the same, finally, in this place of death.

But everyone wanted to help, and there was nothing to do. There was no help from this implacable and grisly harm around us. Ahead, we could see what remained of the mile-long 880 freeway: the viciously undulated steel. Some thing, some beast had stomped on the two-deckered highway, stomped it and squeezed it flat and buckled the concrete and ripped out the steel reinforcements and clawed them and battered them and broke concrete apart and snapped this enormous superstructure carrying commuters home on October 17, 1989, in Oakland, California. And I did not think any of us was meant to see the intestines of any highway, and I did not suppose that any of us was meant to perish in such a sudden but crushing collapse of our supports.

There was no fear in the night in that proximity to that mangled occasion for so much grief. We wanted to rescue anybody. We wanted to hear a call, a cry, a weeping to which we could respond. In fact, there was a crawlspace somewhere in that ruin, and black and white men again and again risked their own lives climbing on that twisted steel and concrete seeking survivors. And they did, at one moment, come upon a six-year-old boy whose mother and father had been crushed in the front seat of their car, and the boy would reach forward to stroke his dead mother's face now and then, and the doctors said they would have to cut through the boy's mother to rescue the boy, and what did rescue mean anymore, and some of the remnants of victim vehicles indicated that the mile-long collapse of 880 had leveled some of the passenger cars to six inches flat and some otherwise crushed trucks compressed to two feet, and who were we looking for, what were we hoping to hear?

After a while, my friend and I left that vigil, and we drove through the crumbling corridors of west Oakland to find the hospital nearest to the collapsed section of 880.

At 1 A.M., the Public Information Officer looks as though three pounds of tears are packed and pushing hard behind her barely open eyes: Phyllis Brown is a petite black woman whose soft-spoken and deliberate manner absolutely blends into the remarkable calm and orderliness of the emergency room where she has been on duty, now, for sixteen hours, and she is tired but steady as a nurse prepared to calm and ease whatever the suffering may require.

"We have been running on emergency mode since 5:15," she explains, "and until two hours ago we had no lights." She tightens her lips slightly, and then she concludes: "It has been difficult."

Around us, as we stand, staff people move about almost silently. You cannot hear anyone's voice, but consultations and reports develop and dissolve, incessantly. It feels like church.

From the orderlies to the surgeons, there is one purpose, and that is to save lives or heal the wounded. The very young black woman who greets every arrival immaculate in jeans and a T-shirt is the triage physician, who is embarrassed by the morally questionable principles that underlie her task: "To provide the greatest care to the greatest good," she explains, "you have to sort through the needs and demands of the patients who arrive by ambulance." Dr. Cherie Hardis is, as she says, "obviously sad." Only forty patients related to the earthquake have come in: To the core of her heart, she wishes there had been a deluge but "the ones who needed a lot of stuff never got to the hospital. They were crushed or killed. They never got here, or anywhere."

And still she waits, erect, and eagerly looking out across the emergency room parking lot; perhaps, after all, there will be more survivors arriving, more help that she can lend, more work for her head and her hands riveted to the deepest promise implied by medical care.

In the desolate half hour that ensues, no new patients arrive.

A contingent of press sweeps into a parking space and reporters pile out. There are so many journalists, now, that Phyllis Brown convenes a press conference in the otherwise empty emergency waiting room.

Dr. Carter Clements is a very young white man standing in jeans with his plaid shirt-sleeves rolled up. He is the assistant chief physician for the emergency department and he reports that the support from the health-care agency and the Board of Supervisors has been extraordinary. Furthermore, so many doctors have volunteered there are almost more doctors than patients available. Of the forty to forty-five arrivals since 5:05 P.M., eight have been judged to have sustained critical trauma aggravations of the "blunt-injury" kind.

He speaks of the loss of power that paralyzed the x-ray facilities that meant that no CAT scans and no angiograms have been possible. He tells us that, yes, in the past, there had been serious earthquake drills but "generally it was assumed that some communications would be intact." For several hours, the hospital had no phones. They have been dealing with the consequences of three-and-a-half foot steel-reinforced concrete slabs falling on cars, wedging cars inextricably into a tangle of fatal mass and crushed-out life.

Everywhere there is an omnipresent and spectacular willing tenderness. "We are helpless," he is saying. "Helpless." Nothing usual applies.

What was needed at the Cypress Section of the 880 freeway was not ambulances, not doctors, not police, not media personnel, but cranes—gigantic capacity cranes to lift and free the victims from their sudden, awful burial.

It will be twenty-four hours before heavy cranes and cherry pickers reach the concrete cemetery of 880. For everyone at Highland Hospital the terrible hope had become just this: that anyone still trapped by that collapse lost consciousness at once and died, unconscious. Otherwise, well, it was to be hoped that there was no otherwise. To hope for death is such a failure for those who would be merciful, and pain marks all the faces of the waiting staff at Highland Hospital.

In the morning light the TV screen persists in its depiction of the devastation of San Francisco: It is the loss of property against the loss of human life in Oakland. It is the cataclysmic disruption of one city against the finality of death in another.

Earthquake damage is estimated at more than $2 billion. People go begging for water and for food and for blankets. Some fifty miles to the south, the residents of Santa Cruz and Los Gatos belatedly receive media attention. There has been vast tragedy and terror. No one can predict recovery time or cost. For an unknown number of human beings, recovery has become irrelevant: They have been killed by the earthquake of 1989.

And the long-neglected animal settles into uneasy sleep, exhausted by the passion of its outrage. And I am waiting for the unidentified young black woman, victim of unpardonable violence, to claim her outrage, claim our love.

Wrong or White

February 1990

We enter this last-ditch decade of the Twentieth Century still staggering from the final revolutionary events of 1989. The astounding spectacle of millions of people in bodily rejection of terror and the abrogation of their human rights must summon each of us from our most cynical inertia. If you missed out on "the Sixties," well, then, here in a brief three or four weeks you could witness entirely comparable, gigantic, and spontaneous maneuvers initiated by ideas of freedom. From Germany to Rumania, a colossal rout of institutional and other tyrannies took place.

And it was white on white: East Germans rushing to embrace West Germans, or Nicolae Ceausescu versus the hundreds of thousands of Rumanians who surged forward to depose him, or Mikhail Gorbachev forced to respond to a Lithuanian challenge to Soviet rule. Nobody powerful in the U.S.A., neither the politicians nor their media echo-men, chose to condemn or chide or advise or trivialize or ignore or threaten or misrepresent or patronize any of these anarchic and mysterious, and, yes, ultimate and sometimes deadly confrontations with a demeaning and cruel status quo. No American with national access to network cameras elected to characterize these wild explosions of fury and unrest as "mob hysteria" or "terrorist" or "lawless" or "riotous" or "violent" or "subversive" and, indeed, the word "communist" suddenly became an adjective equivalent to "tall" or "fat"—as in, "the tall (or fat or communist) shoemaker opened the door." It was white on white.

Unfettered by superpower ideology or manipulation, these localized struggles for autonomy and civil liberties unfolded, day by day. You could see the kindred victories of different peoples left to their own judgments and need. It was white on white.

None of these ordinary heroes would be sneeringly identified as Arabs or Palestinians. They were Poles. Those uproarious hordes overthrowing demands for visas and checkpoint inspections and submission to massive, actual barriers to freedom—they were not seeking to overcome the confinements of apartheid. They were Germans. The people chanting beneath the palace balconies—they did not speak Spanish, they were not citizens of Nicaragua or El Salvador or Panama. These victims of their own passivity and these victories against the docile spirit that allows a tyrant or a tyranny to stand among their lives—these were European components of European history under populist siege. It was white on white. It was right, whatever it was. It was white on white.

And analyzing this European drama, and speaking to the European multitudes here, and there, it was white on white: White men of the American press corps telling the world whatever white European spokesmen told them about what this or that revolutionary scenario meant or did not mean. And, whether spoken in English or shouted out in an unfamiliar European language, the slogans that lifted the arms and the fists and the hearts and the heads of the millions of revolutionaries who would no longer tolerate what has become everywhere intolerable—those slogans carried my own heart back to America, back to a time when we knew what was wrong, when we knew we were right: from our own historic mass demonstrations for "Free-dom Free-dom!" to "Black Power!" to "Make Love Not War!" to the San Francisco candlelight vigil for the meaning of the murdered life of Harvey Milk to the Take Back the Night demonstrations for the safety of women. Like an avalanche of extremely tender memories, these American images of humane revolt engulfed my mind and I could think and feel, at last, a brotherhood and sisterhood of unity with those European strangers enflamed by revolutionary faith and herding themselves into their own new, invincible, and righteous light.

And I noticed that none of the American news media moguls described these astounding developments as "bad" or "dangerous." I noticed that, consistently, from the Oval Office to NBC-TV, these overwhelming facts of European *intifada* came across to us, the regular people of the U.S.A., as unequivocal good news. It was white on white.

It was really striking. Over there, in Europe, as a matter of fact, you could watch the surprise and the lightning speed of structural change that we, Americans of the 1980s, had come to regard as impossible or, at best, as something that the military would or should "quell." Where were the Marines, for God's sake?

And, meanwhile, U.S. support of death-squad government in El Salvador did not abate. U.S. imposition of millions of dollars intended to rig upcoming elections in Nicaragua did not stop. The Administration's and the media's concessions to phony questions about the legitimacy of the leadership of the ANC in South Africa and the PLO on the Gaza Strip and the West Bank—these disgusting tactics of racist oppression—they did not wane or disappear.

These were matters of wrong and white. These issues and broken bones and broken laws and children killed and sovereignty denied and villages brutally occupied—these did not contain the same somehow sacred and intrinsically democratic principles at stake: not the same as East and West Berlin; not white on white; not possibilities for great news. El Salvador, South Africa, Israel—these were categorically different situations of wrong and white. Your nation, your family, your face was neither European nor of European descent. You were wrong. And whether it was Washington, D.C., or Jerusalem, or Pretoria, the wisdom and the virtue and the military force to correct and control your misbegotten miserable existence would be and would remain white power.

It was really striking. And I remembered things. I remembered U.S. obsessions with purported monster-types like Muammar Qaddafi and Yasir Arafat and Manuel Noriega. I remembered Israeli references to Palestinian people as "beasts with two legs." And I sat reading American newspapers that now, and abruptly, informed me about somebody in Rumania, a white man named Nicolae Ceausescu whose regime had slaughtered more than 60,000 Rumanian men and woman, and I wondered: How come the CIA never sent big bucks and probably Rambo himself to topple that atrocious government? How come the U.S. Marines never did anything to "establish democracy" in the context of that European government? But I knew why. It was just another matter of wrong and white.

Neither Qaddafi nor Arafat nor Noriega is a white man. And too bad about that.

Meanwhile, there were women still living on the planet. If you looked closely at the televised crowd scenes in revolutionary Eastern Europe, you could see them, right there, mixed up with the rest of "the people": the white men who would, sooner or later, explain to everybody what was obvious and then say why they, or why some of these white men, would soon replace other white men in the vestments of state power.

And, elsewhere, in El Salvador, the U.S.-supported death squads of Alfredo Cristiani had assassinated six Jesuit priests, plus "a cook and her fifteen-year-old daughter." Okay, no names/no "human-interest" angle/no appropriately reverential feature stories, but what could you expect? Neither that cook nor her fifteen-year-old daughter ever attended a single revolutionary-committee meeting, never received a proper invitation to participate in such a gathering, never learned how to handle an M-16 or hold a political-rally microphone, and anyway, we're talking about one woman and a girl.

And, back home in Berkeley, where I live, some women graduate students had organized a rally against U.S. intervention in El Salvador, and that rally was to be held in People's Park. And it was. It happened just a few days after a white man murdered fourteen young women who were students at the School of Engineering at the University of Montreal.[15] They were there, these young women, mixed up with the rest of the students. And this particular white man looked very closely at the students in order to find the women. He ordered the men to one side of a room and the women to the other side. He allowed the men to leave. Then he shot and killed fourteen women. I think all of them were white. I know they were women. I know that they died because they were not young white men in that School of Engineering. Reportedly, before he pulled the trigger fourteen times, this particular young white man screamed at his female prey. Reportedly, he screamed that they were "all a bunch of fucking feminists."

None of those fourteen young white women was a white man. And too bad about that.

So, at this People's Park rally on El Salvador, the turnout was not terrific. El Salvador is not white. As I stood, waiting my turn to speak to the small and scattered audience, I was chatting with two or three of the young white women organizers. And, suddenly, a particular black man approached us at a methodical, slow pace. As he came abreast of our group, he raised his hands and struck me and the young woman immediately next to me, attempting to knock both of us down. Enraged, I instantly retaliated with a blow between his shoulder blades and, I noticed, he decided not to repeat himself in gratuitous assault upon myself or any other woman on the premises.

And then, as part of her introduction of me, another young white woman asked for a moment of silence to commemorate the murder of the fourteen young white women in Montreal. Some of us kept silent. I could hear the voices of a variety of young men and older men defiling that one hushed minute. And a passionate confusion of aims overtook my mind: Where was the battleground? El Salvador? People's Park? The University of Montreal?

And I could not sort my way among these urgencies. And I refused to choose among these horrors, these attacks of freedom and autonomy and life itself.

I am not a white man. I am not a man. I get emotional about these things—the invasion of my space, my body. I get really upset when somebody kills fourteen human beings because they are not men. I become hysterical when a sexist double standard means nobody totally blows away business as usual whenever any woman is terrorized or raped or murdered.

And I really don't give a damn whether it's one cook and her daughter or one unidentified young black woman or fourteen young white women on a university campus in Montreal, or myself, standing around in Berkeley's People's Park. The sexist double standard that would have us accept that we should not wail aloud and storm the streets on behalf of our own safety, our own womanly, our own female self-determination, well, to hell with that, from Montreal to Rumania, to hell with that.

I am not "a divisive issue." I am not page-twelve material. I want the liberty and the hallowed, full human rights of every woman in the world at the top of the news, right there, mixed up with the East Berliners rushing to embrace the people of West Berlin. And I want this new decade to forswear all double standards. No more of this one standard for white people and then there's Panama. No more "establishment of democracy" courtesy of the U.S. Army. No more official regret for the death toll of "American lives." No more "unknown numbers" of "unidentified" and officially ignored victims of white power. I demand the names of every Panamanian man and woman and child who died because George Bush could not have a merry Christmas unless he tried to eliminate Manuel Noriega, who was trying his best to act like a colored white man with an army at his disposal!

The racist premises for American domestic and foreign policy persist in obscene nudity today. And who is celebrating what, exactly, in Berlin or Poland or Czechoslovakia? And after the huge shopping spree in West Germany, and after the huge, revolutionary glee of Eastern Europe dissipates, and after Archbishop Desmond Tutu returns from his on-site protest against Israeli apartheid to South Africa, and after who wins what electoral office in Nicaragua because of or despite the infusion of millions of American dollars, and after the latest hollow man has been propped into place by U.S. troops in Panama City, there will still be women living on the planet.

There are many wars going on and one of them is universal and it's gender specific against my particular non-European, and female presence in the world and so I'm watching TV, you know, and making these notes, and I'm thinking to myself that it's not necessary, it's possible to end these dictatorships that hate my guts. But, probably, I will have to turn off the TV, even though it's fabulous and fascinating to see how, white on white, a righteous revolution will materialize if people are just left, respectfully, alone to determine where and when they will formulate the deal as "win or die."

And I believe that Rumania can happen here. I believe that the Berlin Wall of psychopathic racism and psychopathic misogyny will fall apart or America will die. It's not complicated. We have no choice. Ours is not a nation state of white on white. And we are not a country of men!

It's 1990. And one of these next mornings I'm gonna rise up and rush right into America and if you look closely you will be able to see me from as far away as Czechoslovakia and I'm not gonna get weary and I'm not gonna give up until it's safe to be here, where I was born, where I belong.

But what will that take?

Mandela and the Kingdom Come

April 1990

The world watches for the face of this man. This is the face hidden and forbidden by force. These are the cheeks and these are the lips and this is the nose and these are the ears and the eyes of the head of a country buried in hatred and blood.

It's 5:35 A.M. when I switch on the TV, and somebody's complaining that Mandela's "really late." He'd been scheduled to appear more than half an hour ago. So he's late. After twenty-seven years in prison, after seventy-one years of imprisonment inside South African apartheid, he is not, the reporter complains, on time. What could possibly explain the delay? Didn't he realize that hundreds of top international media personnel expected and needed him to show up? Didn't he understand that this remarkably elite press corps felt very uncomfortable? It was hot. All morning the sun burned above them and they could find no shade. There didn't seem to be a cold beer available, for miles.

But suddenly the helicopters rose into the sky. And, like a badly lit, slow-motion movie, you could see a short, pale caravan of cars making its approach to the prison gates. Within minutes, it was happening. He was there. He was here. Hand-in-hand with his comrade and wife, he stood still and he did not smile. And then the two of them began to move: He walked like a man who does not take the earth for granted. He took one step after another with obvious care and delight. Right next to him, Winnie Mandela stayed close, attuned and alert, and radiant.

My spirit divided between terror and tears. Would he be shot? In the American tradition of Dr. King and Malcolm X, was I about to see another black man felled and bleeding beyond recall?

But this miracle was no kind of re-run! This Nelson Mandela a.k.a. *terrorist* a.k.a. *communist* a.k.a. *felon* who had vowed to resist violence with violence, to acknowledge respect with respect, and to confront the catastrophe of time with total rebellion against the waste and the weakening that time entails, this same Mandela was returning to near-universal tribute and acclaim: "His freedom," a white man on the radio declared, "is the moment the world has been waiting for."

No one would shoot Mandela. He had outlived the usual meanings of mortality. His resolute endurance of hard labor and three decades of solitude and confinement and love suspended and fatherhood snatched away completely mocked the alleged power of only death. You could shoot Mandela but Mandela could not be killed. He would not die. He would not consent to that. We would not consent to that.

He had borne the unimaginable and so he had become the unimaginable among us: A brilliant, steady lover who will neither fawn nor forgive nor forget. This was the man South Africa had hoped to eradicate. This was the life and the dignity that apartheid means to efface. This was the leader that stone and whips and censorship and stone and night after night of no respite and no remnant caress and stone, and the de facto annulment of marriage, the ridicule of desire, the torture of principled conviction, night after night after night of stone and rock and lifting an ax to the rock and smashing the rock for the stone after stone, this was the leader the lover-in-exile that nothing (not even age) could diminish or destroy.

His voice is not deep. His words do not roll and break, mellifluous. He reads from pieces of paper blow by the wind. He hesitates. The page will not turn. He waits. He tries again. The page turns. He goes on.

He is not young. He does not move easily, or fast. He stands tall. His arms rise, effortless, to the clenched fist salute of black power.

I am crying because I am overwhelmed by victory: The cost is not forgivable. Tears come from someplace uncontrollable and free and right around now anything uncontrollable and everything free looks and feels pretty good to me. I am crying because last week two white men accosted me, calling me "Bitch!" and calling me "Nigger!" and last week Mr. Nelson Mandela was still locked away, a prisoner of racist white men, and I was not sure about the swift and certain demise of apartheid but this morning I am sure. It's over.

His victory is big news. Enemies of his freedom have died or they will die or they must welcome him. This is not about the falling apart of the Berlin Wall. This is white Western hegemony acceding to the non-European future of the planet. You cannot rule somebody who would rather die than kneel. You cannot intimidate somebody seeking his freedom or your death.

His victory is big news. This is an African black man who says, "I stand here before you not as a prophet, but as a humble servant of you, the people." Mandela is not a man of the cloth. The African National Congress is not the Church. Umkhonto we Sizwe, the military wing of the ANC that Mandela founded in 1960, signified and continues to signify armed struggle, here and now, for the kingdom to come, here and now.

He personifies a secular revolt against here and now violations of human rights. He calls on no authority beyond the authority of the pain and the degradation of living in black South Africa.

Mandela's rhetoric avoids religious or other abstract allusions. He remains specific. He speaks a language appropriate to a task-force committee meeting of actual men and women. He proceeds, meticulous, in his matter-of-fact giving of thanks to "Comrade Oliver Tambo" and to the South African Communist Party and to the South African white women of The Black Sash and to "the mothers and the wives and the sisters" and to his "beloved wife and family" and to "the world community" and he does not, anywhere, thank God.

Mandela bodies forth a humanist, democratic vision in which all human life occupies the first and last position of concern. Human beings create tyrannous conditions: Human beings must overthrow these tyrannies. His practical, pragmatic vocabulary does not accommodate delusion or despair. His summoning forth of "a democratic and free society in which all persons live together in harmony and with equal opportunities" resonates as common sense.

There is a man lifting his daughter high above his own head so that she can see the leader who believes she has the power to be free. There is a young boy climbing the rough hard wall of Capetown's City Hall. He never looks down and he never looks behind him as he rises high enough to glimpse Mandela just about to address a world that wants to hear whatever he will say. After twenty-seven years of silence imposed by the innermost prisons of South Africa, Mandela chooses this one word from Xhosa, his native language: AMANDLA! (POWER!)

He hurls the word into the darkness: AMANDLA! (POWER!) And the standing throng of 20,000 instantly responds: NGWETHU! (IT IS OURS!) NGWETHU! (IT IS OURS!) So be it.

Diversity or Death

June 1990

In the beginning was the Indian and no diversity. On this intrepid continent, the rivers and lakes lay underneath one moon. The mountains and the prairies and forests stretched, immeasurable but close, from snowy space to flowering wild trees within two boundaries of one unfathomable ocean. And birds and grizzly bears abounded under one ferocious but supportive solar light. And constellations in the evening skies pursued their dark track cycles and returned, one twinkling mystery forever fixed above this one but ample Earth. And there was no diversity.

In the beginning was the Indian and winters spent in prayerful memories of spring, and summers spent in faithful preparation for perpetual necessities—for fire and for berries and for salmon and for venison preserved against the long nights leading to a final, frozen sleep.

In the beginning was the Indian and there was reverence for mornings, reverence for rocks, reverence for the rain, and obedience to the winds and to the changing temperatures of any day. In the beginning was the Indian and no diversity.

Tribal groupings that exceeded 700 separate but interrelated societies just existed side by side, or distantly: No single Native American nation declared itself the ruling normative social event which would, therefore, determine any other people as deviant or mainstream.

But then, when Christopher Columbus and when the English and when the Germans came to this same continent, they—these invading Europeans—invented ideas about human beings differing from themselves and these ideas allowed these aliens to designate the aborigines as heathen savages deserving genocidal displacement and assault.

In the beginning there was no diversity. Diversity implies a standard. A man is not a standard.

But, to the Europeans who arrived, belatedly, in North America, there were no other men, or women, or children living here. An Indian is not a man.

And so, those emigrating newcomers arrogated privileges of normative identity to themselves. They proclaimed themselves the in-group that defined everyone else, everyone different, as peripheral, at best, or rather more likely, as "uncivilized," and, later, as "three-fifths of a man." By dint of homicidal force, the only valid man and the only valid culture must derive from European history and presence.

For sure, this was an upside-down, imperial process of empowerment: first, attempting to exterminate the Native American occupants of this voluptuous terrain; then proceeding to import a million-fold involuntary African population; and then expanding westward on the strength of bloody conquest of Mexican territories, Mexican peoples, whom we are pleased, today, to acknowledge as Chicanos.

Europeans established themselves on the land of this New World. But not everyone who was not European died. Not everyone not European disappeared from this America. And, lo, the "issue" of diversity arose.

Today, suddenly, it seems, the heterogeneity of these United States has been discovered. Demographic projections for the year 2000 and beyond emphasize the steadily receding prominence of white Americans: Increasingly, the majority American population will neither be "white" nor native speakers of English. Increasingly, in other words, the demographic facts of national life will mirror the racial and ethnic and linguistic realities that obtain, worldwide.

Since our compulsory public school system now fails this impending new American majority, the American business community, for example, has become extremely pessimistic: Who will constitute the American labor force unless deep and immediate changes take place in our classrooms, coast to coast?

In the realm of what's called higher education, here, "diversity" has become a code word for interracial, inter-ethnic conflict heated to explosive levels of intensity. At the University of California, Berkeley, for instance, the most recent entering freshman class, for the first time, ever, did not body forth a white majority: Those demographics accurately reflect the composition of California statewide. At this same university, the faculty remains 91 per cent white and 89 per cent male, and the curriculum maintains its traditional, Eurocentric bias.

Against such an unarguable mismatch, progressive Berkeley students have formed a multicultural and multi-ethnic United Front that recently organized an 80 per cent successful strike. Demanding "diversity" and the hiring and recruitment of people of color, this coalition also called for across-the-board, intensified affirmative action and the establishment of a gay and lesbian studies center.

HONK FOR DIVERSITY, the placards read. Or: HONK FOR ACADEMIC AND SOCIAL EQUALITY.

Some of these student leaders seem to believe that "diversity" is new. But the Earth has always been diversified as to the peoples living, or trying to live, here. Power, on the contrary, has been a peculiar phenomenon concentrated in few places and few families—or interest groups—relative to the whole.

What's new, then, is not "diversity" but, rather, our efforts inside the United States to redistribute power so that people of whatever color or culture or sexual persuasion shall possess equality before the law and due representation in government and due representation in the academic curricula and on the faculties and in the student bodies of our democracy.

If we do not know Chinese, if we know little or nothing about India or Japan, then how will we, Americans, hope to deal in the Twenty-first Century? And on what basis—other than arrogance fortified by the Marines?

If we do not know Spanish, the language of the fastest growing segment of our total population, if we know nothing about Afro-American history and culture, if we persist in the traditional American attitude that the only good Indian is a dead Indian, then who will we, Americans become?

How shall we hope to cohere as a union of disparate but faithful citizens?

How shall we dare to assume any moral authority anywhere?

Either we will redistribute power so as to provide for equality of participation and respect and protection or we will perish as a democratic state at the very moment when, from Berlin to Lithuania to Johannesburg to Tiananmen Square, the fever for freedom under law becomes the global conflagration that burns with a fervor to rival the light of the stars above.

And in this new reckoning with freedom, and with the academic and legal and political and linguistic requirements of freedom inside a democracy, let us not forget the freedom to love: If we even tolerate any oppression of gay and lesbian Americans, if we join those who would intrude upon the choices of our hearts, then who among us shall be free?

Freedom is not divisible. Equality cannot be qualified.

Opposition to diversity is opposition to life itself.

And we who diversify the species *even as we breathe*—ethnically/racially/sexually—we must move, together, for the empowerment of the diversity we prove or we must agree to the consequences of our own docility: our death.

And so I am heartened by such good news as one can find:

- The Madison Plan at the University of Wisconsin, Madison. Instituted by Chancellor Donna E. Shalala, this plan aggressively seeks to transform the fourth-largest state university in the United States so that its faculty and student body and curriculum qualify for the Twenty-first Century, as defensible, democratic public education.

- The American Cultures Requirement at the University of California, Berkeley, which, as of the fall of 1991, will at least recognize the necessity of some knowledge of majority peoples' lives, past and current.
- Progressive students at Duluth, Minnesota, who have organized on the basis of gay and lesbian rights and who have themselves become integral allies of the fight for Native American treaty rights.
- Progressive students at Haverford, Pennsylvania, and at the University of Massachusetts, Boston, who have signed up for direct action on behalf of the Chippewa Indian treaty rights now jeopardized by the Ku Klux Klan kinds of racist propaganda and attack.
- The Great Lakes Indian Fish and Wildlife Commission (P.O. Box 9, Odanah, WI 54861, Phone: (715) 682-6619), which has published "A Guide to Understanding Chippewa Treaty Rights."

I believe this is our chance to return to the beginning of America. In the beginning there was the Indian. In the beginning there was human life and animal life and variegated terrain as infinitely distinct and precious as the cells that underlie existence.

The advent of Europeans to this continent disturbed the just and peaceful equipoise implied by our survival. That happened a long time ago, and that disruption haunts our destiny today.

But we are fortunate. Not all of the currently powerful are blind. Not all of the currently privileged despise the clear commandments of a democratic state. And, not all of all the rest of us have died.

In the Presence of Giants

August 1990

Some things take time.

Exactly twenty-seven years ago, I was twenty-seven years old. My son was five. Martin Luther King Jr. dedicated his "I have a dream" oration to 250,000 Americans standing in one place. Racist maniacs blew up a Birmingham, Alabama, church and, thereby, murdered three black children. South Africa stole Nelson Mandela out of his natural, free life. His wife, Winnie Mandela, began a harrowing and militant vigil, without precedent.

Almost nobody was thinking about trees.

Two years before all of that, in 1961, I found myself sitting on the screened-in porch of a farmhouse in New Hampshire. Just on the far side of the dirt road out front, my father-in-law was bracing himself to cut down a tree. It was not a big tree. It was not especially beautiful. I remember that particular beech tree as somewhat older than a sapling and I can still see the heart-shaped leaves that glittered easily in that mountain-morning light.

As my father-in-law hoisted an ax above his shoulder and brought the blade, heavy and swift, to tell against the slender trunk, my son, Christopher, raced up to him and angrily asked, "What the hell are you doing?"

Christopher's grandfather did not, as I recall, manage to make any sensible reply. Christopher's challenge back then bitterly underlies today's international movement against deforestation, from Brazil to California.

Some things take time.

Violence is fast.

It happens unexpectedly. It comes like a tornado.

It pierces flesh that bleeds. It spills into the water. It calls you a name that is not your name. It knocks you flat. Violence is popular. As 2 Live Crew, the rap group, formulates the issues, it's "nasty as you wanna be." And fast.

Other things take time.

The blasted pelvis of Judi Bari will not heal overnight. A pipe-bomb explosion injured Bari and Darryl Cherney, leading activities of Earth First!, several weeks ago.[16] Incredibly, the local police at first accused these environmentalists of detonating the bombs themselves in order to focus public attention on the redwood trees of northern California. In fact, Bari and Cherney do hope to arouse an impassioned grass-roots opposition in a fashion worthy of the media tag line, "Redwood Summer."

But, obviously, these workers dedicated to survival of trees and, hence, to a life-supporting environment for all of us, would not risk an act of suicidal portent. Altogether consciously, their model for confrontational, saturation protest is the Freedom Summer of 1964, when thousands of black and white college students adopted tactics of nonviolent civil disobedience and then went south, into Mississippi, prepared to die, if necessary, for the sake of black Americans' right to vote.

As shown by the recent attempt to assassinate Judi Bari and Darryl Cherney, opponents of environmental concern mean to imitate the racist savagery that has haunted Afro-American existence: A virulent enmity that will require dauntless legislative as well as direct attack before it will subside and become anything other than usual and unmitigated abuse.

Some things take time.

Before moving west to California,[17] I had never seen redwood trees and, certainly, I had never thought to write about trees of any kind, for any reason. My notion of political urgencies did not encompass the preservation of things as against human beings, although once, on a brief visit to Berkeley, I remember walking through Tilden Park with a friend who had me touch an unmistakably ancient black oak tree. She had described to me a then-current controversy that appeared to pit the future of this tree against the perceived needs of nearby Berkeley residents.

"Of course," I remember her saying, "Of course, if it's a choice between people and a tree, it's the tree that goes, as far as I'm concerned!" I remember feeling uneasy about her certitude: For me, it was not clear that my own interests, for example, should easily supersede the living requirements of the amazing wild "thing" that arched and whirled and rooted down, all at once, so close to where I stood, breathing clean air.

Some things take time.

And I have moved. I am writing these words less than twenty minutes away from that old oak tree. And tonight my mind moves from anxiety about the safety and good health of Nelson Mandela to the safety of our common environment and, hence, to the safety of trees.

Mandela is six-feet, four-inches tall and seventy-two years old. He walks in the world, lucid and relentless and free even as he kept himself lucid and relentless and free despite 10,000 nights in prison.

When I enter a grove of redwood trees, I feel I have slipped inside a cathedral of purity and strength. This hallowed space is not religious: You do not worship anything but what you can see and what that actuality allows. You do not raise your voice. You do not lower your eyes. You do not hurry anywhere. The expansive and compounding significance of age as history becomes a promise you believe your own life will manage to keep. You feel how small you are and you do not feel afraid. In the presence of these giants, you understand serenity as something earned, something integral to the accomplishment of freedom.

I feel this way in the presence of Mandela.

I feel this way inside a grove of redwood trees.

Shortly after the assassination attempt on the lives of Judi Bari and Darryl Cherney, I drove to Mendocino County, the intended site for Redwood Summer. At last I came upon the western offices of Georgia Pacific, one of the two main logging corporations in the area. At the edge of a tiny, nominal lawn, there seemed to be a weird museum exhibit or sportsman's trophy of some sort. The thing lay there, trapped and enormous, behind a chain link fence. What could it be, that huge dead mass captured inside such strange, such smug confinement?

"The is the section of the largest redwood tree known to have grown in Mendocino County."

A large bronze plaque explained everything in boastful detail: *"This redwood was felled in Big Bear Creek, April 18, 1943.*

"Estimated age: 1,735 years.

"Height: 334 feet.

"Diameter of stump: twenty-two feet.

"A saw twenty-two feet in length was used to fell this tree. Actual time required for cutting the tree was sixty man hours."

Some things take time.

Sixty hours is a micro-fraction of a minute in the context of close to 2,000 years.

Violence is fast.

Other things take time.

I faced this appalling memorial and images of black men lynched and images of Native Americans massacred overtook my consciousness and I could hardly stand where I stood.

I had traveled a very long way to live in California and, now, to explore Mendocino County in northern California, but still I was somewhere grisly and familiar: I was somewhere endangered. I was somewhere opposed to the slow and steady reach of a life that grows.

Deforestation is uninhibited, greed-motivated, head-hunting, Western style. And the hunters and the children of the hunters will not escape the meaning of the death of redwood trees.

Our very breath depends upon the preservation of these trees, these accomplishments of freedom. And I know it's late to try and make a sensible reply to Christopher's question of so long ago.

But we'd better try.

A Chance at Grace

October 1990

I never wanted to see a dramatization of *Grapes of Wrath*. One of my forever favorites of political world literature, I thought it should just stay that way: a story to read and reread in private. But so many friends of mine described the award-winning production now playing in New York as faithful to the book and, on its own terms, as harrowing and powerful, I had to go. Perhaps Steinbeck's work would speak to the agony of street people staggering around in the public daylight of urban America, 1990. I had to go.

With the arrival of *Grapes of Wrath* some fifty years ago, our national complacency about food supply and farmers and hardworking whitefolks had been pierced forever with shame. And nobody seemed safe.

If the mythical perfection of an industrious, nuclear, all-white family could be blown by natural disaster, if the government of and for these people could not be moved to rescue their homes and their tractors and their beloved land from depredations of agribusiness, investment speculation, and greed-riveted banks, then who among us could assume security? Who could reasonably claim to enjoy political representation on the serious side?

John Steinbeck's masterpiece telescoped the 1930s demise of hundreds of thousands of farm families into the haunting saga of the Joads who fled west from Oklahoma's dustbowl drought. In a drive-a-wreck jalopy truck, they took off on the road, traveling to California, where, according to various loose handbills, luscious vineyards and orchards lay spoiling under the sun. California meant sunlight and arable earth and all the work a man could manage, day by day, picking oranges or peaches by the bushel. California meant a new and beautiful life of regular, honest toil beneath blue skies.

And so the Joads made that American pilgrimage, crossing the Rockies and coming upon paradise, raggedy but pumped up with hope. They had been duped by agribusinessmen crafty enough to know that 2,000 men competing for 200 jobs would soon reduce to 2,000 men willing to accept otherwise unimaginably low wages: day labor paying too little to provide for a minimal version of normal life. For the Joads, as for hordes of other bitterly evicted "Okies," man-made catastrophe swiftly eclipsed the tragedy of drought they had sought to escape. Now they must outwit and evade or endure savage exploitation, forced vagrancy, and the loss of legal rights reserved for the middle class or, at least, permanent residents of a town.

They were perishing from hunger. Around them, nothing and no one familiar or hospitable remained. In their own country, they had become a homeless people having to steal or beg. And then, Rose of Sharon, a daughter of the Joads, gives birth to a dead baby. In the current Broadway adaptation, Rose of Sharon relinquishes the body of her stillborn infant to her uncle who, horrified by the task, commits the minuscule corpse into the rushing waters of a nearby rising river. At this moment, and engulfed by a terrible rainstorm, the entire family must find refuge. They must reach dry ground.

Rose of Sharon can hardly stand. But she must move or die.

At last the Joads come upon an open barn and inside this haven they discover other people: two black men. Pointing to the motionless figure of his father, a young black man pleads with the Joads for help: He needs a piece/a slice of solid food to save his father's life. But the Joads do not have anything; they have nothing left to give or to share.

And then Rose of Sharon falls to her knees. She undoes her blouse. She lifts the head of the dying black man to her naked breast. She kneels there, center stage, with this dark stranger cradled in her arms.

Lights hold and then fade. The audience rises up. Tears choke my throat. I am breathing the mystery of grace. It is what each of us desires at the utmost depth of consciousness, the saving embrace of grace: that in our most naked need we will be met by comparably naked acts of kindness. This is the motivating wish behind the howl of human life.

And acts of mercy save the merciful as well. For the first time in her miserable existence, that young woman, Rose of Sharon, becomes powerful and necessary even as she kneels to feed a stranger.

And we who saw this mystery enacted, we stood up in gratitude and shock. We had seen something completely realistic that was human yet not monstrous, or narrow, or threatening. We stood because we knew we had been staring at our own desperation and our own power as we beheld that onstage moment of such unexpected tenderness.

We had glimpsed the possibilities of shelter that only we can raise as codes of conduct in the world. And we, the homeless and the affluent, the black kids dancing in the street outside the theater and the theatergoers who turned their backs; we, the women who can find no safety anywhere, and the men who pretend to despise or who destroy domestic conditions of peace; we cannot avoid the always growing harvest of those grapes of wrath.

But we can choose to give ourselves a chance at grace; we can choose to embrace the strangers we must meet in the extremities of common need.

Intifada, U.S.A.

December 1990

The girl looks thin. She keeps her eyes on the ground. To either side, Israeli soldiers lounge, post-massacre. She is Palestinian. She cannot be more than nine years old. How long will she stay alive? Who is prepared to guarantee another week of her life?

Several days before this photo appeared in the papers here, Israeli soldiers and armed Israeli "settlers" shot and killed twenty men.

They were Palestinians. They had gathered to protest Israeli Prime Minister Yitzhak Shamir's announcement of his government's (completely illegal) plan to build a new settlement (15,000 units) in Arab East Jerusalem. They had gathered to defy the announced intention of Israeli Temple Mount faithful fanatics "to lay a cornerstone" for a new Jewish Temple—in Arab East Jerusalem. They had come out, several thousand unarmed men, to rebuke these latest Israeli violations of pertinent U. N. resolutions, Palestinian territorial rights, and human decency.

As documented by the one existing videotape of the entire episode, Israeli worshippers and soldiers, alike, had withdrawn absolutely from the danger-zone, the stone-throwing zone, *for more than fifteen minutes* before, suddenly, Israeli soldiers and "settlers" reappeared, guns blazing, and fatal. The killers were Israelis. The victims were, all of them, Palestinians. This is not a new equation. This equation is not a tragedy. This is the killer plan fully financed, and otherwise tolerated by you and me.

Just, for instance, how do you suppose Shamir will pay for the proposed, and completely illegal, new housing in Arab East Jerusalem? The Bush Administration has guaranteed a $400 million loan for these purposes. The Bush Administration, to my knowledge, has not guaranteed a $400 million anything for the homeless or low-income Americans who need shelter, here.

It must be wonderful to live in Israel. Our American taxes give every single Israeli more money, day after day and year after year, more than every single American suffering from cancer or AIDS would ever hope to receive, week after week, from our Federal purse. And then there are these bonuses, like $1 billion additional for weapons (because George Bush was maybe going to sell $19 billion worth of weapons to Saudi Arabia) plus, of course, they very very recent

$400 million housing deal. And these bonuses arrive on top of $4 billion annual U.S. aid to Israel, a country with barely 3.2 million inhabitants.

And, in case our handouts of money and missiles seem too paltry, Israel expects our unqualified enslavement to something summarily described as a "pro-Israel" position.

Israel continues its military and commercial collaboration with South Africa. Israel refuses international inspection of its nuclear arsenal. Israel refuses to abide by U.N. resolutions that dictate an Israeli exit from the "Occupied Territories"/Palestinian land. Israel expands its illegal "settlements" inside Arab East Jerusalem and the West Bank, the Gaza Strip, the Golan Heights. Israel deports Palestinian nationals. Israel tortures Palestinians, and detains and incarcerates them without trial. Israel closes up Palestinian towns and universities and shuts down Palestinian newspapers, whenever Israel feels like it.

And so, what happens?

Does George Bush rush 250,000 American troops into Jordan, threatening to invade Israel unless Israel relinquishes the "Occupied Territories" that amount to what's left of a homeland for the Palestinian people? Does Bush freeze all loans, aid, and accounts tied to Israel until and unless Israel complies with our Foreign Assistance Act of 1961? (This American law stipulates that no U.S. aid may be provided to countries engaging in a consistent pattern of human-rights abuse.)

No, no, no, no. And why the hell not?

Clearly, a barrel of oil is worth more than any number of Palestinian lives. Clearly, a barrel of oil is worth more than the safety of the 250,000 young African-American and Mexican-American and Latino and poor white men and women now sweltering on the Arabian desert while they await God-knows-what horrible and undue and untimely death.

I say we need a rising up, an Intifada, U.S.A.

I have been circulating a petition where I live and work, and I hope others will circulate their own, and then sponsor rallies, teach-ins, strikes, boycotts, whatever it takes to stand against the Persian Gulf "standoff."

We need to rise up. We need to stand against the "standoff" in the Persian Gulf. We need an Intifada, U.S.A.

At night, I go to bed afraid to close my eyes, or sleep: I ask my soul these questions aching on my conscience: What will happen to that little girl, that child of Palestine? What is happening to you and me

Requiem for Sara

February 1991

She was crossing the street, carrying bags of groceries. She was on her way home. It was 3:30 P.M. on a sunny afternoon. It was not a busy intersection. The driver of the car had been "reckless." And now she lay there on a patch of regular paved road, wounded to extremity. From the collision of the car with her body, she had sustained severe brain damage. Until her death, six days later, she never regained consciousness. Her name was Sara.

She had moved from Brooklyn to Berkeley two years ago, hoping for safety and a somehow easier life. At 9:20 P.M. on a Sunday night, she died. The newspapers said she was thirty-five. I would have guessed thirty-one or thirty-two.

She is survived by her husband, Kent, and their three-and-a-half-year-old baby boy, named Sam. She is survived by her family and Kent's family, and their friends. She's gone. She did not make it through a third year here, where rain hardly ever falls, where cars commonly brake to a halt if a pedestrian even appears to be about to step from the curb.

She is survived by a man intent upon death. She is survived by George Bush. She is survived by an American President trying, in deadly ways, to become, *de facto*, a king: a force unchecked by constitutional or popular edict, a power above Congressional consent or rational debate.

She is survived by Neil Bush who, like his father, will not be asked to risk the ultimate sacrifice for the sake of his father's imperial whims. Neither Neil nor George will be asked to die—possibly, yet, die—for the sake of a territorial, a post-colonial concoction called Kuwait.

She is survived by Secretary of State James Baker, who recently distinguished himself as a functional and talkative lunatic: He was asked, publicly, to respond to one of the numerous peace proposals Saddam Hussein has issued since the King George announcement of the Crisis of Kuwait; Saddam had offered to withdraw from Kuwait if he could retain two uninhabited islands plus one oilfield which straddles the Iraq-Kuwaiti border (95 percent of the oilfield lies inside Iraq). Secretary of State James Baker dismissed that compromise proposal: Not good enough. Saddam must relinquish every last inch of Kuwaiti turf-disputed, uninhabited, or not. A persistent reporter then asked Secretary of State James Baker, if he, Baker, really expects Congress, the American people, and the world community to go to war for the sake of two uninhabited islands plus one oilfield. Secretary of State James Baker said, 'Yes."

Baker and King George survive the accidental, tragic death of Sara Bryson.

I first met Sara several years ago, in a photocopy shop where she worked behind the counter: pony-tail, scrubbed cheeks, lively smile, and an imperturbable, sweet spirit. Her merriment and her gentle but savvy competence anchored the passers-by. I used to stop in once or twice a day, back then, on that neighborhood drag in Brooklyn, and check on various aspects of the universe: Had she seen my lover? What was the World Series score? Did she think the fliers for the birthday party would persuade folks to come or scare them away? And so on.

Sara was always right there, steady and light/tiny and bright. And then, a lot of us noticed something new. Sara had fallen in love. His name was Kent. He was a jazz musician, on the road as often as [he] could get a paying gig. But he would, he did, come back to be with her. And then, a while after that, Sara and Kent got married. And then, after that, she was pregnant.

Sara stayed on her feet, pregnant. Serving customers at the disorganized and crowded copy shop, she stayed on her feet through the first week of her ninth month. She and Kent did not have a lot of money. And they loved each other. They were happy. And then, Baby Sam was born.

I remember feeling so much relief when Sara told me that she and Kent and Baby Sam would be moving to California. Out there, I thought, they will be safe and living under the sun in the sky that you can see, almost everywhere. Out there, it will seem less desolate when she and Baby Sam can took at trees and flowering bushes whenever they are by themselves, waiting for Kent to return from a faraway job.

Last summer, I ran into Sara at the nearby health-food store. As usual, she looked radiant and immaculate and small and sturdy as a rock. They were happy. She was hopeful. Baby Sam was big.

To help piece things together, she'd found work in a day-care center. That meant that she and Baby Sam did not have to separate every day. And, also, she and Kent did not need to invest extra money which they did not have.

She worked hard. She tendered her hopes with all of her young, passionate love. She fought for a decent life for her family. She hated violence. Injustice enraged her. Laziness bewildered her. She's gone.

Does it matter? Does anybody give a goddamn about the death of a young married woman who never threatened anybody, never coveted the title or the territory or the material resources of anyone else?

She was only a woman. She was just somebody shopping for two or three ripe bananas, economy-size detergent, and, for a treat, perhaps fresh strawberries. She was just somebody listening for a cry from her husband. She was only a woman, centered on making an okay breakfast and hoping for peace world wide, plus, sometimes, on special weekends, looking forward to a movie, or Chinese food.

Who cares?

Where is the leader who will lower the flags and declare a national day of mourning for her stolen laughter, her censored intelligence, her interrupted prayer of a willing and eager presence among us?

Who will mobilize this country so that Baby Sam can grow up a gentle, good man among gentle, good men?

And, on the other side of things, why is there no movement to impeach or else to institutionalize those homicidal leaders who ooze onto our TV screens, utter bizarre, bloody pronouncements, and disappear with our destiny clutched inside the pathology of their contempt for a simple human being born only of a woman: just an ordinary woman riveted to the making of a bed, the making of love?

She's gone.

I say it's time to lower the flags and lay down the guns. Sara has been stricken from her easy-going, stubborn stride. It's time to mourn the loss of every possible, joyous life. It's time to honor her hardworking trust in the rest of us. It's time to salvage what's left of this scary place for Sam.

The following poem by June Jordan appears as an inset in the preceding column, "Requiem for Sara" from the February 1991 issue. The poem is dated December 17, 1990. The location of Pajaro Dunes appears under the date.

For Sara:
In Memoriam

Sometimes we say,
"Out under the stars"
meaning someplace different
from the kitchen or the subway
or the grave
but regardless we are
always out
under the stars
as she is Sara
now not far
not gone
but out
under the stars.

The Big-Time Coward

April 1991

On a recent, cold Sunday morning in Kennebunkport, Maine, George Bush and his wife, Barbara, seated themselves inside a small country church of God. (To think about what?)

Alma Powell, wife of the chairman of the Joint Chiefs of Staff of the U.S. armed forces, reports that she likes to keep "comforting foods" like vegetable soup ready, on top of the stove, for Colin, her certainly hard-working husband. Alma adds that, these days, she just "knows" that her Colin doesn't want to hear "little stories" about the children.

Secretary of Defense Dick Cheney, second only to his boss in bloodthirst for arm's-length/armchair warfare, has never served half an hour, even, in the Army, the Navy, the Air Force, or the Marines. (I know; it's not right to pick on him just for that.)

One recent Saturday, at a local antiwar rally organized by the Middle East Children's Alliance, I noted, aloud, that the war, to date, was costing us $56 billion. Every twenty-four hours, the cost was $1 billion, at least. Therefore, I proposed the following to the crowd scattered on the grass and under the trees:

"One billion dollars a day for seven
days for Oakland!
Can you imagine that?
One billion dollars a day!
But to hell with imagination!
This is our city!
This is our money!
These are our lives!
One billion dollars a day for seven
days for Oakland!
(Or) do we accept that there is only
'the will and
the wallet' when it's about to kill or
be killed?
Do we need this money or not?
Do we need it here?

Do we need it now?" And so on.

When I left the stage a reporter came up to me: "You meant one *million* dollars, didn't you?" "No!" I answered him, amazed: "One billion: One billion dollars a day for seven days for Oakland! That's the bill, that's our bill for housing and drug rehabilitation and books in the public schools and hospital care and all of that good stuff: One billion dollars a day.

"It's a modest proposal: In less than three months, those maniacs in the White House and the Pentagon have spent $56 billion in my name and with my taxes, trying to obliterate Iraq and its people and their leader. I'm saying, call home the troops and the bucks! We need these big bucks to make this a homeland, not a desert, right here, for the troops and for you and for me: What's the problem? It's a bargain! Seven billion dollars on the serious improvement of American life in Oakland versus $56 billion for death and destruction inside Iraq! What's the problem?"

But the reporter was giving me a weak smile of farewell that let me understand he found my proposal preposterous: One *million* dollars for life, okay. Billions for kill or be killed, okay. But really big bucks on us, the people of these United States? One billion dollars a day to promote, for example, the safety and educational attainment and communal happiness of 339,000 Americans? I must be kidding!

As I walked away from the park, I felt a heavy depression overtaking me: The reporter, a tall white man with clear eyes, could not contemplate the transfer of his and my aggregate resources from death to life as a reasonable idea. Worse, he could not suppose his and my life to be worth anything close to the value of organized, high-tech, and boastful murder.

But then other people stopped me to ask: "How can we do that? Do we write letters or what?" And so as I write this column tonight, I am reassured because not everybody American has lost her mind or his soul. Not everyone of my compatriots has become a flag-wrapped lunatic lusting after oil/power/the perversions of "kicking ass," preferably via TV.

A huge number of Americans has joined with enormous numbers of Arab peoples and European communities in Germany, England, France, Italy, Spain, and Muslim communities throughout India and Pakistan to cry out, "Stop!"

And when I say "huge" I mean it: If 1,000 Americans contacted by some pollster can be said to represent 250 million people, then how many multi-multi-millions do we, antiwar movement gatherings of more than 100,000, coast to coast and on every continent, how many do we represent?!

And how come nobody ever does that kind of political math?

And tonight, February 22, 1991, when yet again the ruling white men of America despise peace and sneer at negotiations and intensify their arm's-length/ armchair prosecution of this evil war, this display of a racist value system that will never allow for any nationalism that is not their own and that will never allow Third World countries to control their own natural resources and that will never express, let alone feel, regret or remorse or shame or horror at the loss of any human life that is not white, tonight I am particularly proud to be an African-American.

By authorizing the heaviest air assault in history against Iraq on January 15, George Bush dared to desecrate the birthday of Martin Luther King Jr. Tonight, 83,000 bombing missions later, is the twenty-sixth anniversary of the assassination of Malcolm X.

On this sorry evening the world has seen the pathological real deal behind the sanctimonious rhetoric of Bush and Company: The Persian Gulf war is not about Iraqi withdrawal from Kuwait. The war is not about Kuwait at all. Clearly it's not about international law or respect for United Nations resolutions since, by comparison to Washington, Tel Aviv, and Pretoria, "the Butcher of Baghdad" is a minor-league Johnny-come-lately to the realm of outlaw conduct and contempt for world opinion.

What has happened tonight is that the Soviet leader, Mikhail Gorbachev, and the government of Iraq have reached an agreement whereby Iraq would withdraw from Kuwait, and that is a fact—regardless of anything else included or omitted by the proposal. This agreement should provide for an immediate cease-fire, a cessation of the slaughter of Iraqi men and women, and a halt to the demolition, nationwide, of their water supply, their access to food, their securement of shelter.

So what is the response of the Number One White Man in America? He's gone off "to the theater." I guess that means the nearest church was closed. Or that Colin Powell was busy dipping his spoon into the comfort of a pot of soup somebody else cooked for him. And that Dick Cheney was fit to be tied into any kind of uniform so long as it meant nobody would take away his Patriot missiles and Apache helicopters and B-52 cluster-bomb bombers and black and brown and poor white soldiers and sailors and all the rest of these toys for a truly big-time coward.

Confronted with the "nightmare" prospect of peace, Bush goes off to the theater because he'll be damned if he will acknowledge that Saddam Hussein is a man, is the head of a sovereign state, is an enemy to be reckoned with, an opponent with whom one must negotiate: Saddam Hussein is not a white man!

He and his Arab peoples must be destroyed! No peace! No cease-fire! No negotiations!

And I am proud tonight to remember Dr. King and Malcolm X, and to mourn their absence, even as I pursue the difficult challenge of their legacy. Both of these men became the targets of white wrath when they, in their different ways, developed into global visionaries persisting against racism in Alabama, in Harlem, in South Africa, in Vietnam. Neither of these men could have failed to condemn this current attack against the Arab world. Neither of these men ever condoned anything less than equal justice and equal rights. Hence, the undeniably racist double standards now levied against Saddam Hussein would have appalled and alienated both of them, completely.

I am proud to shake hands with the increasing numbers of African-American conscientious objectors.

I am proud to remark the steadfast moral certainty of Representative Ronald Dellum's opposition to this war.

I am proud to hear about the conscientious objections of Representatives Gus Savage and John Conyers and Mervyn Dymally.

I am proud to observe that, even while African-Americans remain disproportionately represented in the U.S. armed forces, we, as a national community, stand apart from all vagaries of popular opinion; we maintain a proportionately higher-than-white level of opposition to this horrible war, this horrendous evasion of domestic degeneration and decay.

And I want to say something else, specifically to you, Mr. President: It's true you can humiliate and you can hound and you can smash and burn and terrify and smirk and boast and defame and demonize and dismiss and incinerate and starve and, yes, you can force a people to surrender what remains of their bloody bowels into your grasping, bony, dry hands.

But all of us who are weak, we watch you. And we learn from your hatred. And we do not forget. And we are many, Mr. President.

We are most of the people on this Godforsaken planet.

A New Politics of Sexuality

July 1991

As a young worried mother, I remember turning to Dr. Benjamin Spock's *Common Sense Book of Baby and Child Care* just about as often as I'd pick up the telephone. He was God. I was ignorant but striving to be good: a good Mother. And so it was there, in that bestseller pocketbook of do's and don't's, that I came upon this doozie of a guideline: Do not wear miniskirts or other provocative clothing because that will upset your child, especially if your child happens to be a boy. If you give your offspring "cause" to think of you as a sexual being, he will, at the least, become disturbed; you will derail the equilibrium of his notions about your possible identity and meaning in the world.

It had never occurred to me that anyone, especially my son, might look upon me as an asexual being. I had never supposed that "asexual" was some kind of positive designation I should, so to speak, lust after. I was pretty surprised by Dr. Spock. However, I was also, by habit, a creature of obedience. For a couple of weeks I actually experimented with lusterless colors and dowdy tops and bottoms, self-consciously hoping thereby to prove myself as a lusterless and dowdy and, therefore, excellent female parent.

Years would have to pass before I could recognize the familiar, by then, absurdity of a man setting himself up as the expert on a subject that presupposed women as the primary objects for his patriarchal discourse—on motherhood, no less! Years passed before I came to perceive the perversity of dominant power assumed by men, and the perversity of self-determining power ceded to men by women.

A lot of years went by before I understood the dynamics of what anyone could summarize as the Politics of Sexuality.

I believe the Politics of Sexuality is the most ancient and probably the most profound arena for human conflict. Increasingly, it seems clear to me that deeper and more pervasive than any other oppression, than any other bitterly contested human domain, is the oppression of sexuality, the exploitation of the human domain of sexuality for power.

When I say sexuality, I mean gender: I mean male subjugation of human beings because they are female. When I say sexuality I mean heterosexual institutionalization of rights and privileges denied to homosexual men and women.

When I say sexuality I mean gay or lesbian contempt for bisexual modes of human relationship.

The Politics of Sexuality therefore subsumes all of the different ways in which some of us seek to dictate to others of us what we should do, what we should desire, what we should dream about, and how we should behave ourselves, generally, on the planet. From China to Iran, from Nigeria to Czechoslovakia, from Chile to California, the politics of sexuality—enforced by traditions of state-sanctioned violence plus religion and the law—reduces to male domination of women, heterosexist tyranny, and, among those of us who are in any case deemed despicable or deviant by the powerful, we find intolerance for those who choose a different, a more complicated-for example, an interracial or bisexual—mode of rebellion and freedom.

We must move out from the shadows of our collective subjugation—as people of color/as women/as gay/as lesbian/as bisexual human beings.

I can voice my ideas without hesitation or fear because I am speaking, finally, about myself. I am black and I am female and I am a mother and I am bisexual and I am a nationalist and I am an antinationalist. And I mean to be fully and freely all that I am!

Conversely, I do not accept that any white or black or Chinese man—I do not accept that, for instance, Dr. Spock—should presume to tell me, or any other woman, how to mother a child. He has no right. He is not a mother. My child is not his child. And, likewise, I do not accept that anyone—any woman or any man who is not inextricably part of the subject he or she dares to address—should attempt to tell any of us, the objects of her or his presumptuous discourse, what we should do or what we should not do.

Recently, I have come upon gratuitous and appalling pseudoliberal pronouncements on sexuality. Too often, these utterances fall out of the mouths of men and women who first disclaim any sentiment remotely related to homophobia, but who then proceed to issue outrageous opinions like the following:

That it is blasphemous to compare the oppression of gay, lesbian, or bisexual people to the oppression, say, of black people, or of the Palestinians.

That the bottom line about gay or lesbian or bisexual identity is that you can conceal it whenever necessary and, so, therefore, why don't you do just that? Why don't you keep your deviant sexuality in the closet and let the rest of us—we who suffer oppression for reasons of our ineradicable and always visible components of our personhood such as race or gender—get on with our more necessary, our more beleaguered struggle to survive?

Well, number one: I believe I have worked as hard as I could, and then harder than that, on behalf of equality and justice-for African-Americans, for the Palestinian people, and for people of color everywhere.

And no, I do not believe it is blasphemous to compare oppressions of sexuality to oppressions of race and ethnicity: Freedom is indivisible or it is nothing at all besides sloganeering and temporary, short-sighted, and short-lived advancement for a few. Freedom is indivisible, and either we are working for freedom or you are working for the sake of your self-interests and I am working for mine.

If you can finally go to the bathroom, wherever you find one, if you can finally order a cup of coffee and drink it wherever coffee is available, but you cannot follow your heart—you cannot respect the response of your own honest body in the world—then how much of what kind of freedom does any one of us possess?

Or, conversely, if your heart and your honest body can be controlled by the state, or controlled by community taboo, are you not then, and in that case, no more than a slave ruled by outside force?

What tyranny could exceed a tyranny that dictates to the human heart, and that attempts to dictate the public career of an honest human body?

Freedom is indivisible; the Politics of Sexuality is not some optional "special-interest" concern for serious, progressive folk.

And, on another level, let me assure you: If every single gay or lesbian or bisexual man or woman active on the Left of American politics decided to stay home, there would be *no* Left left.

One of the things I want to propose is that we act on that reality: that we insistently demand reciprocal respect and concern from those who cheerfully depend upon our brains and our energies for their, and our, effective impact on the political landscape.

Last spring, at Berkeley, some students asked me to speak at a rally against racism. And I did. There were 400 or 500 people massed on Sproul Plaza, standing together against that evil. And, on the next day, on that same Plaza, there was a rally for bisexual and gay and lesbian rights, and students asked me to speak at that rally. And I did. There were fewer than seventy-five people stranded, pitiful, on that public space. And I said then what I say today: That was disgraceful! There should have been just one rally. One rally: Freedom is indivisible.

As for the second, nefarious pronouncement on sexuality that now enjoys mass-media currency: the idiot notion of keeping yourself in the closet—that is very much the same thing as the suggestion that black folks and Asian-Americans and Mexican-Americans should assimilate and become as "white" as possible—in our walk/talk/music/food/values—or else. Or else? Or else we should, deservedly, perish.

Sure enough, we have plenty of exposure to white everything so why would we opt to remain our African/Asian/Mexican selves? The answer is that suicide is absolute, and if you think you will survive by hiding who you really are, you are sadly misled: There is no such thing as partial or intermittent suicide. You can only survive if you—who you really are—do survive.

Likewise, we who are not men and we who are not heterosexist—we, sure enough, have plenty of exposure to male-dominated/heterosexist this and that.

But a struggle to survive cannot lead to suicide: Suicide is the opposite of survival. And so we must not conceal/assimilate/integrate into the would-be dominant culture and political system that despises us. Our survival requires that we alter our environment so that we can live and so that we can hold each other's hands and so that we can kiss each other on the streets, and in the day-light of our existence, without terror and without violent and sometimes fatal reactions from the busybodies of America.

Finally, I need to speak on bisexuality. I do believe that the analogy is in-terracial or multiracial identity. I do believe that the analogy for bisexuality is a multicultural, multi-ethnic, multiracial world view. Bisexuality follows from such a perspective and leads to it, as well.

Just as there are many men and women in the United States whose parents have given them more than one racial, more than one ethnic identity and cultur-al heritage to honor; and just as these men and women must deny no given part of themselves except at the risk of self-deception and the insanities that must is-sue from that; and just as these men and women embody the principle of equali-ty among races and ethnic communities; and just as these men and women falter and anguish and choose and then falter again and then anguish and then choose yet again how they will honor the irreducible complexity of their God-given human being—even so, there are many men and women, especially young men and women, who seek to embrace the complexity of their total, always-changing social and political circumstance.

They seek to embrace our increasing global complexity on the basis of the heart and on the basis of an honest human body. Not according to ideology. Not according to group pressure. Not according to anybody's concept of "correct."

This is a New Politics of Sexuality. And even as I despair of identity pol-itics—because identity is given and principles of justice/equality/freedom cut across given gender and given racial definitions of being, and because I will call you my brother, I will call you my sister, on the basis of what you *do* for justice, what you *do* for equality, what you *do* for freedom and *not* on the basis of who you are, even so I look with admiration and respect upon the new, bisexual politics of sexuality.

This emerging movement politicizes the so-called middle ground: Bisexuality invalidates either/or formulation, either/or analysis. Bisexuality means I am free and I am as likely to want and to love a woman as I am likely to want and to love a man, and what about that? Isn't that what freedom implies?

If you are free, you are not predictable and you are not controllable. To my mind, that is the keenly positive, politicizing significance of bisexual affirmation:

To insist upon complexity, to insist upon the validity of all of the components of social/sexual complexity, to insist upon the equal validity of all of the components of social/sexual complexity.

This seems to me a unifying, 1990s mandate for revolutionary Americans planning to make it into the Twenty-first Century on the basis of the heart, on the basis of an honest human body, consecrated to every struggle for justice, every struggle for equality, every struggle for freedom.

Thomas Was Not the Point

November 1991

The law of the land governs all of our disparate lives. Against the chaos of conflict and above the passions of self-interest, the civilizing power of the law depends upon an ethical consensus on the common good. And because we, the diversity of American people, seldom remain the same from one decade to the next, and because our national condition changes with the history of every day, there can be no absolute law nor any ultimate interpretation of the law.

And yet we must have peace. Within our unstable environment, we search for justice—a commonly accepted, lawful means to the settlement of profound dispute and a commonly accepted, lawful means to the nonviolent allocation, and reallocation, of rights.

The Supreme Court presides over these needs of a democratic state. Since each Justice enjoys a lifelong appointment to the bench, there is provision for stability. And as each presidential nominee submits to Congressional scrutiny, there is provision for reasonably popular and up-to-date input as regards the political and philosophical composition of this highest Court. That would seem to be the ideal plan.

But quite a few things tend to go wrong. Too many Presidents have viewed the Court as a dugout for buddies. Too many members of Congress have abdicated their representative functions: repeatedly they restrict themselves to mock investigation into the personal probity of this or that candidate. Too often, organized citizens have fastened themselves to the task of advocating or assassinating a particular nominee rather than pressuring Congress to resist or to endorse the President, on principle.

This pattern derives, I believe from a surrender to unhappy precedent, and a misunderstanding of the democratic principle at stake.

As a people, we Americans are becoming more heterogeneous. Those who determine the law of the land must, therefore, embody an increasing diversity of background and conviction or, for example, the highest Court will lose its capacity for justice: It will lose its credibility as an agency responsible to and expressive of ethical consensus.

If we cherish rule by law rather than rule by force, then we must oppose the furtherance of a Supreme Court of likeminded colleagues even as the living components of our body politic become less and less homogeneous. Otherwise, there will emerge a dangerous disjuncture between the judges and the judged.

One fact lay embedded in the center of the Clarence Thomas controversy: We have lost a great American jurist, Thurgood Marshall. No one can replace him. The very thought of replacing him insults the brilliance of his career and the exceptional humanity of his intelligence as he reflected upon our most extreme and consequential public debates. And yet someone new had to be appointed to take his seat.

The President made his move. He nominated a man as different from Marshall as George Bush differs from Mahatma Gandhi. He nominated a man whose most striking characteristic seems to be that of satisfied self-hatred, a man whose public condemnation of his sister strikingly revealed his attitude toward the poor and the weak.

For some, the issue became black manhood or the sentimentalized biography of Clarence Thomas. They focused upon who the candidate was rather than what he has done and will do. This was identity politics taken to its lowest level.

On the American Right, however, there was more clarity. Among those who detested Thurgood Marshall and who generally despise black men there was a willingness to promote Clarence Thomas because Clarence Thomas was not the point: The point is to homogenize the Supreme Court. If someone with black skin will serve that purpose, then fine!

But we, the people, must not yield to judgment without representation. If we yield, there will be no justice. And without justice, believe me, there will be no peace.

Can I Get a Witness?

December 1991

I wanted to write a letter to Anita Hill. I wanted to say thanks. I wanted to convey the sorrow and the bitterness I feel on her behalf. I wanted to explode the history that twisted itself around the innocence of her fate. I wanted to assail the brutal ironies, the cruel consistencies that left her—at the moment of her utmost vulnerability and public power—isolated, betrayed, abused, and not nearly as powerful as those who sought and who seek to besmirch, ridicule, and condemn the truth of her important and perishable human being. I wanted to reassure her of her rights, her sanity, and the African beauty of her earnest commitment to do right and to be a good woman: a good black woman in this America.

But tonight I am still too furious, I am still too hurt, I am still too astounded and nauseated by the enemies of Anita Hill! Tonight my heart pounds with shame.

Is there no way to interdict and terminate the traditional, abusive loneliness of black women in this savage country?

From those slavery times when African men could not dare to defend their sisters, their mothers, their sweethearts, their wives, and their daughters—except at the risk of their lives—from those times until today: Has nothing changed?

How is it possible that only John Carr—a young black corporate lawyer who maintained a friendship with Anita Hill ten years ago ("It didn't go but so far," he testified, with an engaging, handsome trace of a smile)—how is it possible that he, alone among black men, stood tall and strong and righteous as a witness for her defense?

What about spokesmen for the NAACP or the National Urban League?

What about spokesmen for the U.S. Congressional Black Caucus?

All of the organizational and elected black men who spoke aloud against a wrong black man, Clarence Thomas, for the sake of principles resting upon decency and concerns for fair play, equal protection, and affirmative action—where did they go when, suddenly, a good black woman arose among us, trying to tell the truth?

Where did they go? And why?

Is it conceivable that a young white woman could be tricked into appearing before twelve black men of the U.S. Senate?

Is it conceivable that a young white woman could be tricked into appearing before a lineup of incredibly powerful and hypocritical and sneering and hellbent black men freely insinuating and freely hypothesizing whatever lurid scenario came into their heads?

Is it conceivable that such a young woman—such a flower of white womanhood—would, by herself, have to withstand the calumny and unabashed, unlawful bullying that was heaped upon Anita Hill?

Is it conceivable that this flower would not be swiftly surrounded by white knights rallying—with ropes, or guns, or whatever—to defend her honor and the honor, the legal and civilized rights, of white people, *per se*?

Anita Hill was tricked. She was set up. She had been minding her business at the University of Oklahoma Law School when the Senators asked her to describe her relationship with Clarence Thomas. Anita Hill's dutiful answers disclosed that Thomas had violated the trust of his office as head of the Equal Employment Opportunity Commission. Sitting in that office of ultimate recourse for women suffering from sexual harassment, Thomas himself harassed Anita Hill, repeatedly, with unwanted sexual advances and remarks.

Although Anita Hill had not volunteered this information and only supplied it in response to direct, specific inquiries from the FBI,

And although Anita Hill was promised the protection of confidentiality as regards her sworn statement of allegations,

And despite the fact that four witnesses—two men and two women, two black and two white distinguished Americans, including a Federal judge and a professor of law—testified, under oath, that Anita Hill had told each of them about these sordid carryings on by Thomas at the time of their occurrence or in the years that followed,

And despite the fact that Anita Hill sustained a remarkably fastidious display of exact recall and never alleged, for example, that Thomas actually touched her,

And despite the unpardonable decision by the U.S. Senate Judiciary Committee to prohibit expert testimony on sexual harassment,

Anita Hill, a young black woman born and raised within a black farm family of thirteen children, a graduate of an Oklahoma public high school who later earned honors and graduated from Yale Law School, a political conservative and, now, a professor of law,

Anita Hill, a young black woman who suffered sexual harassment once in ten years, and therefore, never reported sexual harassment to any of her friends except for that once in ten years,

Anita Hill, whose public calm and dispassionate sincerity refreshed America's eyes and ears with her persuasive example of what somebody looks and sounds like when she's simply trying to tell the truth,

Anita Hill was subpoenaed by the U.S. Senate Judiciary Committee of fourteen white men and made to testify and to tolerate interrogation on national television.

Why didn't she "do something" when Thomas allegedly harassed her?

The Senators didn't seem to notice or to care that Thomas occupied the office of last recourse for victims of sexual harassment. And had the Committee allowed any expert on the subject to testify, we would have learned that it is absolutely typical for victims to keep silent.

Wasn't it the case that she had/has fantasies and is delusional?

Remarkably, not a single psychiatrist or licensed psychologist was allowed to testify. These slanderous suppositions about the psychic functionings of Anita Hill were never more than malevolent speculations invited by one or another of the fourteen white Senators as they sat above an assortment of character witnesses handpicked by the White House staffers eager to protect the President's nominee.

One loathsomely memorable item: John Doggett, a self-infatuated black attorney and a friend of Clarence Thomas, declared that Thomas would not have jeopardized his career for Anita Hill because Doggett, a black man, explained to the Senate Committee of fourteen white men, "She is not worth it."

Why was she "lying"?

It should be noted that Anita Hill readily agreed to a lie-detector test and that, according to the test, she was telling the truth. It should also be noted that Clarence Thomas refused even to consider taking such a test and that, furthermore, he had already established himself as a liar when, earlier in the Senate hearings, he insisted that he had never discussed *Roe v. Wade*, and didn't know much about this paramount legal dispute.

Meanwhile, Clarence Thomas—who has nodded and grinned his way to glory and power by denying systemic American realities of racism, on the one hand, and by publicly castigating and lying about his own sister, a poor black woman, on the other—this Thomas, this Uncle Tom calamity of mediocre abilities, at best, this bootstrap miracle of egomaniacal myth and self-pity, this choice of the very same President who has vetoed two civil-rights bills and boasted about that, how did he respond to the testimony of Anita Hill?

Clarence Thomas thundered and he shook. Clarence Thomas glowered and he growled. "God is my judge!" he cried, at one especially disgusting low point in the Senate proceedings. "God is my judge, Senator. And not you!" This candidate for the Supreme Court evidently believes himself exempt from the judgments of mere men.

This Clarence Thomas—about whom an African-American young man in my freshman composition class exclaimed, "He's an Uncle Tom. He's a hypocritical Uncle Tom. And I don't care what happens to his punk ass"—this Thomas vilified the hearings as a "high-tech lynching."

When he got into hot water for the first time (on public record, at any rate), he attempted to identify himself as a regular black man. What a peculiar reaction to the charge of sexual harassment!

And where was the laughter that should have embarrassed him out of that chamber?

And where were the tears?

When and where was there ever a black man lynched because he was bothering a black woman?

When and where was there ever a white man jailed or tarred and feathered because he was bothering a black woman?

When a black woman is raped or beaten or mutilated by a black man or a white man, what happens?

To be a black woman in this savage country: Is that to be nothing and no one beautiful and precious and exquisitely compelling?

To be a black woman in this savage country: Is that to be nothing and no one revered and defended and given our help and our gratitude?

The only powerful man to utter and to level the appropriate word of revulsion as a charge against his peers—the word was "SHAME"—that man was U.S. Senator Ted Kennedy, a white man whose ongoing, successful career illuminates the unequal privileges of male gender, white race, and millionaire-class identity.

But Ted Kennedy was not on trial. He has never been on trial.

Clarence Thomas was supposed to be on trial but he was not: He is more powerful than Anita Hill. And his bedfellows, from Senator Strom Thurmond to President George Bush, persist—way more powerful than Clarence Thomas and Anita Hill combined.

And so, at the last, it was she, Anita Hill, who stood alone, trying to tell the truth in an arena of snakes of hyenas and dinosaurs and power-mad dogs. And with this televised victimization of Anita Hill, the American war of violence against women moved from the streets, moved from hip hop, moved from multimillion-dollar movies into the highest chambers of the U.S. Government.

And what is anybody going to do about it?

I, for one, I am going to write a letter to Anita Hill. I am going to tell her that, thank God, she is a black woman who is somebody and something beautiful and precious and exquisitely compelling.

And I am going to say that if this Government will not protect and defend her, and all black women, and all women, period, in this savage country—if this Government will not defend us from poverty and violence and contempt—then we will change the Government. We have the numbers to deliver on this warning.

And, as for the brothers who disappeared when a black woman rose up to tell the truth, listen: It's getting to be payback time. I have been speaking on behalf of a good black woman. Can you hear me?

Can I get a witness?

The Fire This Time

January 1992

This is a scary place to live. Beautiful and cultivated and heterogeneous and progressive and temperate and cosmopolitan and comfortable and fragrant with honeysuckle and trim-bodied and vegetarian and wheelchair-accessible, this is more or less urban paradise in America.

This is where more than 40 per cent of Oakland's public high-school students earn Ds or Fs in core courses in reading and math.

This is where the homeless of Berkeley mingle with university students on the sidewalk in front of Cody's,[18] one of the most respected bookstores in the country.

This is where you can leave your car unlocked overnight, or where you drive your car around the corner at your own risk of stray bullets from drug-related arguments.

But it never gets that cold. And it never gets that hot.

And it's not white. You would think something weird had happened if you walked into a pretty swell restaurant and mainly saw white men and women sitting at the tables.

And it's not black. You would know something god-awful had gone down if you didn't see and hear Asian-Americans and Chicano/Chicana-Americans everywhere you turned.

This is the Bay Area of Northern California. Frequently caricatured as fringe-and-freak territory by East Coast media moguls, this, the most populous and the most popular state, this is the U.S.A. in future tense, right now.

And what's bottomline different about those of us who live here is our regular expectation of apocalypse: The premise—our daily guideline—for making love or dressing for dinner is terminal surprise: an indiscriminate, inscrutable, and sudden doom.

Nobody doubts this terrifying promise of impending unimaginable disaster. But no one knows exactly when that emergency will overtake our fat-free, non-smoking, fitness-fixated, spiritualist, contentiously enlightened, roller-blade/back-packing lifestyle. Nor can you find any expert ready to predict that the ending of all that we know will begin under or on the ground, whether we will die by earthquake, mudslide, fire, drought, or whitefly.

Safety from harm and life itself depend upon a roulette grid of variables beyond our control. And we accept the calamity of such an inauspicious, chosen fate with California calm: a sunny and pragmatic attitude that borrows heavily from mainstream American habits of Get Over It and A.S.A.P.

Sunday morning moved in a slow way from blue skies to coffee and lazy thoughts about so many warm and easy hours ahead of me. I stood inside the door to my back yard trying to decide whether or not to water the tomatoes and the begonias, without actually changing my position: I was in no hurry to leave the house. But something seemed strange.

And after a while I noticed a wild wind in the corner weeping-willow tree— the pale, elliptical leaves trembled and they waved and then they whipped about.

I stepped outside. The air felt heavy. I began to sweat. I was standing still. A hard accelerating wind blew gusts of heat that flushed my face. I called to my dog, Amigo, asking him to join me, but he refused to move. He held to his place, away from me. I noticed his hind legs quivering, and I thought, "Earthquake! Shit: There's going to be an earthquake!"

I looked at my watch. It was 10:45 A.M., October 20. From the street I heard yelling, and I ran around to the front. My friend Bacqui stood there, pointing to the southeast: "June! Check this out!"

I raced to his side and looked at the sky. I looked and I could not swallow and I could not say a word. Two or three miles away a huge darkening cloud was rising and darkening as it rose and darkening as it spread on the horizon and the light of the day began to falter and fail and a horrible smell filled my nostrils and I thought, "This is it: This is the way we go out."[19]

I turned away from that colossal darkening cloud and ran back to put Amigo in the house and use the phone. 911 was jammed. I called KPFA and KQED and every one of the TV stations: jammed. I tried 911, again: busy, busy, busy. I switched on the radio and the TV. It was noon, and the day was dark, and the wind was wild, and the heat kept getting worse and worse.

Nothing on the radio. Nothing on the TV. I left them on and began to call my friends. One of them said she thought there was a fire in the Berkeley hills. She said she thought she was okay. She said smoke was beginning to come in the windows. She said there were cinders on the lawn and ashes on her car. I told her to get the hell out. She said she thought she was fine and, besides, she couldn't drive because she'd strained a ligament in her right arm and was carrying her arm in a sling, plus she was home by herself and so on and so forth.

And now the TV kicked in. And now the radio came through. It was fire. It was a wall of fire. The wall of fire was 100 feet high. The wind was pushing the flames at fifty miles per hour. The fire had jumped the freeway. People were fleeing from their cars. Cars exploded. Houses exploded. TV announcers were scrambling with amateur maps and lunatic bulletins of information: If you live here, evacuate. If you live there, evacuate. Don't drive. Don't use the telephone. Close the windows. Close the doors. Stay inside. Please evacuate. These are the numbers to call for help. Please do not use the telephone. Please stay off the road. Fire trucks and ambulances are trying to reach the fire. Please stay inside your house. Please evacuate the area.

I called Berkeley's fire department. A woman answered and said she wasn't sure about the fire: where it was or where it was heading. I should call the Oakland fire department. I called. There was no answer. Friends started calling me and coming by.

One of them insisted that I take ten minutes to pack up everything essential. Ten minutes! There didn't seem to be time enough for ten minutes devoted to thinking about and doing one single thing. I started to pack, and the phone and friends arriving kept interrupting my progress. But finally I had one small bag of unpublished poems, insurance papers, passport, and medicines. And one backpack of things for my dog. And I tore out of the house to buy gallons of drinking water from the nearest supermarket and to fill up the car with gas.

At the gasoline station there was a very long line and everyone went out of his or her way to appear civil and patient and cooperative and California-calm but everyone knew that this very long line was very frightening, in itself, and I looked at the faces of the other people waiting and I wondered who among us might be dead before the end of the day and I wondered who among us would remember her face/his face, or mine.

Loaded up with gas and water I drove back to the home now crowded with friends and loud with TV and radio announcers simultaneously tracking the fire and its consequences. Horror stories superseded horror stories. There was one man who had called his wife to see if she was all right. She had told him she was fine and that he needn't come home. And now he had learned that his wife had burned to death and the house had burned to death and he kept talking to reporters and I kept wondering why.

At 4 o'clock, two friends pulled up outside the house. Packed about with their belongings, they sat there, by the curb, behind the wheel and in the passenger seat, looking dazed and not saying anything coherent. It had taken them two-and-a-half hours to drive a distance that, ordinarily, you can cover in twelve to fifteen minutes. Power generators had blown up in the hills. Traffic lights were down. You could feel the chaos in the pit of your stomach.

I left to look at the fire with my own eyes. I got as far as Ashby and College Avenue before a police barricade made me stop and park. Ahead and above this intersection you could see these flames like Klieg-lit exaggerations of the fires of hell. Gigantic blazing flames of fire lunged and shimmied and dipped and swerved and a roof fell in or a house collapsed and trees turned into torch conflagrations and the word emerging from this unbidden and unbridled horror was rather precise: *inferno*. Temperatures soared way above 100 degrees and even from a mile away you could hear the crackling incineration of yet another home or vehicle or human body.

On Berkeley street corners, a mile or less below the uncontrollable flames, five or six people congregated in T-shirts and sneakers, on bicycles or skateboards. Elderly and teenaged and everlastingly integrated to perfect "quota" proportions of white and Asian and Chicano and African-American and male and female and, everywhere, these clusters stood together, quietly, peaceably.

When I got home again I found my own house transformed: Evacuated friends had brought their sleeping bags and stacks of boxes and bags, and inside the bathroom I nearly stepped on somebody's pet rabbit, and on top of the linen closet was somebody's bird in a large clean cage, and the kitchen was cluttered with redundant supplies of fruit and vegetables and bread and juice and Diet Pepsi.

It was crowded but somber, now. The fire was not expected to subside before the middle of the next morning. Given the ferocity and the breadth of its rage, no one wanted to think about the human implications of that forecast. No one had anything much to say. The windows were shut. The doors were closed. But still you could smell the fire and still you could feel its dreadful heat.

At about 9 P.M., I went out again to see the fire, this time using my press credentials to get closer. In the darkness, it was difficult to breathe: The air felt clogged and granular. The fire looked like enormous fireplace logs aglow with memories of flame. You could watch the firelit decomposition of a tree or of a building. Black and electric orange colors flickered and flared and disappeared. You could hear nobody calling for help. There were no cries rising out of that firelit night. I wondered at the silence and at the apparent futility of a human scream for rescue or for relief from physical agony.

Within the next few days, a fabulous variety of people had materialized to run the emergency shelters or to donate food and money or to collect and deliver baby clothes and textbooks. Sometimes the volunteers outnumbered the victims.

Two days later, on campus, students talked about apocalypse. And I wondered if we are trying to live on an accursed tract of land: What have we done? I thought about the California calm and the California friendliness and how we do seem like decent, basically well-intentioned men and women and, yet, something really is not right with us.

And then some numbers began to monopolize media attention: $600,000 homes or $2 million homes, and somehow the fact that half of the households lost to the fire had incomes of less than $35,000 never made it to the headlines and a kind of class war battled against the simpler, gentle instincts of most people. And sometimes some of the shelters attempted to separate the homeless from the (newly) homeless. And the old homeless might be given a can of Coca-Cola and told to beat it while the newly homeless received free counseling and hot food and fresh salad stuffs and treatment for shock and soap and showers and unlimited use of a phone. And the uncontrollable chaos of tragedy brought you to tears, unexpected and everywhere.

Everyone alive was a survivor of "The Great East Bay Firestorm" that killed twenty-five people, burned out more than 3,500 homes, left more than 6,000 people homeless, and forever altered the way any one of us would look at the sky and at each other.

The fire ravaged more than three square miles of roadway, hillside, trees, bush, flowers, glass, iron, concrete, wood, and flesh and bone, leaving behind a rubble and ash of twisted, pulverized, melted down, charred, dismembered, and unrecognizable, oozing, crusted landscape. It was the worst wildfire in U.S. history.

And I thought about the Indians to whom this land belongs, this terrifying and beautiful land of California. And I thought about the Mexicans to whom this land belongs. And I thought maybe we are cursed because, mostly, I do not remember them, the dead to whom the earth belongs. And what would it mean to remember them?

The genocidal conquest of the Indians and the Mexicans: That happened so long ago. Like slavery: That happened so long ago. Like the Holocaust: That happened so long ago. Like the bombing of Baghdad: That happened so long ago. Like the Great East Bay Firestorm: That happened so long ago.

We get over it. We forget as soon as we can. We move right along. And we do not remember because we do not love the Indians. We not love the Mexicans. We do not love the Africans. We do not love the Jews. We do not love ourselves. We do not know anything about true love and so we kill or we die but we do not suffer from the loss of human life.

And without the connection of love, there is no reason for grief. And without grief we will not remember and so we will not understand the human meaning of "gone," and we will not enter that human community of bereavement.

And because, most of the time, we strive to live rational, passionless lives, we succumb to the easy appeal of violence instead, and we may even crave that wretched extremity of experience. But violence is not the same as love. Violence will force you to forget or forfeit your sanity. Only love will let you grieve and, therefore, remember.

The Great East Bay Firestorm is no longer news. Its victims include wealthy and working poor and middle income and white and black and Asian-American men, women, and children. They will need our help for at least the next ten years. Please do not forget.

Toward a Manifest New Destiny

February 1992

Three of the four Noble Truths articulated by Buddha, upon his enlightenment, in his first sermon:

"The First Noble Truth is that all beings are subject to suffering. No one escapes...suffering is universal.

"The Second Noble Truth is that the cause of suffering is ignorance. And ignorance of oneself is the greatest ignorance.

"The Third Noble Truth is that ignorance, the cause of suffering, can be overcome."

c. 428 B.C.

"Manifest Destiny"

First used in the U.S. Congress on January 3, 1846, by Representative Robert C. Winthrop of Massachusetts, who spoke on the subject of "the right or our manifest destiny to spread over this whole continent."

Thirty years ago, white publications loved to headline stories about my neighborhood, my family, and me, with three words: "The Negro Problem."

I remember rapid adjustment of my mind from a state of plain puzzlement to anger. I'd be passing by a subway newsstand and there I'd see it, that incendiary formulation that implied that we, "Negroes," had created our own difficulties and, further, that we, "Negroes," were the only ones who could, or should, give a damn. So many Americans succumbed to that game!

Again and again, slick magazines and daily papers blamed the victim and erased, or exculpated, the perpetrators of the crime. This was all the more remarkable as the context was one of wild white violence, which meant that Negro "difficulties" might well include catching a bullet in the brain if your local sheriff discovered you trying to register to vote.

What finally blew away these print media fabrications—what finally replaced them with factual knowledge leading to a national and worldwide uproar that, in turn, led to the Civil Rights Act of 1960 and other pivotal laws—was the camera: Regardless of the caption beneath the photograph, regardless of the text read by the (white) voice-over on film, visual reports of our history carried the day. You could not watch a white man screaming as he overturned, set afire, and burned up a Greyhound bus and then still be confused about who, exactly, had done what, where, and when.

I wonder what it will take to blow away an equally fictitious, an equally venomous print-media construction of our time: the so-called Politically Correct or PC Controversy.

I would like to assume that an eyeball basis for analysis and opinion could decide things. And perhaps, at the last, that will happen. But I cannot forget going on a lunch date, once, with Victor Navasky, editor of *The Nation*.

We met at his office above the congestion of 14th Street in Manhattan. As we walked to the restaurant of his choice, a few blocks away, we moved among and around crowds of black and Puerto Rican as well as white New Yorkers. I was asking Victor how come *The Nation* had never hired a single black columnist. He seemed exasperated by my inquiry. He could not comprehend how anything calling itself *The Nation* but staffed entirely by white men could seem peculiar, if not offensive, to anyone. He could not imagine that an American who was different from himself in serious, immutable ways—he could not imagine that such an American writer might bring to *The Nation* something important: information and perspectives that he and his white associates could not otherwise encounter or possess.

"Are you saying," he asked in an avuncular tone, "are you implying that there is A Black Point of View?"

I answered him—"Yes"—and I attempted to explain that there is an absolute difference between his white male history and my own. I argued that such a chasmic separation in experience must produce significant divergences of viewpoint, expectations, and the like.

But Victor was not interested. Comfortably seated at his regular table inside his restaurant of choice, he knew something I was only beginning to understand: There is difference, and there is power. And who holds the power shall decide the meaning of difference. Victor held the power, and he had decided that ideas and opinions and feelings that belong to anybody markedly different from himself are ideas and convictions that do not count.

Victor embodies a one-man definition—a big part, the American media part—of the problem of knowledge in the United States. Too much of what we know or don't know depends upon unaccountable individual values and the sometimes whimsical happenstance of one man's or one powerful family's or one corporate CEO's political biography. In the case of Navasky, here was a white man blind and deaf except to a mirror universe of his kin and kind. And what could I do about it?

I have worked here, inside this country, and I have kept my eyes open, everlastingly. What I see today does not support a media-concocted controversy where my life or the lives of African-Americans, Native-Americans, Chicano-Americans, Latin-Americans, and Asian-Americans amount to arguable fringe or freak components of some theoretical netherland. We have become the many peoples of this nation—nothing less than that. I do not accept that we, American peoples of color, signify anything optional or dubious or marginal or exotic or anything in any way less valuable, less necessary, less sacred than white America.

I do not perceive current issues of public education as issues of politically correct or incorrect curriculum. In a straight line back to James Baldwin who, twenty-eight years ago, begged us, blackfolks, to rescue ourselves by wrestling white people out of the madness of their megalomania and delusion, I see every root argument about public education turning upon definitions of sanity and insanity. Shall we submit to ceaseless lies, fantastic misinformation, and fantastic omissions? Shall we agree to the erasure of our beleaguered, heterogeneous truth? Shall we embrace traditions of insanity and lose ourselves and the whole real world?

Or shall we become "politically correct" as fast as we can and defend and engage the multifoliate, overwhelming, and ultimately inescapable actual life that our myriad and disparate histories imply?

In America, in a democracy, who shall the people know if not our many selves? What shall we aim to learn about the universe if not the entire, complicated truth of it, to the best of our always limited abilities? What does public education in a democratic state require if not the rational enlightenment of as many of the people as possible? But how can you claim to enlighten a child and then tell him that the language of his mother is illegal?

Barco de Refugiados
by Lorna Dee Cervantes

Mamá me crío sin lenguaje.
Soy huérfano de mi nombre español.
Las palabras son extrañas,
tartamundeando en mi lengua.
Mis ojos ven el espejo, mi reflejo:
piel de bronce, cabello negro.

Siento que soy un cautivo
a bordo de un barco de refugiados.

El barco que nunca atraca.
El barco que nunca atraca.

Refugee Ship

Mama raised me without language.
I'm orphaned from my Spanish name.
The words are foreign, stumbling
on my tongue. I see in the mirror
my reflection: bronzed skin, black hair.

I feel I am a captive
aboard the refugee ship.
The ship that will never dock.
El barco que nunca atraca.

(Reprinted by permission of Lorna Dee Cervantes).

White warriors for the preservation of the past and for a mythical status quo, white warriors for the insane, invoke supposedly scary scenarios in which Platonic Dialogues disappear from the core of academic studies and students instead examine the teachings of Buddha or the political writings of Frederick Douglass. I look at these mainly conjectural outbursts and I say to myself, "What's all the fuss about?"

The favorite, last-resort accusation of these white warriors for the insane, for the traditional white-male-dominated canon of required readings in American higher education, is this: That the barbarian leadership of us, the barbarian hordes, basically aims to subvert and challenge and eliminate the intellectual icons of Western civilization. Commonly, this accusation produces a good deal of apologetic shuffling on the part of the alleged barbarians, the so-called Politically Correct. Well, I am one barbarian who will not apologize. You bet that's one of my basic aims! Why would anyone suppose that I or any Native-American or any Asian-American would willingly worship at the altar of traditional white Western iconography?

The white man killed my father
Because my father was proud
The white man raped my mother
Because my mother was beautiful
The white man wore out my brother

in the hot sun
of the roads
Because my brother was strong
Then the white man came to me
His hands red with blood
Spat his contempt into my black face
Out of his tyrant's voice:
"Hey boy, a basin, a towel, water."
    -David Diop, "Le temps du martyre."

As the contradiction among the features
creates the harmony of the face
we proclaim the oneness of the suffering
and the revolt
of all the peoples on all the face
    of the earth
and we mix the mortar of the age
    of brotherhood
out of the dust of idols.
    -Jacques Roumain, "Bois-D'Ebene."

(The Diop and Roumain verses are reprinted from Frantz Fanon's *Black Skin, White Masks*, by permission of Grove Press.)

The gods of the white Western world, from Jahweh ("Vengeance is mine, saith the Lord") to Jesus ("Blessed are the meek") to Dante to Nietzsche to Milton to T.S. Eliot to Wallace Stevens: What have they done for me? Show me one life saved by any of these gods! Show me one colored life!

As you descend deeper and deeper into media hysteria about alleged or impending "violations of the canon" and "rape of the foundations of Western civilization," the smell of brain rot and unmitigated white supremacist ideology becomes unmistakable.

Suppose, for example, suppose I skipped English literature and Shakespeare altogether and instead I studied Chinese: Chinese history and Chinese literature. A quarter of the human beings on the planet are Chinese. And I know next to nothing about them. I do not really understand why my friend who was born in the Year of the Dragon cannot marry her beloved who was born in the Year of the Dog. But I can recite to you a score of beautiful lines from Elizabethan sonnets. And I do not altogether fault what I know, but I do not view my ignorance as acceptable. And if I had to choose between those sonnets and Chinese history, and if I chose Chinese history, who could criticize me, and on what grounds?

It depends, of course, on the purpose of education. Uncontested, until now, the purpose of American schooling has been to maintain the powerful in power. And so, traditional materials for the American classroom have presented every war, every battle, every dispute, every icon of knowledge required by "higher" education in the image of the powerful so as to serve the interests of the powerful who need the rest of us to believe they are really nice guys who take off their boots before they take over your house and your land.

Reinforcing the skewed effects of traditional materials is the homogeneous identity of teachers and faculty who persist, increasingly out of sync, with the heterogeneous student bodies whose intellectual development they must oversee. For example, in California public schools, teachers remain 82 per cent white while so-called minority students occupy 54 per cent of classroom seats. Such a dramatic disjuncture does not bode well for imperative curricular change that will serve the cultural and historical needs of these new (young) Americans.

Supreme Court Justice Clarence Thomas—whose four law clerks are, every one of them, white men, and whose accomplishments as former head of the Equal Employment Opportunity Commission do not cleanly distinguish him from David Duke—wonderfully illustrates the results of traditional "higher" American education. So do those Japanese-Americans who cannot proclaim, too fervently or too frequently, how lamentable was the Japanese bombing of Pearl Harbor.

If you're not white, if you're not an American white man, and you travel through the traditional twistings and distortions of the white Western canon, you stand an excellent chance of ending up *nuts*: Estranged if not opposed to yourself and your heritage and, furthermore, probably unaware of your estrangement, your well-educated self-hatred.

The last seven days leading to the fiftieth anniversary of Pearl Harbor were particularly difficult. At moments, I felt overwhelmed as the coast-to-coast unanimity of know-nothing, racist blatherings about December 7, 1941, grew louder and ever more obviously self-righteous and unbalanced by even a respectable modicum of trustworthy scholarship or unbiased inquiry into the Japanese side of the story.

Of course, any concern to secure the Japanese side of the story would represent a concern that is Politically Correct. It would mean supposing that the Japanese people are not some subspecies of the human race, alias homo Americo, or whatever. It would mean supposing that the Japanese government did not lapse into a psychotic military fit that fateful morning but that, in fact, the Japanese government had its reasons for attacking that rather far-flung U.S. naval base, Pearl Harbor.

And I have been nauseated by the unmitigated, ignorant, hate-mongering sanctimony of American leaders these past seven days. Is there, after all, another country as militaristic, as predatory, as imperial, as deadly as our own? Does the average American even have the glimmer of an adequate, sane education to respond to that question?

The lunacy of racist America, the insanity of Politically Incorrect education in racist America means that it's okay to advertise the atomic bombing of Hiroshima as "revenge" for the Japanese bombing of Pearl Harbor.

Asian peoples are the largest group of human beings on the planet. This kind of pathological, complacent Asian-bashing is truly not all right: not morally or intellectually or, in any wise, defensible, sane behavior. And when I must wallow in this latest display of America's latest racist target—a target jeopardizing most of the human beings on the planet—then, yes, I get pretty damned upset. Here is a quote from the front page of *USA Today*, December 6, 1991:

"By 1941, Japan's campaign of Asian conquest was ten years old. Over Western protests the Japanese war machine had occupied Manchuria and invaded China. After the occupation of French Indochina, the United States, Britain, and the Netherlands imposed a trade embargo, cutting Japan's oil supplies by 90 per cent. Japan quickly turned its attention to expropriating oil fields in the Dutch East Indies. To prevent U.S. interference, Tokyo mounted a bold plan to wipe out the U.S. fleet at Pearl Harbor, Hawaii, on December 7, 1941."

Okay. "By 1941, Japan's campaign of Asian conquest was ten year old." By 1941, how old was America's and England's and the Netherlands' campaign of Asian conquest? And what in the hell are you talking about when you say "French Indochina" and the "Dutch East Indies"?

Here is a poem that no English major in the U.S.A. will ever be required to read: It was written by the Japanese-Canadian poet and novelist Joy Kogawas, and it's entitled "Hiroshima Exit."

> In round round rooms of our wanderings
> Victims and victimizers in circular flight
> Fast pursuing fast
> Warning leaflets still drip down
> On soil heavy with flames,
> Black rain, footsteps, witnessing—
>
> The Atomic Bomb Memorial Building:
> A curiosity shop filled with

Remnants of clothing, radiation sickness,
Fleshless faces, tourists muttering
"Well, they started it."
Words jingle down
"They didn't think about us
        in Pearl Harbor."
They? Us?
I tiptoe around the curiosity shop
Seeking my target
Precision becomes essential
Quick. Quick. Before he's out of range.
Spell the name
American?
Hiroshima?

Air raid warnings wail bleakly
Hiroshima
Morning.
I step outside
And close softly the door
Believing, believing
That outside this store
Is another door

(Reprinted, with the permission of Greenfield Review Press, from *Breaking Silence: An Anthology of Contemporary Asian-American Poets*, edited by Joseph Bruchac.)

The annual American commemoration of Pearl Harbor offers as hateful a case history of racist miseducation according to the canon as any: Is there any other occasion on which the United States catapults into national acrobatics about having been caught off guard, caught by an enemy first strike?

If December 7, 1941, is "A Day of Infamy," what should we call August 6, 1945?

Why is the Japanese attack on Pearl Harbor so particularly galling and humiliating as to merit racist designation as a "Black Day" in American history?

Why do we remember Pearl Harbor and not V-J day? Why do we forget February 19, 1942, *that* Day of Infamy, when Franklin Roosevelt signed Executive Order 9066 whereby 100,000 innocent Japanese and Japanese-Americans were sentenced to American concentration camps? What is the difference between A Sneak Attack or A Terrorist Attack and, on the other hand, A Surprise Attack, A Brilliant Military Maneuver, A Pre-emptive Strike, or A Massive Allied Air Assault?

Is there a difference between the U.S. military base of Pearl Harbor and the Japanese civilian city of Hiroshima?

Is there any difference between a wartime buddy of George Bush—a buddy flying a naval attack plane on a wartime mission against Japan—and 130,000 Japanese men, women, and children, civilians living in the civilian city of Hiroshima, where they were mass murdered, mass burned to death or deformed into a living death within five minutes of the United States' dropping the "Unthinkable Weapon," the atom bomb? Is there any difference?

What was the difference between official U.S. treatment accorded to German-Americans, Italian-Americans, and Japanese-Americans during World War II?

What's the difference between a German, an Italian, and somebody Japanese? Why were Germans and German-Americans and Italians and Italian-Americans *not* rounded up and sent to American concentration camps in World War II? Why were only those Japanese-Americans living on the West Coast sent to concentration camps?

Did you ever learn/did your teachers ever tell you that a higher percentage of Americans of Japanese ancestry ended up serving in the U.S. Army during World War II *than any other racial group?*

Did you know that until 1943 Federal law prohibited foreign-born Chinese from becoming American citizens? Did you know that until 1952 Federal law prohibited foreign-born Japanese from becoming Americans?

Did you know that, having already segregated Chinese and Korean children, the San Francisco School Board in 1907 voted to segregate the total of the *100* Japanese children living there?

Is it possible that the Japanese government copped an attitude, at any point, toward the racist American policies and laws imposed upon Japanese people trying to live and work hard in the United States?

Question: Why am I always talking about racism, anyway?

Did you know that the Naturalization Act of 1790 decreed that only white people could become naturalized citizens of the United States?

Did you know that the Naturalization Act of 1790 fused all peoples of color into the damned and the despised and the legally unprotected American "underclass" now clamoring to overthrow The Canon that doesn't ever mention Hiroshima while it most certainly requires you to read Matthew Arnold, the Nineteenth Century poet, essayist, and arrogant jerk who pretty much invented White Poetry—or the notion of touchstones of Great Poetry—all of the touchstones being, as it happens, white male poets: Dante, Goethe, Pound, Eliot, Stevens, Heaney.

Because most well-educated Americans would have to answer, "I don't know" or "I didn't know" in response to that foregoing batch of test questions, a virulent Oreo phenomenon like Clarence Thomas becomes a probability rather than a shock.

And, on another level, Japan-bashing/Asian-bashing continues to flourish and intensify, even among other despised American groups who should know better.

How can anybody get past the ignorance that the American media and the academic canon guarantee? It's not easy. A friend of mine, the preeminent scholar of Asian-American history, Ron Takaki, was recently told by Howard Goldberg of *The New York Times* that *The New York Times* was feeling "frankly over-Japanned." Moreover, Goldberg summarily dismissed Takaki as "dead wrong" because Takaki had dared to disagree with Goldberg about Pearl Harbor. Takaki had argued that there is both American and Japanese responsibility for that attack, and for the commencement of the Pacific war. Accordingly, Goldberg characterized Takaki's op-ed piece as "revisionist history" and, therefore, decided not to allow Takaki to appear on *The New York Times* op-ed page.

It's not easy. But most Americans are not even distant relatives of the nice guys who run the country. And so there's not a lot of emotional blur to our perceptions. We've had to see them as clearly as the hunted need to watch the ones who hunt them down. Even without the overdue and radical reform of American education that sanity and democracy demand, some of us have learned more than we ever wanted to know about those nice guys.

Some of us sit in front of a young man, a member of the Creek nation, and we hear his voice break and we feel his hands trembling and we avoid staring at the tears that pour from his eyes as he tells us about the annihilation of his ancestors, about the bashing of babies' heads against trees, and about the alternate, nearly extinct worldview that his forefathers and foremothers embraced. Between convulsions of grief, he speaks about the loss of earlier, spirit relations between his hungering people and the foods of the Earth.

Some of us must devise and improvise a million and one ways to convince young African-American and Chicana women that white skin and yellow hair and blue eyes and thin thighs are not imperative attributes of beauty and loveliness.

Some of us must reassure a student born and raised in Hong Kong that we do not ask her to speak aloud in order to ridicule her "English" but in order to benefit from the wisdom of her intelligence.

Some of us search for avenues or for the invention of avenues for African-American boys to become men among men beyond and without surrendering to that racist offering of a kill-or-be-killed destiny.

And we move among the peoples of this nation on an eyeball basis. We do not deny the heterogeneity that surrounds our bodies and our minds. We do not suppress the variegated sounds of multiple languages spoken by so many truly different Americans all in one place, hoping for love.

Over the last three semesters, I've been teaching a series of experimental poetry classes at the University of California-Berkeley. As of last spring the enthusiastic, diverse, campus-wide student response led me to offer what I call Poetry for the People.[20] Centered on student writings, this course publishes student poetry and presents these new poets in public readings of their work.

The ethnic, racial, intellectual, and sexual diversity of these students has forced me to attempt to devise a syllabus that is, for me, unprecedented, and even unwieldy, in its range. And for the first time I've had to ask for help from a diverse number of student teacher poets as well as other faculty, in order to handle the course materials responsibly.

The idea behind Poetry for the People is that every man or woman can be enabled to use language with the precision and the memorable impact that poetry requires. In this way, the writing and publishing and public presentation of poetry becomes a process of empowerment for students as well as a catalyst for coalition politics of a practical and spontaneous nature.

Student readings have been attended by standing-room-only crowds, without exception. Required books for the course include Native American, Chicana/Chicano, white poetry, African-American poetry, women's poetry, Asian-American poetry.

And so I am trying to become Politically Correct. I am just one among an expanding hard-core number of American educators who believe that an American culture requirement, for instance, is not a laughable or subversive or anti-intellectual proposal: On the contrary! We are teachers running as fast as we can to catch up with the new Americans we are paid to educate.

In 1987, the Hudson Institute released a report entitled "Workfare 2000." According to the *San Francisco Chronicle*, "the report stunned American business leaders with its projection that in the remaining years of this century, *only 15 per cent of the entrants into the workforce would be white males.*" (My italics.)

That's nationwide.

By the year 2010, California's population will nearly double, and this will be the racial breakdown: overall, 61 per cent people of color; 39 per cent non-Hispanic white; 38 per cent Hispanic; 16 per cent Asian; 7 per cent black.

From that total population, we will have to publicly educate nearly twice as many students as the total number in 1991. What will we teach these new Americans? How will we seek to justify every lecture, every homework assignment?

In 1992—right now—this is the composition of the freshman class at UC-Berkeley, reputedly the best public university in the United States: 30 per cent white; 31.5 per cent Asian; 20.5 per cent Hispanic; 7.5 per cent black; i.e., 59.5 per cent people of color.

And so, walking across this American campus, you will see, as I have seen, on an eyeball basis, that this America of ours is changing faster than fast-although the faculty at Berkeley remains 89 per cent white, which represents only a 2 per cent decrease of white faculty members during the last ten years.

The current distribution and identity of power will have to change, as well, or we will have to laugh the word *democracy* out of our consciousness forever.

And that is the political crisis that each of us personifies, one way or the other:

Since the demographics of our nation state do not even forecast English as the usual first language of most of our future children, what is the meaning of "English Only" legislation, for example, in the state of California?

What does that reveal besides the politics of culture?

And who shall decide what these many peoples of America shall know or not know?

And what does that question underscore besides the political nature of knowledge?

And what shall be the international identity and what shall be the national identity of these United States when a white majority no longer exists inside our boundaries even as a white majority has never existed beyond these blood-and-gore-begotten boundaries of our nation state?

I do not agree that I am a statistical component of some alarming controversy. The indisputable value of each and every one of our lives is not debatable, is *not* politically correct or incorrect.

In this crisis of American power, in this conflict between power and human life, *there can be no canon, there can be no single text for the education of our multicultural, multilingual, multiracial population!*

Some thirty years ago, in his "Letter to My Nephew," James Baldwin wrote the following:

"Know whence you came. If you know whence you came, there is really no limit to where you can go. The details and symbols of our life have been deliberately constructed to make you believe what white people say about you. Please try to remember that what they believe, as well as what they do and cause you to endure, does not testify to your inferiority but to their inferiority and fear."

And, in that same letter, he wrote: "If the word *integration* means anything, this is what it means: That we, with love, shall force our brothers to see themselves as they are, to cease fleeing from reality and begin to change it."

And so I propose that we undertake to make of the teachings of public education in America a politically correct, a verifiably sane basis for our multicultural, multiracial, and two-gendered lives on this infinitely multifaceted, multilingual planet. I propose that we undertake this awesome work with imperturbable pride and, yes, fanatical zeal.

It seems to me that this Year of the Ram, this moment or ours, is just an obvious, excellent moment to declare for Americans, and for ourselves, a Manifest New Destiny: a destiny that will extricate all of us from the sickness of egomania and ignorance, a destiny that will cherish and delight in the differences among us, a destiny that will depend upon empowerment of the many and merciful protection of the young and the weak, a destiny that will carry us beyond an eyeball basis of knowledge into an educated, collective vision of a really democratic, a really humane, a really really good time together.

Valentine's Day, 1992

March 1992

It's a little bit hard to focus on lace and flowers in the wake of Clarence Thomas and George Bush. I mean you feel a little bit stupid choosing mellow music, lighting candles, and planning a long hot bubbly bath with somebody wonderful when the head nitwit in charge of the whole show says he was offended by "the filth" and "the indecency" of the televised trials of Patricia Bowman and Senator Kennedy's nephew.

I am offended by the filth and the indecency of rape. It's not television that bothers me: It's the brutality of trial proceedings based on the assumption that women regularly lie about rape because we love all the attention we get when everybody examines our underwear/our diaries/the length of our skirt/the height of our heels/our attitudes toward sex. For example: Is it or is it not true that you have been known to want and to enjoy sex with somebody you were meeting for the first time (who was, of course, also meeting you for the first time and who also wanted and who also enjoyed sex with you on that same basis)?

Anyway, thanks to Clarence and thanks to George, I am unequivocal, this year, about what (not who) I want for Valentine's Day: I want power! I want truly enormous political power: I want power proportionate to the needs and proportionate to the numbers of women in these United States. And any leader, any candidate, any platform, any feminist agenda, any women's studies' curriculum that fails to nail itself to the task of empowerment of women contributes to the enemy environment in which we barely stay alive.

For instance, here at the University of California-Berkeley, there's a worsening income disparity between men and women on senior-rank faculty levels, and not even 10 per cent of the faculty is female. Nationwide, the gender disparity in income holds firm against us. In the U.S. Senate and the U.S. House of Representatives, you will find not even 10 per cent female representation.

And then there's the huge number of families headed by women who, because they are women and because day care is a "woman's issue," must battle against poverty with less and less Federal and state aid. (In California, Governor Wilson proposes as much as a 25 per cent reduction of benefits for already desperate AFDC households.)

And everywhere in America, the number of children subjected to poverty rose from 16 per cent to 20.1 per cent during the last decade.

And there's the growing assault upon our right to choose whether we will have the children our Government refuses to shelter and feed.

And every year the violence of the war against women becomes more harrowing and the statistics become less abstract and the songs rappin' out hatred of women advance to a popular big beat.

And in 1991 the demand for emergency food increased 100 per cent in Boston and 70 per cent in Philadelphia.

And every single year 175,000 American women learn they have breast cancer. This year, alone, 45,000 American women will die of breast cancer. And yet the National Cancer Institute allocates only $90 million for research into this tragedy.

In Brazil, one woman in nine is an AIDS victim.

In Africa, the number of orphans created by AIDS will increase, during the next eight years, to ten to fifteen million, while the number of infants born with the HIV infection will rise from the current 750,000 to four million.

How many women dead from AIDS do these terrible facts imply? This is the ground on which we stand. It's political ground. And if we do not think, bottomline, David Duke—if we do not mobilize to stand our ground against David Duke and his closet competitors in the White House and in the state capitols across the country—then we will not only lose the ground under our feet: We will be buried there.

But let me close with a more traditional Valentine salutation: This is my Valentine to Tom Holt, history professor at the University of Chicago. In October 1991, Holt sent out a letter asking for 1,000 black men to join with him and donate $26.50 each to defray half the cost of a full-page New York Times ad composed by "African-American Women in Defense of Ourselves"—against the public humiliation of Anita Hill and the Supreme Court seating of Clarence Thomas.[21] This historic coming together of black women and black men was conceived and organized by Barbara Ransby, Ph.D candidate, University of Michigan, Professor Elsa Barkley Brown, University of Michigan, and Professor Deborah King of Dartmouth College. I send my Valentine greetings to these three women, as well.

I take heart from this altogether happy precedent: We can politicize our strength. Yes! We can learn how to love each other enough to seize and determine the everyday/everynight politics of our beleaguered, wistful lives.

Requiem for the Champ

April 1992

Mike Tyson comes from Brooklyn. And so do I. He grew up about a twenty-minute bus ride from my house. I always thought his neighborhood looked like a war zone. It reminded me of Berlin—immediately after World War II. I had never seen Berlin except for black-and-white photos in *Life* magazine, but that was bad enough: rubble, barren, blasted. Everywhere you turned, your eyes recoiled from the jagged edges of an office building or a cathedral, shattered, or the tops of apartment houses torn off, and nothing alive even intimated, anywhere. I used to think, "This is what it means to fight and really win or really lose. War means you hurt somebody, or something, until there's nothing soft or sensible left."

For sure I never had a boyfriend who came out of Mike Tyson's territory. Yes, I enjoyed my share of tough guys and gang members who walked and talked and fought and loved in quintessential Brooklyn ways: cool, tough, and deadly serious. But there was a code as rigid and as romantic as anything that ever made the pages of traditional English literature.

A guy would beat up another guy or, if appropriate, he'd kill him. But a guy talked different to a girl. A guy made other guys clean up their language around "his girl." A guy brought ribbons and candies and earrings and tulips to a girl. He took care of her. He walked her home. And if he got serious about that girl, and even if she was only twelve years old, then she became his "lady." And woe betide any other guy stupid enough to disrespect that particular young black female.

But none of the boys—none of the young men, none of the young black male inhabitants of my universe and my heart—ever came from Mike Tyson's streets or avenues. We didn't live someplace fancy or middle-class, but at least there were tencent gardens, front and back, and coin laundromats, and grocery stores, and soda parlors, and barber shops, and holy-roller churchfronts, and chicken shacks, and dry cleaners, and bars and grills, and a takeout Chinese restaurant, and all of that kind of usable detail that does not survive a war. That kind of seasonal green turf and daily-life-supporting pattern of establishments to meet your needs did not exist inside the gelid urban cemetery where Mike Tyson learned what he thought he needed to know.

I remember when the City of New York decided to construct a senior housing project there, in the childhood world of former heavyweight boxing champion Mike Tyson. I remember wondering, "Where in the hell will those old people have to go in order to find food? And how will they get there?"

I'm talking god-forsaken. And much of living in Brooklyn was like that. But then it might rain or it might snow and, for example, I could look at the rain forcing forsythia into bloom or watch how snow-flakes can tease bare tree limbs into temporary blossoms of snow dissolving into diadems of sunlight.

And what did Mike Tyson ever see besides brick walls and garbage in the gutter and disintegrating concrete steps and boarded-up windows and broken car parts blocking the sidewalk and men, bitter, with their hands in their pockets, and women, bitter, with their heads down and their eyes almost closed?

In his neighborhood, where could you buy ribbons for a girl, or tulips?

Mike Tyson comes from Brooklyn. And so do I.

In the big picture of America, I never had much going for me. And he had less.

I only learned, last year, that I can stop whatever violence starts with me. I only learned, last year, that love is infinitely more interesting, and more exciting, and more powerful, than really winning or really losing a fight. I only learned, last year, that all war leads to death and that all love leads you away from death.

I am more than twice Mike Tyson's age. And I'm not stupid. Or slow. But I'm black. And I come from Brooklyn. And I grew up fighting. And I grew up and I got out of Brooklyn because I got pretty good at fighting. And winning. Or else, intimidating my would-be adversaries with my fists, my feet, and my mouth.

I never wanted to fight. I never wanted anybody to hit me. And I never wanted to hit anybody. But the bell would ring at the end of another dumb day in school and I'd head out with dread and a nervous sweat because I knew some jackass more or less my age and more or less my height would be waiting for me because she or he had nothing better to do than to wait for me and hope to kick my butt or tear up my books or break my pencils or pull hair out of my head.

This is the meaning of poverty: When you have nothing better to do than to hate somebody who, just exactly like yourself, has nothing better to do than to pick on you instead of trying to figure out how come there's nothing better to do: How come there's no gym, no swimming pool, no dirt track, no soccer field, no ice-skating rink, no bike, no bike path, no tennis courts, no language-arts workshop, no computer-science center, no band practice, no choir rehearsal, no music lessons, no basketball or baseball team? How come neither one of you has his or her own room in a house where you can hang out and dance and make out or get on the telephone or eat and drink up everything in the kitchen that can move? How come nobody on your block and nobody in your class has any of these things?

I'm black. Mike Tyson is black. And neither one of us was ever supposed to win anything more than a fight between the two of us.

And if you check out the mass media material on "us," and if you check out the emergency-room reports on "us," you might well believe we're losing the fight to be more than our enemies have decreed. Our enemies would deprive us of everything except each other: Hungry and furious and drug-addicted and rejected and ever convinced we can never be beautiful or right or true or different from the beggarly monsters our enemies envision and insist upon. How should we then stand, black man and black woman, face to face?

Way back when I was born, Richard Wright had just published *Native Son* and, thereby, introduced white America to the monstrous product of its racist hatred. Richard Wright's Bigger Thomas did what he thought he had to do: He hideously murdered a white woman and he viciously murdered his black girlfriend in what he conceived as self-defense. He did not perceive any options to these psychopathic, horrifying deeds. I do not believe he, Bigger Thomas, had any other choices open to him. He was meant to die like the rat he, Bigger Thomas, cornered, and smashed to death, in his mother's beggarly clean space.

I never thought Bigger Thomas was okay. I never thought he should skate back into my, or anyone's community. But I did and I do think he is my brother. The choices available to us dehumanize. And any single one of us, black in this white country, we may be defeated, we may become dehumanized, by the monstrous hatred arrayed against us and our needy dreams.

Poverty does not beatify. Poverty does not teach generosity or allow for sucker attributes of tenderness and restraint. In white America, hatred of blackfolks has imposed 360 degrees of poverty upon us.

And so I write this requiem for Mike Tyson: international celebrity, millionaire, former heavyweight boxing champion of the world, a big-time winner, a big-time loser, an African-American male in his twenties and, now, a convicted rapist.

Do I believe he is guilty of rape?

Yes I do.

And what would I propose as appropriate punishment?

Whatever will force him to fear the justice of exact retribution, and whatever will force him, for the rest of his damned life, to regret and to detest the fact that he defiled, he subjugated, and he wounded, somebody helpless to his power.

And do I therefore rejoice in the jury's finding?

I do not.

Well, would I like to see Mike Tyson a free man again?

He was never free.

And I do not excuse or condone or forget or forgive the crime of his violation of the young black woman he raped!

But did anybody ever tell Mike Tyson that you talk different to a girl? Where would he learn that?

Would he learn that from U.S. Senator Ted Kennedy?

Or from hotshot/scot-free movie director Roman Polanski?

Or from rap recording star Ice Cube?

Or from Ronald Reagan and the Grenada escapade?

Or from George Bush in Panama?

Or from George Bush and Colin Powell in the Persian Gulf?

Or from the military hero flyboys who returned from bombing the shit out of civilian cities in Iraq and then said, laughing and proud, on international TV: "All I need, now, is a woman"?

Or from the hundreds of thousands of American football fans?

Or from the millions of Americans who would, if they could, pay surrealistic amounts of money just to witness, up close, somebody like Mike Tyson beat the brains out of somebody else?

And which university could teach Mike Tyson about the difference between violence and love? Is there any citadel of higher education in the country that does not pay its football coach at least three times as much as its chancellor and six times as much as its professors and ten times as much as its social and psychological counselors?

In this America where Mike Tyson and I live together and bitterly, bitterly, apart, I say he became what he felt. He felt the stigmata of a prior hatred and intentional poverty. He was given the choice of violence or violence: The violence of defeat or the violence of victory.

Who would pay him what to rehabilitate inner-city housing or to refurbish a bridge?

Who would pay him what to study the facts of our collective history?

Who would pay him what to plant and nurture the trees of a forest?

And who will write and who will play the songs that tell a guy like Mike Tyson how to talk to a girl?

What was America willing to love about Mike Tyson? Or any black man? Or any man's man?

Tyson's neighborhood and my own have become the same no-win battle-ground. And he has fallen there. And I do not rejoice. I do not.

The Light of the Fire

June 1992

Fire everywhere! Across the miasma of Los Angeles, the flames lift into the night and they proliferate. They rise, explosive, from my heart.

Is there horror? Is there heat unbearable? And is there light where, otherwise, we could not see ourselves? Is there an unexpected, unpredictable colossal energy alive and burning, uncontrolled, throughout America?

Behold my heart of darkness as it quickens now with rage! Behold the hundred—no, a thousand—young black men whose names you never knew/whose neighborhoods you squeezed into a place of helpless desolation/whose music you despised/whose backwards baseball caps and baggy jeans you sneered at/whose mothers you denied assistance/whose fathers you inducted into the Army or you broke to alleyways where, crumbling at the marrow of their spine, they aged in bitterness.

Behold them now: revengeful, furious, defiant, and, for hours on end, at least, apparently invincible: They just keep moving, and the fires burn. And white kids and Chicanos and Chicanas join them, yes! And Asian-American teenagers join them, yes! There they stand or run, beside and among these young black men who will not bow down. They will not say, "OK. I am nobody. I have nothing. And you hate me and that's fine! Where should I sign, now, for service to my country? Show me how to worship at the shrine of law and order."

What happened? How come we finally woke up? Why would a jury's verdict of "Not Guilty"[22] galvanize and rescue so many from protracted, profound passivity, suicidal torpor, and fratricidal craziness? How come all of the steady, punitive, self-righteous, and official attacks on poor people didn't get us going?

How come Presidential vetoes of civil-rights legislation and the unspeakable onslaught of Clarence Thomas as replacement for Supreme Court Justice Thurgood Marshall didn't push us into the streets?

How come the *senseless* and racist throwaway of $42 billion on Operation Desert Storm didn't pack the highways with a 3,000-mile-long caravan of fired-up folk determined to evict killer lunatics from the White House and the Pentagon?

How come?

We had seen the eighty-one-second videotape of Los Angeles police attacking Rodney King.

We thought, we believed, that this time, and for once, the cops could not escape. Their brutality was clear. Their brutality was nauseating. The case was opened and would soon be shut. We viewed the trial as a procedural nicety. We would actually live to see one important episode of equality before the law! And then the jury found for the defendants. The jury concluded that there never came a moment when they felt, as they watched four cops attack an unarmed black man—there never came a moment when they felt "enough is enough."

And get this straight: The jury watched police surround Rodney King. They made him lie down on the street, face down on the street. They beat him. They stomped him. They hog-tied his hands and feet. They shot him four times with a Taser gun that injected 50,000 volts of electricity into his nervous system with each shot.

But that was not too much. That was never excessive force: not for that jury. Not one member of the jury was a black man or a black woman. Rodney King was denied due process according to the law. He was not judged by a jury of his peers.

And what was the crime of Rodney King? He was a young black man, not yet dead, and not yet ready, and not yet willing to die: He was black. He should have been dead. He should not have been born.

Or, as defense attorneys for the police explained, Rodney King kept getting up on "all fours." He wouldn't stay down. He kept raising up his head. He kept rising and rising. He would not lie down. He never assumed "a compliant mode."

And now we have Los Angeles in flames. The mode is nowhere compliant. People of color run around, or walk, without fear. We're off our knees. Heads up, fists in the air, and fire everywhere.

I condemn and deplore the violence of poverty and the injustice of hatred and the violence of absolute injustice that makes the peaceful conduct of our days impossible or cowardly.

Twelve years ago, when Miami police murdered Arthur McDuffie and black people rose up,[23] I wrote:

"It was such good news. A whole lot of silence had ended at last! Misbegotten courtesies of behavior were put aside. There were no leaders. There were no meetings, no negotiations. A violated people resisted with violence. An extremity of want, an extremity of neglect ... had been met, at last, with an appropriate, extreme reaction....

"And why should victims cover for their executioners? Why should the protesters cooperate and agree to discuss or write letters?...

"But this has been the code, overwhelmingly for the oppressed: That you keep cool and calm and explore proper channels and above all that you remain law-abiding and orderly precisely because ... it is the power of the law of the terrorist state arrayed against you to force you to beg and bleed without acceptable recourse except for dumb endurance or mute perishing....

"If you make and keep my life horrible then, when I can tell the truth, it will be a horrible truth, it will not sound good or look good, or God willing, feel good to you, either...."

Twelve years later and I understand that anarchy is not about nice. I understand that the provocation for anarchy is always and ever the destruction of every reasonable basis for hope. And tonight I know that the Simi Valley, California, jury's verdict of "Not Guilty" feels like the destruction of any reason for hope.

But I must conclude that "the good news" of the 1980 Miami uprising was politically indefensible as such because it did not lead to something big, new, humane, and irreversible. Today, for example, there is another victim of state violence: Rodney King.

And I believe we must take care not to become like our enemies: I do not accept that we should fall upon a stranger, outnumber him or her, and beat and possibly kill our "prey."

And I believe we must take care to distinguish between our enemies and our allies, and not confuse them or forget the difference between a maniac and a potential comrade.

And I have learned about the histories of Native Americans and Chicanos and Asian-Americans and progressive white peoples in these United States and I know that we have more in common than our genuine enemies want us to realize.

And on this evening of the first day after the jury's "Not Guilty" verdict, I attended and I spoke at a rally across from the Superior Court Building, here in Oakland. And the 500-plus Americans gathered there embodied the full racial and ethnic and class and age and sexual diversity that will give us the political and moral strength that we need for successful revolution.

And, as the graffiti proclaimed on the lone wall still standing after flames gutted an L.A. bank, LA REVOLUCION ES LA SOLUCION.

This enormous moment belongs only to each of us. Now we can choose to free ourselves from cross-cultural ignorance and second-hand racist divisions of thought and response. We can unite in our demands for equal human rights and civil liberties.

We can secure further prosecution of lawless police in L.A. We can change the nature of official power. We can gain a second Bill of Rights that will deliver at least as much money to support every African-American child as we spend on the persecution and imprisonment of young black men.

I am talking just for starters. Obviously, a second Bill of Rights should, and would, bring new entitlements into the life of every kind of American citizen. But these necessary, humane, and irreversible, and democratic gains cannot be won without political and moral unity centered on principle rather than identity.

And I am writing tonight by the light of the fire everywhere. The begging body grows cold.

I am beginning to smell something clean. I am beginning to sense a victory of spirit risen from the death of self-hatred. I am beginning to envision our collective turning to the long-term tasks of justice and equal rights to life, liberty, and the pursuit of happiness right inside this country that has betrayed our trust repeatedly. Behold the fire everywhere!

Willing and Able

August 1992

Last June, Charlie Lubin graduated from Berkeley High School. Three days a week you can catch him at work in the cafeteria of his alma mater. Other times he's busy at a local silkscreen shop, producing T-shirts to order. Or he's out playing softball, or he's studying to become a clown.

Charlie Lubin is twenty-two years old. He was born with Down syndrome. Right after his birth, hospital doctors and nurses counseled his mother with these words, "Don't see it!"

But Barbara Lubin refused to surrender her child into those waiting, professional hands of death. "That crazy woman with a retarded son" fought to keep him alive, and she kept fighting all the way to Lubin v. Berkeley Board of Education, a 1978 landmark legal battle that established the rights of disabled children to an appropriate, and fully conceived and fully delivered, public education.

> He says, "Excuse me, I don't mean
>   to be rude
> But I do not know what to call you.
> Is it physically challenged, mobility
>   impaired?
> wheelchair bound, wheelchair user?
> Handicapped, handicapper,
>   handicappable?
> crip, crippled, confined?
> deformed, defective, disabled?
> Inconvenienced, invalid?
> sick, special, survivor?
> Please tell me, whats the word?
>   What...."
> I say, "Wait! How about calling me
>   by my name?"

His name is Johnson Cheu. Twenty-two-and-a-half years ago, Johnson arrived, premature. He was placed inside an incubator for eighty days and, at some awful moment, a technical malfunction deprived Johnson's brain cells of oxygen.

"I've just been very fortunate," he tells me. "I have a very light case of spastic cerebral palsy. That means that a lot of my muscles never relax from varying states of permanent contraction."

I have never seen Johnson out of a wheelchair and I ask if spastic cerebral palsy dictates the use of such support. "Not exactly," he says. "I can, actually, stand and walk around. But I'm limited by the fact that one of my steps is the energy-expended equivalent of 265 steps of yours. The chair increases my endurance, my mobility."

In his last semester as an undergraduate, Johnson served as a voluntary tutor for Berkeley High School students. Today he teaches four different English classes there and, once or twice a day, he breaks for a cup of coffee or a bottle of juice from the cafeteria where Charlie Lubin is gainfully employed.

Besides teaching, Johnson writes poetry and leads a University of California-Berkeley poetry workshop. He will enter Stanford University next September and pursue an accelerated graduate-studies program to receive secondary teaching credentials and a Master's in the Art of Education.

Charlie Lubin and Johnson Cheu are two of the forty-three million Americans who persist among us despite the burdens of mental or physical disability.

Day after day, Charlie and Johnson meet with ignorant/fearful/indifferent and cruel stupidities of response that most of us commit whenever we notice somebody markedly different from ourselves. Terms such as "retarded" or "crippled" plainly express our panic or our disdain.

Johnson Cheu has written a poem about the daily indignities he faces, describing the "hateful grimace" or the "sad pity eyes" that meet him when he goes shopping. He refuses to ask for assistance because he knows people will respond "in baby talk/pat my head." "I am not a dog," he writes.

On campus one afternoon, I stood chatting with Johnson Cheu. Suddenly a huge moving van began to back into us. We yelled as loud as we could, but the van wheezed and rolled closer and closer. Johnson had to execute some almost magical, swift maneuvering of his wheelchair in order to escape. We were both breathless and furious when, finally, we could stop scrambling for safety.

People don't give a damn. People do not think about the stamina demanded of anyone disabled. We hardly ever bother to imagine what it takes to get dressed, or to cook, or to eat, or to learn algebra, or to cross the street, if you are not 100 per cent able-bodied. Disability means difficult and tedious and isolated and outcast.

But Charlie Lubin and Johnson Cheu have won for themselves a way out of no way. In 1991, the Americans with Disabilities Act (ADA) became law. ADA easily compares to the most important civil-rights legislation of the 1960s. Most situations of employment and public facilities (from schoolrooms to hotels to airport telephones) must no longer discriminate against disabled persons. Legal concepts of discrimination now include physical design and redesign requirements as well as new consumer and/or employee and/or citizen-at-large policies. The intent of the law is to fully enable the disabled to function on a competitive, decently self-sufficient basis. This is the best anything to emerge from the U.S. Congress since I don't know when.

And so I hope we get on with the next task of enforcement, and make that happen fast. I hope we properly perceive this legislative precedent as solid ground for the shock of further good news: further revolutionary legislation that, for example, will enable the homeless and the sick to acquire the help they need, without humiliation.

If we will pay attention to the achievements of Charlie Lubin and Johnson Cheu, and if we will embrace and build upon the ADA, then, maybe, we will become part of some national good news that will lessen our national reasons for shame.

This Time I'll Vote

November 1992

Editor's Note: June Jordan was asked, along with other writers, editors, and regular columnists to contribute to a symposium in The Progressive by commenting on her presidential preference in the 1992 U.S. presidential election. The following is Jordan's contribution. It is located within an article titled "What, Me Vote?"

This year's Presidential election will be very difficult for a lot of good people. You have four white men running for power. One of them is the father of at least two criminals. All of them are white, male, Christian, heterosexual, married, English-speaking, and rich. It is not a pretty picture. It is not a picture representing most of us who live here. If anybody cared to examine the relevant statistics, she or he would discover that the rich, the well-to-do, or, for that matter, middle-class folks with job security, constitute an overbearing, offensively concentrated, and fast-shrinking minority.

Today more Americans qualify as poverty-stricken than anytime since 1964. Back then, Lyndon Johnson responded with his War on Poverty. Our current Grand Wizard of the White House deletes the subject of poverty from his cue cards altogether and, instead, attempts to take us into War on Iraq, Round Two.

Next, there's gender.

In this media-declared Year of the Woman, both political parties have opted to omit the female from their most serious consideration. Hence there is no woman candidate for President or Vice President. And, despite the female majority of the population, and even if all women seeking elective office were to emerge victorious, women—most Americans—remain outrageously underrepresented or not represented.

Next, there's race.

If you add Native Americans and African-Americans and Latino-Americans and Chicanos and Asian-Americans together you do not come up with four white men. You do not come up with a homogenous critical mass. You do not come up with one English-speaking Voice of America.

Next, there's sexuality.

Unlike the Vice President, I am not prepared to say that heterosexuality is right or wrong. But what's good about it? Can anybody tell me that heterosexuality will stop unconstitutional and fascist intolerance and hate crimes?

Next, there's religion.

Thanks to the Republican platform and the Republican Convention, religion has become a political issue: Shall there be separation between Church and State? What if you don't go to church? What if you're Jewish? Or Muslim? Or Buddhist? Or nothing? Is God on our side against the Arabs, the Japanese, the European Community? And whose Holy Tablet shall set forth the Commandments in a democracy?

Next, there's democracy.

Thanks to the Republican platform and the Republican Convention, democracy has become a political issue: From the many shall we become four white men? Shall we become Barbara or Marilyn? Or blonde? Or fighter pilots flying the skies over South Central Los Angeles?

Next, there's marriage.

A strong, increasing number of Americans of voting age or older remains verifiably single—i.e., not married and/or never married. Divorce rates suggest that conventional conjugal arrangements often lack something attractively compelling. So what? In Seattle, it rains a lot. In California, hardly ever.

When I think about my country I try to stay with the facts. I try to stay home, first of all, and mind my own business. Kuwait, for example, is far from my mind working overtime to understand drugs and so-called budget crises and the taking away of food and clothing from American families and the evaporation of Federal aid to our cities, which are where most of us have to walk and look for work and try not to dread the cold ending of another day on the streets. When I think about my country I do not pretend that everyone else is a lot or exactly like me. I accept and I want to understand the stranger histories and languages and kitchen-table rituals and romantic inventions of other Americans.

And now I am afraid for my life. I am afraid that this election year it is my life that has become the target. It is my skin. It is my body furious for freedom. It is my heart that will not submit to hatred or dictatorship. It is my head that will not bow to priorities of power versus priorities of justice and domestic, equitable redistribution of our national wealth.

And so I will choose two of the four white men. Two of them have not yet proven themselves inhumane and besotted by fantasies of faraway conquest. Two of them have attempted to speak about trees and jobs and the rich. Two of them have yet to go on public record against the necessity and the preservation of public education. Two of them apparently regard national health care as a desirable entitlement rather than a neo-communist threat. Two of them have yet to veto civil-rights legislation. Two of them espouse a woman's right to abortion.

And so this time there will be no jokes. This time there will be no cynical baloney about "the lesser of two evils." When somebody decides that you, in fact, are evil incarnate--because you're not white or not middle-class or not married or not heterosexual or not English-speaking or not crazy about armed force— then it's not about "the lesser of two evils": It's about absolutely eviscerating the evil of the insolence of those who categorize other Americans, other people, as "wrong." It's about throwing the Republicans out.

This time I am voting for myself and my family values: I am voting for war against poverty, AIDS, breast cancer, hate crimes, and censorship. I am voting against the war against people of color inside and outside the U.S.A. I am voting for choice. I am voting Democratic.

On the Night of November 3, 1992

January 1993

There was great rejoicing all over the land. George Bush was out. And inside my little house, the mood fluctuated between stunned reverence and invincible joy.

Moving easily among the nonfat, non-cholesterol chocolate-chip cookies, or cakes, and three flavors of frozen yogurt, my friends finished off their champagne and started up (decaffeinated) coffee and I could not remember feeling so much at home before; so safe!

My friends looked like big America writ small in loving needlepoint: African-American men and women and Chinese- and Vietnamese- and Irish- and English- and French-Americans and one black teenager and one white child and Jewish and gentile and heterosexual and gay and lesbian and married and single and Southern and East Coast and Middle Western and nine years old to fifty-six, and nobody fighting and nobody bitter and nobody mad.

In the justified euphoria of that American moment, it was easy to let go of the horror and dread and shame of the last twelve years. Everything good and necessary seemed possible.

We could fathom and then destroy the reasons for the righteous fires of the Los Angeles revolt.

We could memorialize and never again countenance anything like the Salem, Oregon, hate-crime incineration of Hattie Cohen, a twenty-nine-year-old black lesbian, and her white, gay housemate, forty-five-year-old Brian Mock.[24]

We could do away with the stupidity of the so-called "politically correct" debate and, instead, undertake the creation of a new American core education worthy of the old and the emerging majorities of Americans who already fill or drop out of our public schools.

We could properly fund and enshrine our public libraries as the open doors to accurate, multicultural, multiracial, multiethnic, multilingual information that they must become.

We could terminate the awful absurdity of a national argument about who controls a woman's body and her mind.

We could make terrific Grade A PG family-value movies about the hero and the heroine doctors who perform abortions and who provide contraceptive advice despite death threats and bully picket lines and blown-up clinics.

We could cure AIDS.

We could cure breast cancer.

We could learn to praise and lavishly remunerate the nurses and the neighborhood volunteers who comfort and who feed the victims of these killer afflictions.

We could halt and forever forswear the demonization of Arabs and of everybody else who may very well hold different, "un-American" ideas about how things should be in a "new world order."

We could invest the cost of three or four B-2 bombers into the complete, redemptive, *onsite-resident-rebuilding* of our inner cities.

We could do this. It could happen. We were here to testify. As a people, we had spoken and we had won!

But now it was growing late. And one of my friends, Adrienne, sat down at the piano and began to play. And then another of my friends, André, joined her in a love song he'd written years ago—"There may come a time when hunger's not known/and we'll stop the abuse of the Earth, our home...." And then Adrienne modulated from that R&B ballad mode into a Gospel takeover of the keyboard and suddenly André was singing, "O beautiful for spacious skies, for amber waves of grain/for purple mountain majesties above the fruited plain...." I looked over my shoulder and I could see André's son, seventeen-year-old Mike, standing, loose, and listening to his father, and checking out the gorgeous, daring trust that underlay the whole impromptu delivery of the music:

"... and crown thy good with brotherhood...."

And I was thinking, "Bet: Bill Clinton doesn't know the half of what all his energetic rhetoric about change and hope has started up and set ablaze!"

André is a black man in his thirties. He works full-time at one job, and part-time at another regular job as well. Three years ago, he abandoned his career as an R&B singer/songwriter/performer to become the full-time single parent of his only child, Mike. In fact, André rescued his son from an abusive home situation and has dedicated himself to activist parenting of a teenager who, among other things, is homophobic.

André is gay. His son, Mike, is not. André sings and writes R&B ballads. Mike writes rap. And I had been getting to know him and some of his ideas about rap when the Simi Valley verdict of "not guilty" exploded everything. This happened close to the end of Mike's last semester in high school, so he just decided to quit, because "school was messed up, too. They had lost my transcript.

And I did my homework but the teacher said I didn't ... so I left. It was like a burden off my shoulders, really.

"And that same week of the Rodney King thing and this man broke into the lady's house right downstairs from us. And all of a sudden there was this pounding on the door and the lady said what was going on. So I picked up a stick and I went downstairs and I went outside and I was looking for the robber a little bit. Then the police come and they rush up and they grab me. They throw me to the ground: A black lady and a Chinese man. And they ask me for identification. But I never carry no ID. So I said, 'Well, I live here!' And they ask me to prove it! And they still trying to lock me up and the black lady police she put handcuffs on me and push my face in the concrete, and man that hurted me too, and she stuck her leg in my back. And around that time my Dad look out the window and he come down and talk to the police and I was hellified mad but Andrè tell me to go inside and he stay out there and talk to the police, I guess."

Not long after this, Mike split from his father's house. And Andrè searched and walked the streets, but could not find him. Mike had disappeared. And Andrè lived crazy with fear: Where was his boy? Who would listen to him? ("Well, I live here!") Who or what would bring him back alive?

After a couple of months, Mike came home. Maybe he thought that the deal that Andrè offered him—a home and financial support as long as he stays in school—was as good a deal as anything out here, or better. Maybe he just missed his father and their ongoing arguments about most of the things teenagers fight with their parents about. Maybe he thinks Andrè has the best damned family values he ever heard of.

Whatever the reason, Mike was back. And his eyes were soft as he stood, listening to the song about America.

And when I asked Mike how he felt about the Clinton victory, did he feel hopeful, he said, "Kinda. Sort of." And then he let me hear snatches from a rap he'd recently stopped working on:

Now I'm not really a political rapper
But this new shit is just as fishy as a
        snapper
1992 the year of correction the
out-with-the-old-in-with-the-new
        election

Will he clean up health care
wipe out welfare?
All I really wanna know

what's he gonna do for me
stop the drug problem; clean
up my community

Constitution after Constitution after
   Constitution
is broken
It's time to leave the courthouse smokin
Go to the corner store/buy me some gas
C'mon back and throw some flames on that ass
Cause that's the only way/all this madness
   gone cease
I said it before/No Justice: No peace!

Mike reiterated that he was no longer working on that rap. And maybe he won't bother to finish it. Or maybe he will. But he's back. He's in school. And, on the night of November 3, 1992, he was here, in my house, with his father. And he stood around, drinking Diet Pepsi, and polishing off the food on his plate, and watching the rest of us do instant analysis, and celebrate.

And when his father's soul baritone merged with Adrienne's gospel rendition of that prayer about our "spacious skies," Mike did not leave. He did not disappear. He stayed where he was standing, at ease. And he stood there, willing to listen and to see what would happen next.

And I don't know what will happen. But Andrè, Mike's father, has never given up on this country, or his son. And he's working hard. And he plays by the rules.

And looking at him, and looking at Mike, and resting my eyes upon Adrienne and David and Carolyn and George and Ben and Temu and Margaret and Minh-Ha and Jean-Paul and Fran and Daniel and Evelyn and Amy and Roberta and Lauren and Will—all of my friends who came into a happy and diverse American community of our own making—I could almost touch the infinitely deep and delicate hope that a landslide of election results had given birth to.

And because revolution always takes place on the basis of great hope and rising expectations, I am not too worried about the future. One way or the other, a whole lotta change is gonna come. Through happiness realized or through and beyond the pain of betrayal, we will become the beneficiaries of our faith.

And even without revolution, we will prevail because we have proven to the world, and to ourselves, that we are not "fringe elements" or "special-interest groups" or so-called "minorities." Without us there is no legitimate majority: We are the mainstream. We have become "the people."

And let our elected leadership beware the awesome possible wrath of a mighty, multifoliate, and faithful people whose deepest hopes have been rekindled and whose needs have not been met.

Islam and the U.S.A. Today

February 1993

The woman weighs forty-six pounds. She is too thin to breathe. What's left of her flesh barely covers her bones. Her eyes persist as soft as they are large and brown. She is African. She is probably Muslim. She is dying in Somalia, the country of her birth. In the last six months, hundreds of thousands of Somalis have already died. Children have perished in huge numbers difficult to admit.

Or, those who were captured were twelve to twenty-five years old. Some of them managed to escape from vile detention camps where more than 10,000 girls and young women remain, repeatedly raped by day and by night. Many of them are Muslim. They are casualties of an "ethnic cleansing" that imperils all of the Muslims alive in former Yugoslavia.

Or, on barren land between Lebanon and Israel, 400 men arrived in winter and emptiness. They had been blindfolded and pushed into buses that traveled through the darkness, with illegal speed. They had been seized inside their homes and driven away, at gunpoint, into sudden unimaginable exile. From their enemies each of them received a blanket, a paper bag of food, and $50. They are Palestinians. Most are Muslims. They may not survive. No man can live on no man's land.

Or, roughly two years ago, we launched one of the most relentless and savage bombing assaults in human history. Our target was the city of Baghdad, home to 6.5 million people, mostly Muslim. Even now, that voiceless and beleaguered population must contend with the ferocious consequences of our attack: widespread disease, severe malnutrition, contaminated water, and nationwide cultural and technological wipeout.

Or, during the holiday transition from 1992 to 1993, one of the mainstays of local entertainment was Walt Disney's animated feature film, *Aladdin*. Except for the hero and the villain, all the men are corpulent and ugly. All the women, including the heroine, appear, throughout, half naked and/or clad in nearly transparent "harem" attire à la Hollywood. The villain turned out to be "a dark man" thinking "dark thoughts." Given the ostensible storyline, one assumes that every character is an Arab and, therefore, Muslim. I cannot imagine black people, or Jews, or anybody other than Arab men and women, drawn in such repulsive, frightening, vapid, and inaccurate fashion, today, without enormous popular and political uproar.

Or, the media gave far more coverage to the "amicable" break between Charles and Diana than they devoted to the terrifying and internecine explosion of violence and counter-violence between the Hindu majority and the Muslim minority of India. Nowhere could you find any depth of analysis or appropriate background information. For example, how many Americans understand Britain's colonial responsibility, as regards this latest bloody and tragic outbreak of intraracial hostilities? How many of us know that more Muslims live in India than in Pakistan?

And what does that matter?

While he was spokesman for the Black Nation of Islam, Malcolm X aroused the self-respect of black folks otherwise impervious to organized appeals for unity and discipline. After his pilgrimage to Mecca, Malcolm became an orthodox Muslim and, among other things, his experience of Islam deracialized his basic take on moral reality.

Who is Muslim and what is Islam?

Or, where does Islam fit "inside" American objectives for the Twenty-first Century?

As religion rises into the incendiary realm of world affairs, we should take care to detect and oppose, de facto and aforethought, U.S. wars against the people of Islam. In the instance of Somalia and former Yugoslavia, we can verify the impact of our aggression through inertia. In the instances of Iraq and the Palestinians, White House perspectives have led to overt assault, decimation, and unacknowledged, awful suffering.

The first so-called Christian crusade was anything but holy, anything but benign. In the name of their exclusive beliefs, Western white men, again and again, invaded distant Muslim towns and cities. These first "Crusaders" slaughtered all of the "infidels" they encountered in these "infidel" homelands. What is happening now?

The hour is already dreadful, and late, for self-examination of the unfolding, unholy nature of regular American response to Muslim men and women in various extremities of need or self-definition and affirmation. Islam will not fit itself into White House daydreams of "a new world order." Accordingly, we had better get ready to decide, on an altogether public and conscious level, what we, what the U.S.A., plans to do, or not do, about that.

At the moment, we pretend to ignorance of our crimes and we proceed on the basis of racist ignorance of the victims of our crimes.

And the Muslim woman of Somalia weighs forty-six pounds. What is her name? Why is she starving to death? And what names will she call you and me if she ever regains her strength to speak out loud?

And how shall we defend to ourselves our behavior in the context of her needs/her human rights? What is the moral meaning of our own gods?

I Am Seeking an Attitude

May 1993

Until now, I have never said, "I am a woman." I'm not sure why. I guess I'm not sure exactly what those words mean.

And yet my gender identity is as basic, as incontrovertible, as my racial identity. I have written the sentence "I am black" innumerable times. I have thought that sentence, and I have felt its meaning all the way to the bone of my self.

What is the difference between gender and race? Why do I feel perfectly comfortable saying, "I am a black woman," or "I am a woman of color," but then something inside me pretty serious balks/blanks out when it comes to the more elementary declaration: "I am a woman"?

Or why do I write without hesitation about the injustice that freed the cops who beat up Rodney King, and then I keep to myself my qualms about the fact that he has been charged with beating up his wife?

Maybe it has to do with the human necessity of pride.

We women are the majority of every people on the planet. But, everywhere, we are most lacking in political representation, least compensated for the work we do, most illiterate, most impoverished, most lacking in legal protection and recourse, and most concentrated in the lowest paying, least secure, and least valued sectors of the labor force.

In addition, we are, everywhere, subject to physical and social violence. On our own: On the streets of the world and in the dwelling places we call home, we are not safe. And, even in the realm of medicine and medical research, we, women, in general, do not exist: Most tests are conducted on men for diseases affecting primarily men. Men are regarded as the universal body, the universal voice. From cholesterol to literature, you just have to hope that your female organs and/or your female perspectives do not differ importantly from those organs and viewpoints of the universal male.

While this state of affairs can have readily comical results, it can also kill you—if you happen to be somebody who needs to say, "I am a woman."

For example, given the popular perception and sentiment on the horrifying crisis of AIDS, you would probably run into real trouble trying to educate people to the fact that breast cancer kills far, far more Americans every year. Over the past ten years, roughly 140,000 Americans have died of AIDS while close to 600,000 Americans have died of breast cancer. And yet, when President Bill Clinton got around to something specific about health care, in his budget speech to the nation, he rightly declared himself determined to greatly increase funding for AIDS research, but he did not so much as mention breast cancer.

Of course, breast cancer kills only women.

I am a woman. I am looking for reasons for pride in my gender identity. Given the international and the whole human historical context of female inequality, where can I find them?

Why did it take my mother so long to defend herself against my father? Why was suicide her final defense?

Why have we taken so long to defend ourselves against the brutality, derision, and economic subjugation that have been our regular female experience?

Where are the reasons for pride?

Where are the woman-songs comparable to "... and before I'll be a slave I'll be buried in my grave"?

And what about those of us asked to become—or bullied into becoming—the slave of the slave? What about we, women of color, who have been pained into a false choice between unconditional loyalty to our men (themselves despised by white men) and our own need to escape from despicable "bitch" status and treatment?

And why do men hate us, anyway? And why do we, nevertheless, and always, continue to love them as lovers and husbands, and fathers, and why do we women, as mothers, raise boys into a manhood that then endangers our own lives?

I am seeking an attitude. Twenty years ago, I thought I was proving something terrific and really big deal when I decided I would, without exception, move through the corridors of Yale University in high heels and in as fashionable an array of dresses as I could almost afford on my unequal, woman's salary as an assistant professor. That was a weird episode of considerable discomfort. And it is curious to me, today, to realize that I thought I needed high heels and dresses to confirm my gender identity inside that ossified space of male values—and that I thought that such gender confirmation of myself, as a woman, would naturally mean something positive and good.

Boy, was I young!

Twenty years later, and I look through my file folders: Africa, Clinton, the Budget, African-American Issues, South Central L.A., Gay and Lesbian Issues, Foreign Policy Issues, and, yes, here is one labeled, WOMEN.

As I riffle through newspaper clippings kept under that heading, I can feel a kind of pitiless nausea overtaking me. Here is the African woman of Somalia who weighs forty-five pounds. Here are Muslim women clutching at such protection as they can find inside traditional Islam. Here are young black teenagers (female), 62 per cent of them likely to live below the poverty line once they drop out of high school—compared to 37 per cent of young black teenagers (male).

And, in any event, according to *The New York Times,* "Students sit in classrooms that, day in, day out, deliver the message that women's lives count for less than men's." Here are American women 50 per cent more likely to be raped inside the military than in civilian life.

And here are more than 20,000 mostly Muslim women systematically suffering gang rape around the clock in the former Yugoslavia. And here is nobody powerful in this country, from President Clinton up or down, opening his—or her—mouth to decry these atrocities and to make them stop happening.

I mean, I am a woman.

And I am living and I am paying serious taxes inside this country that took us into an unholy, barbarous, unpardonable war against the people of Iraq for the sake of an inarguably plain old rotten dictatorship called Kuwait. And this country where I live and pay serious taxes murdered way more than hundreds of thousands of Iraqi human beings and spent way more than the total allocation for education on the delivery of such a savage rescue of such a stupid and intractable dictatorship as the one that still holds power in Kuwait. And yet—and yet!—the elected leadership of this same country where I live and where I pay serious taxes cannot even open its mouth to condemn genocidal rape!

This country cannot suddenly shoot its Patriot missiles and fly its Stealth bombers the hell into Serbian turf because why? There is no oil in former Yugoslavia. And another thing: The only people being raped are women.

I am a woman. And I am seeking an attitude. I am trying to find reasons for pride.

I was proud when we elected four new women to the United States Senate.

I was proud when we elected the first black woman to the United States Senate.

I was proud when a woman became Secretary of Health and Human Services.

I was proud when a woman became Attorney General of the United States.

But where are they now? Is it possible that not one of these illustrious women could find two minutes in which she could lay down humanitarian and, yes, military demands in behalf of the 20,000-plus mostly Muslim girls and women in former Yugoslavia?

Maybe they don't remember rape. Maybe when you get to be powerful you lose your gender identity above the neck and you just can't remember the very common horror of rape.

I am a woman. I have been raped twice in my life. And I remember. And I go through the hours of a Monday or a Tuesday and I do not forget what is happening to all the victims of so-called ethnic cleansing and, particularly, I do not forget the women victims of so-called ethnic cleansing. And I do not and I will not forgive the elected leadership of my country for its inertia and its silence and, therefore, its complicity with the evil of so-called ethnic cleansing.

Where are my reasons for pride? One of my colleagues, in a manner of speaking, Anna Quindlen,[25] recently published a column arguing for intervention in behalf of these female victims of rape. Ordinarily, I respect and admire Anna Quindlen's writing. But for her, rape was not the point. Rather the tragedy is this: Having been raped and raped and raped and raped, again and again, these thousands upon thousands of young mostly Muslim girls and women may never become receptive to any future proposition of heterosexual intercourse and, hence, these rape victims may be unable and/or unwilling to serve a procreative function for their people.

And, hence, these people, 100 per cent, may perish.

I guess I should say, "Thank God Quindlen managed some justification for the rescue of these female casualties of so-called ethnic cleansing."

But is it not remarkable, is it not appalling, that she, evidently, does not believe that rape, by itself, is quite sufficiently something to interdict because rape, by itself, is horribly destructive, violent, and wrong?

Where are her reasons for pride?

Or mine—when, in the past, I have argued for our equality and empowerment mainly by emphasizing our indispensable procreative and then our nurturing functions?

How low can we go?

Pretty damned lowdown when I must present the issues of my freedom and my rights primarily in the context of my ongoing usefulness to somebody else!

I am a woman. And that's not easy.

Crazies out here want to tell me all about my body. My body! Tell me no abortion. Try to kill any doctor who could help me. Went and killed one. Finally. Blew him away. Three bullets shredding the flesh of his back. Crazies out here blowing up/closing down abortion clinics. Call me Welfare Queen if I go ahead and have the babies when I don't have no job and no way to get a job and nowhere to leave the babies if I do find something anyhow.

Crazies out here tell me I can't love no woman. Want to kill me if I do. Went and killed one. Hattie Cohn in Salem, Oregon. Burned her to death.[26]

Crazies out here tell me I can't love no man unless he have himself a big-time income and reliably conjugal inclinations. Crazies out here tell me I can't love no man unless we married anyway. The Pope say just abstain. The Pope himself abstain.

Crazies out here like to drive me crazy.

But I'm not crazy. I am seeking an attitude.

Out of these histories of horror and impositions of shame and degradations of a rising freedom spirit, is there a pathway to my pride? Behind that question is another one. Is there a will to power?

For me, the problem of gender identity stems from its usual estrangement from ambitions of power. Usually we push for things to change in our favor, yes, but usually we push in the most courteous and reasonable and listening fashion imaginable. We want or we need whatever it is because that would be the right thing, the moral case, and because, otherwise, we are left in danger and in pain.

Hardly ever do we enter the realms of righteous rage! Hardly ever do we formulate the matter so that whoever opposes or impedes or ridicules our demands will understand that if he does not get out of our way and/or get rid of that smirk he will be the one in danger: He will be the one in pain!

Hardly ever do we make it clear that by "rights" we mean power: The power of deterrence and the power of retaliation and the power to transform our societies so that no longer and never again shall more than half of every people on the planet beg for dignity and safe passage and political and economic equality!

Usually we try to persuade or seduce or defuse the anxieties or deflect the violence of our opposition. Usually we try to fool ourselves, as well: The War Against Women surely does not require War Against the Enemies of Women— be they male or female. And so we neither win nor lose; we persist—and too often we perish. At the very least, we perish in the spirit.

For me, the problem of gender identity is our evasion of the implications of power and our may-I-say-"feminine" inclinations to make nice. War is not nice. And it's hard to embrace something alive and yet powerless. It's even a bit creepy as an idea: something alive without power. But female gender identity, per se, has been presented like that, to me. It has been given to me as a certificate of suffering: I am one of those who could have been thrown away or suffocated or drowned at birth because I was born a girl.

But pride does not arise from suffering. Pride develops as we resist our misery, as we revolt against, and as we exorcise all misery from our days and nights.

And so I know pride as a black woman and as a woman of color because black people and people of color resist oppression and because we loathe, actively, every source of our unequal liberty, our unequal entitlement under law.

We behold our racial identity as a call to arms, a summoning of ourselves into battle for power and territory and wealth and happiness and well-being.

We declare war against our enemies. We wage war for the sake of our self-determination.

"We," in this case of colored peoples, includes me.

But have we, women of these United States, for example, have we declared war against our enemies? Are we ready to live and die for the sake of our self-determination?

Show me the nationwide day of absence by women so that, for starters, the Equal Rights Amendment shall become law.

Show me female vigilante patrols keeping city streets and country roads safe for our passage at any time and in any attire of our choosing.

Show me national flying furies who confront and who overpower crazy Operation Rescue gangsters wherever they dare to raise their ugly killer heads.

Show me proportional political representation of women by women on every level of government.

Show me women loving women absolutely without persecution and absolutely without death.

Show me overdue changes so that everyone who does such "women's work" as day care of children and night care of children and teaching and nursing and peace-making and converting the wilderness of our humanly mixed attributes into a benign environment for human beings—everyone who does this so-called women's work shall receive more money and more perks than General Colin Powell or your nearest college football coach.

Show me emergency Federal commitment to cure breast cancer.

Show me our feminist faxorama to jam White House machinery with our demands for crisis intervention against rape in former Yugoslavia and against violence against women in our own country.

Show me the power and I will feel the pride!

I am a woman. And I think I have found my attitude. And I think, really, it's about: "Let's get it on!"

The Truth of Rodney King

June 1993

April 17, 1993, and a Federal jury has found two Los Angeles policemen guilty in the beating of Rodney King twenty-five months ago. This same jury found the other two police defendants not guilty. And, immediately, attorneys for the convicted have declared their intention to appeal. So, today, there is less than a full-fledged national disgrace recurring in Los Angeles.

But we would be ill-advised to assume that even this partial delivery of justice will stand. And we would be oblivious to brutal colonial attitudes if we did not note and decry that the overwhelming state response to the first miscarriage of justice has been paramilitary, at best. There has been no top priority of focus and think-tank frenzy to relieve the beleaguered citizens of South Central Los Angeles with money and programs that could lift them out of the violence of poverty and the violence of unequal protection under the law.

Nothing basic has changed. And so my spirit remains riveted, still, with grief and misgivings, to one year ago: On April 29, 1992, the whole world learned of the Simi Valley verdict of "not guilty" in the first trial of the Los Angeles policemen accused of brutally beating an unarmed African-American man named Rodney King.

My own initial reaction to this terrible and completely shocking news was to burst into tears of bitterness and terror: In my lifetime, will violence ever be made to stop inside the national black community? In my lifetime, will the American system of justice ever deliver anything besides injustice to the black community?

Because there had been a videotape documentary of the police assault on Rodney King, I had expected, along with millions of other African-Americans, that for once the guilty would be punished and the victim would be protected by due process under the law. But the visual documentary evidence of unlawful police violence—evidence that was sickening to watch even at the remove of a TV set—that evidence did not carry the day. Racism carried the day.

According to a defense attorney, hideous, monster images of black men as wild and depraved subhuman creatures motivated Los Angeles police to attack one unarmed African-American man with nauseating and relentless savagery.

And where did the police acquire such racist images?

Is it not the case that American media coverage of young black men promotes such violent, such vicious fantasy?

Is it not the case that, as Malcolm X observed, media coverage of blackfolks serves to criminalize the black community in the minds of white America and, having criminalized our community, police violence against our communities appears justified and necessary to most Americans?

Is it not the case that the lamentable nature of our usual school curriculum is such that most white Americans, most Asian-Americans, most Latino-Americans, and even a sadly significant number of African-Americans, ourselves, do not learn anything important and accurate about African-American history, or culture, and so in the absence of coherent, valid, historical instruction, all of these various Americans accept the cultural perversities of media coverage as objective, reliable, and truthful information?

It was that very same one unarmed African-American man, Rodney King, the victim of inarguable and unlawful police savagery, it was he who said through the microphones of the press that rushed to cover the L.A. uprising against the injustice of the Simi Valley verdict, "Please can we get along here.... We all can get along. I mean, we're all stuck here for a while. Let's try to work it out."

These were the words of the black man who, allegedly, so terrified the L.A. police that they could not help but beat and stomp him almost to death. You would think that, perhaps, the truth of his being that spoke to his countrymen beginning with the word "please" might well explode and exorcise the racist fantasies and misinformation and ignorance that underlay the police assault upon his defenseless body.

But that would be a woeful underestimation of the racist nature of Rodney King's predicament. That would be a willful blindness to the racist nature of the national response to the L.A. uprising against the depravity of judgment that led to the "not guilty" verdict in the first trial.

The truth of Rodney King and the truth of African America is not anything that racist America intends to allow, or learn, or teach, or protect.

The truth of Rodney King and the truth of African America is an integral part of the truth of the emerging new majority of these United States: a majority that is neither white nor necessarily English speaking. In less than sixty years, most Americans will be descendants of the peoples of Africa, Asia, the Pacific Islands, the Hispanic world, and Arabia, not Europe.

Where is the public-school curriculum that is ready to teach all of these new Americans what they need and deserve to know about themselves, and about each other?

How can anybody justify compulsory public schooling and yet deny the racial and ethnic reality of the students compelled to sit inside our classrooms?

Despite media coverage of the L.A. uprising, it is a fact that most of the people arrested were Hispanic, not black. Forty per cent of businesses destroyed were Hispanic, and most of the rest of the businesses destroyed were owned by Korean-Americans.

Where is the public school curriculum that is ready to teach these three communities—African-Americans, Asian-Americans, and Latino-Americans—how our histories intersect and how our bound-together destinies depend upon our ignorance or our knowledge of our connections: our common oppressor, as Malcolm X would put it?

If we could gather together the political force of African- and Asian- and Latino-American communities, if we could coalesce these peoples into one lobby for educational reform, a national housing program, and job training for jobs that exist, we could empower the numerical new majority of Americans and become the political new majority.

Since 1970, twenty million Asians and Latinos have emigrated to America. But, so far, the necessary American redefinition of race and the necessary American revolution of public education in America—a redefinition and a revolution required by this enormous infusion of new, non-European human life into our mainstream—so far these transformations have not happened. And so far these communities have competed and contended for a pitiful slice of leftover pie. Coalitions have yet to come together.

And so I would like to respond to Rodney King. I would like to say, yes, we can all get along—but first we will have to coalesce in order to enlarge that pitiful slice into a whole, big, massive pie. And second, we will have to coalesce in order to secure the revolution of America's public schools so that the faces and the names and the languages of our children demand that we change the meaning of "we" and that justice and equality in the courtroom, in the streets, on the job, and in the classroom are, as Martin Luther King Jr. would say, the best guarantors—the only guarantors—of our "getting along."

First, let me deal with the pie:

In Ron Takaki's brilliant forthcoming book, *A Different Mirror*, he cites these lines written by a Japanese immigrant describing a lesson learned by Mexican and Asian farm laborers in California: "People harvesting work together unaware of racial problems." But as we know only too well, since 1970 there has been less and less to harvest, here in America.

Since 1970, we have had to survive a calculated Federal withering of every program capable of ending poverty, or mitigating the misery of poverty. Since 1970, we have been forced to survive huge Federal cuts in aid to our cities, cuts in public education, cuts in the care of the sick, cuts in drug rehabilitation.

And we have had to survive the massive deterioration of our bridges and our roadways and our public facilities even as we have had to survive the massive deterioration of the best hopes of our young people and the massive deterioration of our economy as a means of support and purpose and security for our American lives.

Those twenty million new Americans who arrived from 1970 onward came here from Mexico and from El Salvador and from Vietnam and from Korea and from Japan because, just like the Seventeenth Century pilgrims, they were desperate for a better life. But they arrived just as an official white backlash against African-Americans was going into high, inhuman gear.

And so these past two decades have seen an enormous swelling of citizen need coincident with an entirely cruel, shortsighted, unjust, and always racist construction of citizen opportunities and citizen entitlement.

This is why there is just a pitiful slice of leftover pie.

Secondly, we will have to coalesce in order to secure the revolution of America's public schools. We must demand recognition of the faces and the names and the languages of our culture. Those of us who have been designated for so long as special interest/fringe group/minorities—we have the happiness now of realizing that we have become the mainstream; we are the people.

We: African-Americans and Latino-Americans and Asian-Americans and Native Americans and Pacific Islanders and Arab-Americans and women and gay Americans and lesbian Americans and Americans with disabilities—that is the new American meaning of "we," that is the de facto coalition that put Bill Clinton into the White House. We constitute a de facto coalition responsible for electing the current President of these United States.

We are truly powerful! And now we must move from de facto coalition to self-conscious, aggressively activist coalition and take over the classrooms and take over the American core curriculum of public education.

This means, for one thing, that we must laugh or fight the so-called controversy over so-called politically correct instruction out of our lives.

And if we could provide these new Asian and Latino-Americans with the accurate and coherent historical information that they need—if we could properly educate these new Americans, then they would know, for example, that their own heartbreak predicament of rejection and hate crime and taxation without representation and poverty and startlingly high rates of tuberculosis and suicide-their newfound American predicament—directly derives from the ongoing, hateful predicament of African-Americans against whom racist white America raised a Federal backlash meant to whip blackfolks into invisibility and silent suffering.

And if we could provide African-Americans with the accurate and coherent historical information that they need, then African-Americans would understand the completely legitimate, kindred aspirations of these new immigrants, understand the persecuted histories their emigration bespeaks, and understand our heavy, real connections to these new Americans.

But can we provide such an education?

I say we must. And I say we can, absolutely.

We must organize the parents of our students. We must teach the parents of our students so that they will join hands with us to defeat every single so-called "school voucher" proposal that comes up—wherever it comes up!

We must organize and teach the parents of our students what that school-voucher brainstorm is all about. We must make it unmistakably clear that the idea behind that brainstorm is this: Since the American public is changing so that the so-called minorities now constitute the majority population in our public schools, it is time to eviscerate public education in order to protect the new white minority of Americans: Take away the money, and we will have to close the schools and/or close the libraries and/or use completely obsolete and indefensible textbooks and/or crowd the classrooms so that teachers must resign for the sake of their sanity.

When public education served the powerful, it was compulsory, and money flowed into the coffers of our schools. Now that public education must challenge and displace the currently powerful—or else betray its obligations to its new American clients—the currently powerful oppose and seek to weaken and to destroy the validity of public schools on which the overwhelming majority of young Americans must rely for their empowerment.

Today we have California Governor Pete Wilson saying ridiculous things like, we must increase community college tuition by 300 per cent. Today we see teachers in Los Angeles bullied into a so-called vote about whether to take a 10 per cent cut or lose their jobs altogether. That, I submit, is not a vote, not a choice. That is a shameful episode in our state and in our country.

We must reject outright any and all pay cuts for teachers. Let's get serious about who is doing the work. Let the members of Congress and the governors and the chancellors and the football coaches—let them take a 50 per cent pay cut!

It is lunatic to ask of teachers any further sacrifice. It is lunatic to tolerate any further erosion of the well-being and capability of our public education system in America.

Just as President Clinton recently pledged $17 billion in new money to the high-tech industry, he needs to commit an additional $20 billion to the industry of public education.

Yes, but where is the money to come from? President Clinton has said that there are no sacred cows in his budget. But I beg to differ:

The 1992 Defense Department received $307 billion of our money. That's 20 per cent of the total budget. And the $307 billion stipulated does not even include veterans' benefits.

And what about education?

The 1992 U.S. budget allocated $45 billion to education—and job training, too, that is.

I say there is a sacred cow in the picture.

A B-2 bomber costs $2 billion—each. Let's have a B-2 bomber for the public school system of every single city in America: $20 billion in additional money for education would mean only ten fewer B-2 bombers on the runway to nowhere.

President Clinton has said it is time to invest in America. I agree, complete-ly. Which is the better investment: ten B-2 bombers, or $20 billion in additional money, our money, for the physical refurbishment and democratic reform and academic revolution of American education?

At this point we put 20 per cent of our total budget into bomber planes and missiles while Germany and Japan put 5 per cent of their respective budgets into "defense." Where is the mystery of our inability to compete?

The Cold War is over, the Berlin Wall is down. What the hell are we de-fending against?

We need to call our own Senators and Representatives. We need to call Ron Dellums, who now chairs the House Armed Services Committee. We need to call Bill and Hillary Clinton and tell them to cook that sacred cow. We are starving out here!

Now, supposing we get a B-2 bomber for every public school system of every city in America. That's $2 billion a pop.

Then supposing we use that money to duly remunerate American teachers of American children so that, at last, our teachers receive the financial and social respect they deserve—as the literal, designated mentors for our national destiny.

And supposing that we succeed in transforming ourselves in our minds and in our deeds from minority and special or fringe-group members into an ag-gressive majority coalition of Americans determined to get real about this new America in our hands—and in our classrooms.

And supposing we successfully devise a core curriculum that includes the whole world and all of America rather than something else—something quite familiar and dangerous and useless and wrong.

And supposing then that we learn what we need to learn in order to teach our students about themselves—that is to say, teach them about American diversity that is the beginning and the test-ending truth of these United States.

Then, can we all get along?

In Martin Luther King's essay, "A Testament of Hope," which was published after his assassination, he wrote:

"When millions of people have been cheated for centuries, restitution is a costly process. Inferior education, poor housing, unemployment, inadequate health care—each is a bitter component of the oppression that has been our heritage. Each will require billions of dollars to correct. Justice so long deferred has accumulated interest and its cost for this society will be substantial in financial as well as human terms. This fact has not been grasped, because most of the gains of the past decade were obtained at bargain prices. The desegregation of public housing cost nothing; neither did the election and appointment of a few black public officials....

"The black revolution is much more than a struggle for the rights of Negroes. It is forcing America to face all its interrelated flaws—racism, poverty, militarism, and materialism.... It reveals systemic rather than superficial flaws and suggests that radical reconstruction of society itself is the real issue to be forced."

I propose that we begin by facing the political nature of education, the political nature of knowledge, and our collective power to change what our children know about themselves and about each other so that we can get along with the business of saving the world for human life.

I propose that we underscore to ourselves and to our elected representatives and to our students and to our civilian police force that the achievement of a great society depends upon securing justice and equality for all of its citizens.

I propose that we redesign our political and our academic and our social lives so that we can finally answer that one unarmed African-American man, Rodney King, saying to him, well, yes, we can all get along as soon as we take care of some serious business—on your behalf and mine, and ours.

We have to join with every American who would love justice and equality more than a law-and-order status quo of hidden but combustible inequities and chasmic, silent suffering.

And, then, yes, we can all get along.

Yes, please God: I believe we can.

Bosnia Betrayed

September 1993

I used to wonder what it must have felt like to be a grownup living in Germany or in the United States during World War II. How did anybody hear about the Nazis? Did everyone believe the news? Did anybody care?

I always wanted to imagine that only bad people didn't know what was happening; only bad people could choose to ignore or else accommodate to evil. This had to mean that regular good people locked arms within minutes of the first reports and then powerful good people went without food and sleep until they figured out what to do. And then, of course, they did it: They moved whatever and whomever needed to be moved to stop the genocide.

But today was cloudy. And tonight it's raining. At dinner, I had to accept or reject a small piece of lemon pie, and then I had to decide for or against a second slice. Mostly, this is the way I live: watching the weather, and making decisions of extremely little consequence.

My friends are not much different. One of them just flew back from a boring job interview in Colorado, and to celebrate his return, we played tennis for an hour. Another friend turned fifty, and well-wishers came around for birthday barbecue.

But every night, I keep waking up. There is now a visible rash on my neck. Is this the trivial big picture in which yet another Muslim girl is savagely attacked and raped? Is this the pedestrian frame of reference in which yet another Muslim village explodes in flames? More than 20,000 Muslim girls and young women repeatedly and repeatedly raped!

Systematic rape makes me nauseous, even as an idea. And I am dark. I'm black, in fact. And a whole lot of folks find me and mine definitely undesirable. And I do not require some megadose of anything to imagine me and mine the object of "ethnic cleansing," and I really have a problem with a program like that. I really do.

And I cannot understand why people wonder about what kind of health care Bill Clinton will finally propose, or if he will ever forget about the deficit and focus, for example, on South Central L.A. If "ethnic cleansing" doesn't get to you, if the comic-book specter of Ross Perot is more disturbing to you than the documented and relentlessly ruinous assault of Muslim girls and young women, then things are pretty clear. There is nothing to wonder about.

Bill Clinton, who cravenly capitulates his constitutional civilian power to the military, utterly lacks a value system hinged to the survival of human life and dignity, which is why he buddies up with Colin Powell.

And Powell! Did he luck out or what? When Clinton was elected, he probably thought he had become the dutiful employee of a President with whom he might regularly disagree. But no! Now he finds himself the Big Boy in the picture: the man to be mollified and coddled and photographed with.

Powell was a poor student at City College years ago, and today, in the context of gay and lesbian rights, he clearly does not remember Harry Truman ordering the military to integrate. That made possible Powell's very own j-o-b. But his job is the least of it.

Evidently, Powell does not remember the Middle Passage that carried millions of Africans captured for slavery to these shores. He does not remember how many more millions of his African forefathers and foremothers perished during that bedeviled voyage. He does not recall how, once the surviving victims reached America, a national policy of "ethnic cleansing" beginning with slave codes beleaguered our days and our nights from that awful moment of arrival to this moment. Does he?

Isn't he the humanitarian genius who concocted the plan to deliver food to Bosnian Muslims by dropping ten-ton packages from jet planes thousands of feet up in the sky?

Isn't he the tough guy whose idea of a good fight is Grenada or another round of infernal bombing of Baghdad, in famished, disease-ridden Iraq?

Isn't he the courageous military counselor advising Clinton to stay out of former Yugoslavia because maybe there might be an American fighter plane shot down or American troops wounded, and so forth?

Thank God Powell and Clinton did not head the country during World War II. We were unconscionably slow getting into it but, at last, and at least, we did get into it.

To coexist with genocide is to collaborate with genocide. "Ethnic cleansing" implies and glorifies genocide. More than 120,000 Bosnian Muslim men, women, and children slaughtered! More than a million and a half Muslims terrorized into refugee flight!

What will compel national and international commitment of every kind of resource available to stop the brutality and the genocide?

If we do not rescue Bosnian Muslims from their rapine executioners, if we do not restore to them their rightful, sovereign territory, then how shall we justify our military might and our think-tank capacities?

Is there any cause more clear, more summoning, than the cause of human life?

Apparently, yes. And, therefore, there is no safety for any of us: no safety. Nor do we deserve to suppose that we should be safe when the intended extermination of another people does not disturb our routine preoccupations.

Yes, but if we went into Bosnia what about other situations of similar horror? Wouldn't we have to intervene all over the place? ...

You bet. And so what about that! I mean, excuse me, but are we or are we not talking about "ethnic cleansing"? Are we or are we not talking about somebody violently seizing space that belongs to someone else—*someone not clean enough to live?*

Exactly who is clean enough to stay alive? Exactly who should decide who's clean and who's dirty/wrong/off/dark/undesirable?

Hey, I would like to return to my quandary about slices of lemon pie. And I would like to devote myself to loving somebody who loves me. And there is music I need to hear. And flowers I need to see. And children I want to hold close to my heart. And these homely desires define a delicate human condition that cannot withstand our indifference, our inertia, our insensibility when somebody else is screaming for help in his and her house.

At the least and at this horribly late date I say it's time to retrieve our national moneys from our armed forces: Armed forces not at the disposal of human life are indefensible.

Let us aggressively retrieve those ill-spent moneys and spend them in ways that may begin to enable us to be and act like human beings down and dirty for the rightful, dignified survival of us all.

Freedom Time

November 1993

A million years ago, Janis Joplin was singing, "Freedom's just another word for nothing left to lose." I found that puzzling, back then. Or, "white."

To my mind, freedom was an obvious good. It meant looking at an apartment and, if you liked it, being able to put down a deposit and sign a lease. It meant looking for a job and, if you found something for which you qualified—on the basis of education and/or experience—being able to take that position. Freedom had to do with getting into college if your grades were good enough. Freedom meant you could register to vote and live to talk about it.

A lot of other Americans felt the same way, thirty years ago. And black and white, we sang militant songs and we tested public transportation and restaurants and universities and corporate hiring policies and nice, clean neighborhoods for freedom. And we rallied and we marched and we risked everything for freedom because we believed that freedom would deliver us into pride and happiness and middle-class incomes and middle-class safety.

Thirty years later and freedom is no longer a word that most folks remember to use, jokingly or otherwise. And the declining popularity of the word is matched by our declining commitment to protect, and to deepen, and to extend, the meanings of freedom in the United States.

Today we know that "black and white" does not adequately describe anything real. Individual, economic, racial, ethnic, and sexual realities defy such long-ago simplicity. "Black" has become Nigerian or Afro-Caribbean or Senegalese or African-American or Zulu. "White" has become Serbo-Croatian or Bosnian Muslim or Irish Republican or Italian-American or Greek or Norwegian. And, even as collective identities inside America have multiplied, our political presence here has intensified as well: women, Latino, Asian, Native, gay, lesbian, senior citizen, and so-called legal and illegal aliens. (As for the very popular concept of "aliens," you would think that, by now, anybody other than Native Americans or Chicanos/Mexicans would be pretty embarrassed to mouth such an obnoxious pejorative.)

But rather than recognize galvanizing intersections among us, too often we yield to divisive media notions such as women's rights, for example, threatening the rights of black folks or Chicanos. There is a dismal competition among

Americans who should know better and who should join together for their own good. There is an acquiescence in the worst knavery of the mass media, as those top TV shows and those major weekly magazines inflame our most egocentric and paranoid inclinations. In consequence, we are muddling through a terrifying period of atomization and bitterness and misdirected anger.

What the new emerging majority of these United States holds in common, at its core, is a need for freedom to exist equally and a need to become the most knowledgeable, happy, productive, interconnected, and healthy men and women that we can. Ours is a need for freedom that does not omit any racial, gender, ethnic, sexual, or physical identity from its protection. But unless we will, each of us, reach around all of these identities and embrace them even as we cherish our own, no one's freedom will be assumed.

In Margaret Atwood's novel *The Handmaid's Tale*, the reader comes upon this remarkable one-liner: "Nothing changes instantaneously: In a gradually heating bathtub, you'd be burned to death before you knew it." I think we're jammed inside that bathtub and the water's getting hot.

About five weeks ago, I was walking my dog, Amigo, along the rather quiet streets of North Berkeley when a young white man yelled something in my direction and asked me to stop. I stopped. He bolted in front of me and, excitedly, inquired whether I had seen "anything or anyone unusual." I said no, and waited to hear him out.

It seems that twice on that one day, somebody had "delivered" an anti-Semitic bound book of neo-Nazi filth to the lawn in front of his house. He, Eric, was the father of a newborn baby and his Jewish wife, he told me, was completely freaked out by these scary events.

"How about you?" I asked him. Eric shrugged, and kept repeating that he "didn't understand it" and "couldn't believe" that none of his neighbors had seen anything. We talked a little while and I gave Eric my name and telephone number, as well as the numbers of some active people who might rally, fast, against this hatefulness.

In subsequent weeks, Eric invited me (and Amigo) into his house to meet his wife and to see their new baby boy, but I never had the time. Or, I never made the time to visit them.

Shortly after the first delivery of neo-Nazi literature to my neighborhood, I got on a plane bound for Madison, Wisconsin. *The Progressive* was putting on a benefit show and the editors arranged for me to join the celebration. Madison, Wisconsin, is a lot like North Berkeley except Madison gets cold, and stays cold, during the winter. Similar to my Northern California habitat, there are abundant public indications of environmental concern and civility: sheltered bus stops, wheel-chair-accessible street crossings, bike lanes, public tennis courts, fabulous public libraries, a wonderful public university, and bookstores and backpackers all over the place.

I stayed with Dr. Elizabeth Ann Karlin during my visit to Madison. The morning after my arrival, Dr. Karlin and I sat at the dining table looking at newspapers, drinking coffee, and pushing bagels away from the butter and the cream cheese. At some point, Dr. Karlin stopped talking, and I glanced at her face: It was flushed, and she fell silent. Now her dogs were wild with barking and ferocious agitation.

I got up and went to the windows. Outside, two white men were marching back and forth carrying placards that said, ABORTION, A BABY CAN LIVE WITHOUT IT, and LIBERTY AND JUSTICE FOR SOME.

Breakfast was over.

I located my press pass, my ballpoint pen, yellow pad, and I tied my sneaker shoelaces and went outside to interview these members of "Operation Rescue" and "Missionaries to the Pre-born." Why were they there?

"We're picketing Elizabeth Karlin's house because she kills babies in her Women's Medical Health Center."

I talked with Kermit Simpson and David Terpstra for more than two hours. It was eerie. It was familiar. They spoke about the futility of the courts, the brutality of the police, and their determination, regardless, to rescue "innocent babies" from "murder." It was familiar because their complaints and their moral certitude echoed the regular complaints and the moral certainty of the civil-rights movement.

But these groups were white. These groups were right-wing religious fundamentalists. And the only freedom they were concerned about was the freedom of the "unborn."

In fact, throughout our lengthy conversation, neither one of these men ever referred to any woman or anything female: "The baby" had to be saved from murder. That was the formulation. No woman's mind or body or feelings or predicament, at any moment, entered their consideration. What mattered was "the baby."

As I listened to David Terpstra, a good-looking white man in his twenties, it occurred to me that he was the kind of person who might have shot and killed Dr. Gunn.[27] Certainly he would see no reason not to kill a doctor who "kills babies." David told me there are twenty-two warrants out for his arrest, and he keeps moving.

He has no wife and no children and nothing special besides his mission to save "the baby."

Inside Dr. Karlin's house, the day was ruined. Even if the sun had returned to the sky (which it refused to do), there was terror and dread palpable, now, in every room.

And where were the good people of Madison who love their civil liberties and who hold Dr. Karlin in highest esteem as a warrior of our times and who used to understand that individual freedom depends upon a mass demand for its blessings and opportunities?

And what could I do for my friend, the doctor, before I got back on a plane, and left the scene of her clear and present danger?

The next weekend was a memorial reading for Tede Matthews, a gay white American who had managed the Modern Times bookstore in San Francisco, and who had died of AIDS in July. Tede Matthews had also distinguished himself as an activist for human rights in Central America. And he had helped many, many writers and poets to acquire a community of support. He was/he is much beloved. And he died of AIDS.

In the overflow audience of several hundred people who came to honor Tede Matthews's life and to establish a Tede Matthews fund for civil rights for gay men and lesbians in Central America and in the United States, there were many gay men and lesbians.

And I heard in my brain the helter-skelter of selective scripture that the Operation Rescue guys hurled into that Wisconsin silence. And I reflected on the tragedy of Tede Matthews's death, and the death of thousands upon thousands of young men whom we have loved and lost. And I wanted to rise from my seat in a towering, prophetic rage and denounce any scripture/any construct of divinity that does not cherish all of the living people on earth and does not grieve for the cruelties of daily life that afflict every one of us if basic freedom is denied.

But this was a memorial service. And Tede Matthews is no longer alive.

On my return to U.C. Berkeley, one of my students alerted me to a forthcoming issue of *Mother Jones* that would trash Women's Studies in general and our department in particular.[28] This student, Pamela Wilson, had been quoted out of context and she explained things to me. And she was mad.

The *Mother Jones* article proved to be a juicyfruit of irresponsible, sleazy journalism: a hatchet job with malice towards every facet of the subject under scrutiny and entitled, "Off Course."

Since its appearance, several other national publications have chimed in, applauding the "exposure" of "fraud" perpetrated upon students beguiled into taking courses that let them study themselves and sometimes sit in a circle of chairs.

The head of Women's Studies, Professor Evelyn Glenn, called a special departmental meeting. The faculty decided to respond to the attack, in writing, and on national public radio.

One student, Catherine Cook, has received hate mail from loquacious bigots who believe that women's studies, along with ethnic studies, make it clear that public education is wasting taxpayer money. Furthermore, these "non-academic" studies "debase" the minds of young Americans who, instead, should "get a job," and so forth.

As a matter of fact, this latest assault on freedom of inquiry and the pivotal role of public education within that categorical mandate, this most recent effort to roll things back to "the basics" of white men studies taught by white men with the assistance of books written by and about white men has upset our students. The young woman who received hate mail because she thought she had a right to pursue her (women's) studies had trouble breathing, and her hands shook, as she brought those items of hatred into our faculty meeting. Students in my class, Coming Into the World Female, seemed puzzled, at first, and then stunned, and now furious with brilliant energies as they prepare for a press conference, a mock Women's Studies class, and a demonstration that will take place just outside the entrance to the office building of *Mother Jones*.

The students voted to create those public reactions. They have spent hours and hours in solemn, wearisome research and composition. They believe that the truth of their intentions—and the truth of the necessity for women's studies and ethnic studies and African-American studies—will become apparent to most of America if only they, the students, do all of this homework into the facts, and if only they give the design and the wording of their flyers maximal painstaking and meticulous execution.

They believe that there is a mainstream majority America that will try to be fair, and that will respect their courage, and admire the intelligence of their defense. They believe that there is a mainstream majority America that will overwhelm the enemies of public and democratic education. They believe that most of us, out here, will despise and resist every assault on freedom in the United States.

And I hope they're right. With all my heart, I hope so. But the water's boiling. And not a whole lot of people seem to notice, or care, so far.

Freedom is not "another word for nothing left to lose." And we are letting it go; we are losing it. Freedom requires our steady and passionate devotion. Are we up to that?

A Good Fight

December 1993

I was nine years old at Robin Hood Camp for Girls. Two and a half hours north of Brooklyn, by bus, and mountains and woods and lakes suddenly came together as a real-world situation for me.

I was short for my age, and very young.

It never seemed odd to me that our camp boasted the name of a rather notorious male hero.

I never wondered about the absolute difference between my regular concrete street life in Bedford Stuyvesant and the idyllic circumstance of our summertime cabins and dirt trails and huge, hearty, community meals on the outside deck of the rec hall.

I don't remember puzzling over my experience of seasonal integration, which meant that ten months of the year I lived and played in an entirely black universe, and then for eight weeks I became a member of a minority of three or four black girls in a white vacationland of seventy-five to eighty other kids coming from neighborhoods and schools quite different from my own.

I was nine years old and free! I was far away from home, and I was hellbent on having a great time. We played softball and we learned archery and we went on wilderness hikes, overnight, and we burned our tongues on hot chocolate in tin cups and we rode horses, English saddle, and we swam and we made things for our parents in arts & crafts.

I was nine years old and some of the counselors gave me *The Razor's Edge* and *Tender Is the Night* to read after lights out and some of them tried to take away what they called "that filthy rabbit's foot" that my best friend, Jodi, gave me to wear for good luck.

And we sat around campfires and sang under the stars. But best of all, we played softball and I supposed that when I grew up I'd probably become a professional shortstop for some terrific softball team, and then, maybe, after lights out, I'd write my own *Tender Is the Night*, or *Time Must Have a Stop*, or *Magic Mountain*.

Those were my plans. But, in fact, the most exciting thing that happened was that Jodi and I became Blood Brothers. Of course, it never occurred to us that maybe we should become Blood Sisters: We were thinking of David and

Jonathan when we each cut the inside of our wrists with a penknife and mingled blood to seal our pact of eternal friendship. Not satisfied with that, we formed an elite club, The Dare Devils, and we hammered overlapping capital D's into our silver bracelets that we now could hardly wait to finish in arts & crafts where, formerly, we laconically wove lanyards or beaded belts or painted jewelry boxes for the "old folks" back home.

And, having mingled our blood, and, having hammered our bracelets into distinctive emblems of our bond, our tribe of Dare Devils leaped across big splits in the earth or we set loose the rowboats in the darkness or we swam across the lake, secretly, by moonlight, or we raced each other, on horseback and on foot, and we looked for the highest trees to climb and we played out our days with utmost heart and utmost hilarity and we—nine- and ten-year-old little girls—thought we were young gods fully blessed by all of our lives full of energy and love and an insatiable appetite for danger. We were daredevils loose on a beautiful planet. We were nine- and ten-year-old little girls and we thought we were free.

Toward the end of that summer, we had a final campfire down by the boats, and the song we sang was, "For all we know—we may never meet again—before you go—make this moment sweet again." We were so young. We could tell that was supposed to be a sad song but we felt no sadness ourselves. We tried not to giggle. We tried to sit in sadness out of respect for the grownups sprinkled among us. And I remember wondering if I would sometimes feel sadness, too, when I got old enough to become a counselor.

But I wasn't sure. Back then I could not imagine the sadness reserved for girls, everywhere.

I would have been amazed by any societal surprise at our Dare Devil/Blood Brother activities.

I would have been dumbfounded to hear that every fifteen seconds a woman is battered in the United States.

I would never have believed that people kill babies if they're female.

Or that white people despise black people.

Or that half of all black mothers have no or inadequate prenatal care.

Or that one out of every eight women in the United States has breast cancer and that before this decade is out, 500,000 American women will die of breast cancer.

Or that only 5 per cent of the money spent for cancer research is spent on finding a cure for breast cancer.

Back then, my ideas of daredeviltry did not conjure up the taking of my black body into a roadside luncheonette for a forbidden cup of coffee.

I never would have imagined that my loving a white man or that my loving any woman or that my raising my son by my own wits would constitute high risk and certain jeopardy.

And I never would have supposed that the biblical story of Ruth and Naomi held as much heroism, or more, inside its humble womanly narrative as the story of David and Jonathan.

And I would have laughed at anybody who said that someday I'd have breast cancer and that, even after going through a mastectomy, I'd have only a 40 per cent chance of survival.

Then, last year, one early morning, there was my friend, Dr. Alan Steinbach, bending over me in the recovery room at Alta Bates Hospital, and Alan was saying, "There's bad news!"

I thought, immediately, that he must mean something godawful had happened to my son, or to one of my friends, but he meant there was bad news for me. They'd performed a biopsy and found an enormous amount of cancer in my right breast.

And so I became one of the millions of American women who must redefine courage and who must redefine the meaning of heroic friendship if we will survive.

And my son and my lover and my friends gathered around like Dare Devils daring themselves and their devotion and their walking of my dog and their changing of the dressing and their seamless and hilarious system of around-the-clock support to save my morale and to save my life.

And it was not easy. And it was not brief. And it is not over.

In between surgery number three and number four, I wrote this poem:

> The breath continues but the breathing
>   hurts
> Is this the way death wins its way
> against all longing
> and incendiary thrust from grief?
> Head falls
> Hands crawl
> and pain becomes the only keeper
> of my time
> I am not held
> I do not hold
> And touch degenerates into new
> agony

I feel
the healing of cut muscle/
broken nerves
as I return to hot and cold
sensations
of a body tortured by the flight
of feeling/normal
registrations of repulsion
or delight

On this meridian of failure or recovery
I move
or stop respectful
of each day
but silent now
and slow

I swear to you I never ever expected to write anything like that, my whole life, but I had to try to tell that truth.

The Women's Cancer Resource Center of Berkeley and the National Black Women's Health Network and Dr. Craig Henderson and Dr. Susan Love and Dr. Denise Rogers and Christopher and Angela and Adrienne and Dianne and Stephanie and Martha and Haruko and Amy and Sara and Pratibha and Lauren and Roberta and Camille and my colleagues and students at school and the neighbors next door and Amigo, the Airedale who lives with me—they dared me to make this cancer thing into a fight: They dared me to practice trying to lift my arm three or four inches away from my side. They dared me to go ahead and scream and cry but not to die. And so I did not die. But I have faced death. And I know death now.

And in the mornings when I walk out into the garden and I see the ninety-seven-year-old willow tree and the jasmine blooming aromatic and the honeysuckle bulging into the air and Amigo gulping at a bumblebee and a stray bluebird lifting itself in flight above the roof of my little house, I am happy beyond belief.

And when I may join with men and women to end the disease of breast cancer and the disease of race hatred and the disease of misogyny and the disease of homophobia and the disease of not caring about the victims of ethnic cleansing and the victims of our malignant neglect, I am happy beyond belief.

Because this is a good fight. It feels good to me. And, yes, now I know about sadness but I do not live there, in sadness.

And I am happy beyond belief to be here and to join with you to make things better.

Give Me Two Reasons

March 1994

Dear Bill Clinton:

If you think about what can happen in less than thirty seconds, then a year seems like a real long time. That's about as long as you've been holding title to more power than any other individual on the planet. I know you're a man and not a natural resource or a natural disaster. But you're President of these United States, and that should mean something about safety for those of us who put you in the Oval Office.

Whether earthquake or fire or hurricane or corporate "downsizing" or juries arriving at idiot-incendiary conclusions or affluent and fanatical hatemongers standing tall, the big guy in the big house on Pennsylvania Avenue is supposed to protect us, the people, from harm or, failing that, deliver us from desperation. You're the big guy. That's your job. That's what national security requires: our domestic safety from harm and desperation.

If I remember correctly, most women who voted cast their ballots for you, as did most elderly Americans, most young Americans, most African-Americans, most Mexican-Americans, most Asian-Americans, most Chicanos, and most gay and lesbian Americans. Our *de facto* coalition of choice gave you the major-league boost you needed to move out of Little Rock, Arkansas. And so, the way I see things, you owe us, the new majority of American citizens, a whole lot—as a matter of reciprocity, if nothing else.

Can you give me two reasons why any one of the original Clinton supporters should vote for you again? Or even speak to you? Can you give me two reasons why I should not call you Spineless Sam or confuse you with George Bush?

Given your track record of equivocation, cowardice, and retreat on one hand, plus active humiliation, appeasement, betrayal, and blustery inertia on the other, why should we—folks who celebrated November 3, 1992—believe anything good can come of you, except, perhaps, by accident?

Your failure begins and continues with your willing coexistence with genocide: Your refusal to stop so-called ethnic cleansing and the concomitant mass rape of Muslim women in Bosnia.

Then there are your broken promises—to the Haitian refugees, to pro-choice Americans, to gay and lesbian Americans, and to city dwellers ("inner" or "outer" be damned).

Then there is your eating of the defeat of your anyway heavily diluted proposal for jobs.

There is your silence on American poverty except to blame the victims of Federal and state neglect and abandonment.

There is your acquiescence to racist and unconstitutional anti-immigrant uproar and proposed legislation.

There is your beating up on the neediest among us: families that qualify for the miserly assistance our welfare programs use as an excuse to belittle and castigate the poor.

There is your absolute zero performance as regards hungry homeless Americans, who daily increase in number.

Then there is your savage, gratuitous, and unforgivable insult to law professor Lani Guinier.

And, finally, there was that incredible moment of complacency and insolence when you stood in the pulpit of a black church and presumed to speak on behalf of Dr. Martin Luther King Jr. Your arrogance was matched only by your ignorance of Dr. King who, relentlessly, made it clear that Americans will have to pay billions and billions of dollars in order to reverse this country's pathological, 400-plus years of racist impact on black people living here and dying here.

Yes, I know that more than a year ago, your closest advisers had written, "It's the economy, stupid!" on the wall of your "War Room." But I had voted for you because you had actually said: "We cannot afford to waste a single life."

And I had taken you at your word. But you have failed to keep faith with those of us who wanted to trust you.

And that, Mr. President, is the State of the Union today. We are reeling from unnatural and natural disasters without benefit of the rescue and the relief that follow from true executive commitment to the safety of every single life.

Because you have broken so many promises to so many of us, there was only one "brother" in Los Angeles you could call. Rather than creating a new democratic community of inclusion and justice and mercy, you have surrounded yourself with millionaire white men who remain as completely out of touch with the majority of Americans as you are.

But we, the new majority, we exist. And you will learn, Mr. President, that without us, you will become, for good and for evil, beside the point.

A Powerful Hatred

May 1994

What a sunny day! Plum trees in pastel bloom. Jasmine in fragrant flowering display. What I'd like to do is fall asleep listening to Prince, or wake myself up, completely, with the energies of Pearl Jam, or walk my dog for three miles in every direction under that very blue sky above me. But other things are happening.

There is a powerful hatred loose in the world. And everything and everyone we cherish is endangered. And so I would have to be some kind of really nearsighted fool to wallow in what's left of the world that's gorgeous and freely given and natural and sweet and hot and unpredictable and delicate and good for growing things. I'd be a wallowing fool unless I also tried to eliminate, or reduce, that hatred that can take all that we have away from us.

But how should I stage my fight? Who will listen to what I have to say?

Except for those occasions when the media smell a possible chance to pit black folks against other black folks, when do I get calls asking for my thoughts and opinions about anything whatsoever? If the media wanted to know what mainstream black folks think and feel about white folks, for example, they would regularly interview the head of the A.M.E. (African Methodist Episcopal) Church and chairs of African-American Studies Departments and a representative sampling of black students at your nearest high school, and black writers and thinkers such as Adolph Reed and Angela Davis and Manning Marable and Cornel West and Bell Hooks.

And what the media would discover is that whether they're looking at somebody separatist or not, most black folks are very clear about one thing: who endangers their lives. Most black folks know he is a powerful white man, such as the President or the Governor or the distinguished U.S. Senator from almost anywhere. And that's how most of us feel most of the time about white men: that they are powerful and dangerous.

And we are not racist. We simply do not have power; white men do. And they—and the few black men invited in, such as Ron Brown, Clarence Thomas, Colin Powell, and Shelby Steele—use that power in ways that cause us enormous harm.

For two decades, Federal and state policies have combined to ensure a statistical tragedy of huge magnitude now unfolding in the national black community. Whether we use indices of unemployment or homelessness or drug addiction or domestic violence or levels of education never attained or official designation as a family on or below the poverty line, our people face a future deformed by boastful government neglect and by hysterical moves to further criminalize and further incarcerate greater and greater numbers of our young men and women. And our people face an uninhibited scapegoat campaign to stigmatize and invalidate the neediest among us: welfare families dependent on AFDC support that amounts to an average of $370 a month for a mother and her two children.

Is it not hateful to equate "crime" and "welfare" with "black"? That is the equation promoted by Bill Clinton and Pete Wilson, both of them white men who never tire of blathering about these issues they deliberately distort.

As the President tells it, welfare dependency (black) is a first-priority problem to be eliminated for the sake of good character and the budget. He mouths these sentiments despite the fact that the total percentage of our national budget available for welfare assistance is less than one half of 1 per cent. (And, incidentally, most recipients of welfare aid are white, not black.)

But Bill Clinton knows nothing about good character; good character doesn't follow from working a nine-to-five shift, as he suggests. Good character has to do with honesty and reliability and kindliness.

Clinton and other powerful white men impugn the character of (black) women on welfare, but where did these men get the idea that raising children is something other than full-time, supremely important, hard work? And exactly what kind of "workfare" are they talking about for single mothers when even white male college graduates cannot find employment? What kind of workfare do they have in mind besides some hideous update of legalized slave labor?

Then there is "crime," which means, according to Clinton and his powerful white cohorts, young black men. Well, it seems that the Almighty Budget will not tolerate help for the poor, and the Almighty Budget has no money for job creation or for rescue and revitalization of our public schools or for drug rehabilitation or for development and implementation of effective, grass-roots community planning, or for social and psychological counseling: No funds available in the Almighty Budget!

But, hey! Bill has a plan: three strikes and you're out forever. And what will that cost California, alone, every year? More than $6 billion! And so, suddenly never mind about the budget. To punish/derogate/imprison/destroy, there are multibillions of dollars in hand, evidently. But to salvage/teach/train/enlighten/empower? No money in the bank!

Now, if you jail somebody at age twenty-five and sentence him to life, that will cost—supposing he lives another forty years—$1 million ($25,000 a year times forty years). So Bill Clinton and Pete Wilson have $1 million per black man to spend and it's the God's truth that they're putting that kind of money into his imprisonment, his $25,000-a-year retirement from society.

There is a powerful hatred loose in the world. And most black folks know it. Most of us know it's white, not black. It's white, not Jewish. It's white and it's male, not female. It's white and it's male and it's heterosexual, not gay or lesbian. We who are weak make it our business to figure out who's strong—strong enough to help us or to crush our lives.

And so we pay attention to truly powerful white men. We notice that the guys who worship at the altar of Pentagon priorities (at a time when the former Soviet Union would not be able to muster a credible threat to Grenada) and who dump all over our human needs in the name of reducing the deficit are the very same guys who think up obscenities like how about taxing food stamps or what about three strikes and you're gone even from the potential for a useful, self-respecting life.

We notice that these are the same guys eagerly collaborating with racist wannabe gatekeepers to America: powerful white men whose ancestors for sure never asked permission to come to this country but just came hell-bent on owning slaves, exterminating Native Americans, and grabbing gold. These powerful white men now conspire to stop immigration to America by anybody who does not resemble themselves. These same powerful white men are the ones who waffle on or ignore women's issues and who betray and/or attack gay and lesbian Americans. These same powerful white men are the ones who will not broach the subject of education except to propose and/or execute additional cutbacks of funds accompanied by the jacking up of student tuition.

These same powerful white men apparently manage to sleep very well at night, thank you, even though their verifiable executive decisions mean that we coexist with absolutely documented genocide, a.k.a., ethnic cleansing in the former Yugoslavia.

There is a powerful hatred loose in the world. And it's obvious to most black people that this hatred is based upon a white supremacist ideology that determines domestic and foreign policies alike. We see American inertia vis-à-vis genocide in Bosnia as part of one horrible continuum that guarantees no action/ no deliverance/no beautification/no justice/no peace in South Central L.A. And that continuum is controlled by a white racist value system that does not regard human life as valuable because it's human, because it's alive.

The ruling racist value system of these United States asks three questions of each of us:

1) Does this citizen and his or her group look like somebody I would allow my daughter to marry?
2) Is this citizen and his or her group cheaply available for the enhancement of my profit margins?
3) What can I get away with? In other words, is it "safe" to condemn or ignore or impoverish or imprison or belittle this citizen and his or her group?

There is a powerful hatred loose in the world. And the most powerful practitioners of this hatred do not deploy a hateful rhetoric. They do not declare, "I hate black folks," or "I hate women," or "I hate Jews," or "I hate Muslims," or "I hate homosexuals." They make "civil" pronouncements, such as:

"The Defense Budget must not be cut further"

or "I made every effort to introduce a jobs bill to the Congress but...."

or "Top military experts advise against our active intervention in Bosnia"

or "I do not feel comfortable with the writings of my friend, Lani Guinier"

or "The White House is anxious to get past the uproar over gays in the military in order to put its best efforts behind healthcare reform"

or "Crime is our number one domestic concern"

or "Illegal aliens threaten to bankrupt state treasuries."

And most black people notice something else. We notice a virulent, racist double standard. We notice how long we had to wait before the United States adopted any sanctions against South Africa. We notice that the United States has never even considered sanctions against Israel. We notice that the American media got all excited and riveted by Minister Louis Farrakhan when one of his lieutenants spewed forth loathsome anti-Semitic (and also, by the way, homophobic and misogynist) remarks. We notice that the American media absolutely failed to broadcast or telecast the news of Minister Farrakhan's December 4, 1964, column in *Muhammad Speaks* when he described Malcolm as "a dog returning to its vomit" and when he, Farrakhan, declared that Malcolm was "worthy of death."

Anti-Semitism is wrong. Anti-Semitism is evil. All scapegoating of any kind of people is evil and wrong. Farrakhan and Khalid Abdul Muhammad fulminate about white people, and they trash and vilify that most vulnerable segment of white America: the Jewish population.

I have already turned away from Farrakhan. I was never there. He was never on my side.

Farrakhan runs on hatred. His targets change. But the hatred continues. His views and preachments are not easily distinguishable from those of David Duke. But Farrakhan does not possess a fraction of the power invested in and represented by David Duke.

We notice double standards.

We notice no uproar remotely comparable to the Farrakhan controversy when U.S. Senator Ernest Hollings describes African heads of state as cannibals, or when Jesse Helms utters another unconstitutional commandment, or when Republican Presidential candidate Patrick Buchanan lets loose rabid scattershots against black folks and gay and lesbian Americans and women daring to dream of a life besides and beyond motherhood and vacuum cleaners.

And where were the media and Congressional calls for public repudiation of Baruch Goldstein[29] and the rabbi who officiated at his funeral, the rabbi who said, "One million Arabs is not worth a Jewish fingernail," and "We are all Goldstein"?

Why is Baruch Goldstein "a lone, violent madman" and Farrakhan, on the contrary, Public Enemy Number One?

We notice double standards. And we do not like what we see. We do not like what that means. And so, yes, there is fury and there is rage in Black America today. For all of these two decades of terrible reasons, there is black fury and there is black rage.

Today the black community is victim to a national scapegoat campaign that promises to wreck our prospects as a people, irreversibly. And Farrakhan is a distraction, a calculated media distraction of our energies from the real deal: the power of white supremacist ideology here, and everywhere.

Is it conceivable that the media could open up to other black voices concerned by issues such as government responsibility and equality and justice and building political coalitions and exposing truly powerful white men such as Clinton and Wilson as ambassadors of programmatic hate?

I think it's inconceivable because American media uphold a racist agenda alongside Bill and Pete and Tom and Dick and Harry.

The media construct of Minister Farrakhan leads progressive white Americans and even some Americans of color to believe that the problem is black racism when, actually, the problem is racism and hatred of any color or kind. And the problem behind that is the problem of who has the power to make whose lives miserable or whose lives over or whose lives fresh and hopeful again.

There is a powerful hatred loose in the world. And there is a savagery of racist double standard ruling our lives. And the way to escape this horror of powerful hatred is to get serious and real clear.

What powerful white man, what powerful white Christian male heterosexual in America today will raise up the model of his lifework as an example opposite to that of Baruch Goldstein, Louis Farrakhan, Bill Clinton, Pete Wilson?

Where can we find a value system seeking to make rather than break connections among our various, frail lives? Where can we find such values invested in any man or woman wielding great political and/or corporate power?

When will we extirpate self-hatred as well as our hatred of folks weaker than we are from our own personal days and nights?

And what is to be done about the really big deal? The President? The governors? The U.S. Senator from almost anywhere? And you and you—whoever you are—perilously interposed between Sarajevo and South Central L.A., what are you going to do?

Injustice and contempt breed hatred.

Hatred reaps hatred.

We need, each of us, to begin the awesome, difficult work of love: loving ourselves so that we become able to love other people without fear so that we can become powerful enough to enlarge the circle of our trust and our common striving for a safe, sunny afternoon near to flowering trees and under a very blue sky.

We Are All Refugees

July 1994

This is a moment of enormous and demanding contradiction. In South Africa, Nelson Mandela has become the president of the country that held him in prison for more than twenty-seven years. In South Africa, the new Bill of Rights prohibits discrimination against anyone on the basis of race or gender or class or age or sexual orientation. In South Africa, where 5 per cent of the population controls 88 per cent of the national wealth, President Mandela has appointed a cabinet committed to a five-year plan carrying forward three key proposals: the construction of one million new homes, a vast public-sector employment program, and universal, free, compulsory education.

In South Africa, where for more than 350 years white racist ideology has enjoyed enforcement by tyrannies of the law and the whip and the bullet, the first democratically elected president, Nelson Mandela, has pledged himself to *nonracial* principles of justice and equal citizen entitlements for all.

Meanwhile, in these United States where common nouns such as democracy and liberty have long known bumpersticker popularity, the notion of a black man or a woman becoming the President remains a joke/a dopey idea/a theoretical construct of small or no plausibility.

In these United States it is difficult to find executive respect for any principle whatsoever except the principle of leadership by following the polls, and that other, most lamentable principle of allocating the least to those in greatest desperation.

Rather than living in a sovereign state in which someone wrongfully imprisoned may nevertheless rise above injustice and one day occupy the highest office, we suffer from budget policies that crush public education up against our ill-considered rush to criminalize and incarcerate and stigmatize and impoverish and deport those men, women, and children among us who possess the most meager array of options.

Rather than the "new world" invoked by President Mandela, our politicians and their media flunkies in these United States spout disinformation designed to bring about an Old World faithful to a Eurocentric, patriarchal history that drags a pretty poor track record into view.

And so you will not hear White House or Sacramento declarations of a five-year plan to meet basic human requirements for housing and employment and knowledge. Instead you will hear White House and Sacramento presentations of a racist slant on public issues of crime, drugs, and so-called welfare, and so-called illegal aliens. Rather than "child care," you will hear "border patrol." Rather than "rehabilitate," you will hear "three strikes and you're out."

And in the absence of a civilizing humane leadership, and in the presence of a leader who contemplates taxation of food stamps, and in the presence of a leader who can betray his promise to Haitian refugees and who can sleep very well in verified co-existence with genocide in Bosnia and who can desecrate the legacy of Dr. Martin Luther King Jr. by daring to misrepresent Dr. King's analysis which, contrary to Clinton's galling and appalling assertions, in fact called for billions of dollars to be invested in human salvation undertakings inside South Central L.A. and inside every other city of these United States—in the quandary of such terrible leadership absence and such awful leadership presence, is it any wonder that a ten-year-old boy recently assisted his fourteen-year-old buddy in the killing of a woman for $80 and the hell of it?

In a country where Dan Quayle is reportedly making a comeback no doubt related to the victory of Richard Nixon's burial of Tricky Dick's real life, is it any wonder that the ten-year-old willing accomplice to murder could say something so stupid as: "It wasn't supposed to be like that. It was a game, right?"

And then there is the forgotten issue of the woman, Elizabeth Alvarez, who was the mother of three children and married and now she's dead and *The New York Times* devoted a whole page-and-a-half to her killers:[30] What "the boys" said or didn't say, and what various experts think or do not think about "the boys" and all you ever know about Elizabeth Alvarez is that she was pregnant, she was married, and she's dead.

But how old was she? How come she didn't kill anybody? Did she ever dream or do anything besides get married and have children? Why does *The New York Times* refer to her simply as "a mother of three"? Was she never anybody's sister/friend/teacher/confidante/employee/partner or somebody's dearest person in the whole wide world?

I want to know how come Elizabeth Alvarez never killed anybody. I want to know how come boys and men commit 87 per cent of all violent crimes. And no, I don't think Elizabeth Alvarez is dead because the two killer boys were raised by "women on welfare." But I do think that the fact that the father of one boy abandoned him and his fourteen-year-old mother, and I do think that the fact that the father of the second boy regularly beat up that boy's mother—I do think that these misogynist facts of paternal irresponsibility and violence led to their fatal choice of "a mother of three" as victim.

As I think about the stories of women—from my students all the way back to my maternal grandmother—again and again I am struck by qualities of hesitation and restraint. Some might interpret these characteristics as facets of mere modesty. But I would disagree. Modesty is something calculated or fake. And it leads nowhere except to the lowering of your eyes. But hesitation and restraint make tenderness and generosity and altruistic interaction possible and even likely.

Hesitation and restraint quiver quietly alive someplace opposite to violence and domination. And I wonder about that apparently unequal equation.

Is that the problem, worldwide?

Is the female of the species some kind of noble/virtuous set-up for her male counterpart?

How come Elizabeth Alvarez never killed anybody?

If she ever imagined boy-killers under development and wanted to evade a violent death, where could she go? Where could she find sanctuary?

As a woman, married or not, and pregnant or not, and mother of one/two/three, or none—where could she find political or economic asylum that would mean safety and respect and equal access to freedom *and to the power* to guarantee her own safety and her own equal access to freedom?

Instead of Mandela's New World, our politicians and their media flunkies busily and viciously strive to resurrect an Old World in which there will be no safety, no asylum, for anybody but themselves. These men, direct descendants of other men who came to America never asking anybody's permission to arrive or to invade or to conquer or to exterminate or to enslave or to betray or to exploit and discriminate against those who preceded them and those who, willingly or not, came after them—these men now contrive a so-called immigration crisis and they invent and then promulgate pathological-idiot terms like "illegal aliens."

But, as a matter of fact, the planet is not entirely white, or male. And the United States is no longer mostly white, and it will never be more than 50 per cent male. And today's wannabe gatekeepers are having themselves a holy-cow fit about this in-your-face situation of their inevitable decline. And so they castigate every one of the varieties of colored peoples seeking entry into our beloved American experiment of a multi-racial/multi-ethnic/multi-cultural body politic. And, as usual, the punishing burden of this hateful effort to exclude and to reject people clamoring for refuge and relief, the brunt of this hatred falls upon the weak: 80 per cent of the 100 million displaced people on the planet are women and children: 80 per cent! Overwhelmingly, the face of displaced humanity is a female face. Overwhelmingly, her female predicament of multifaceted oppres-

sion remains not recognized as a political predicament. And, so, overwhelmingly, most refugees do not qualify for political asylum.

But what if we women everywhere arose to demand political asylum from
the personal and the institutional violence and domination that scar our existence everywhere? What if we demanded political asylum for ourselves—on the
job, on the block where we live, in the bedrooms where we want to find and
make love?

What if we declared ourselves *perpetual refugees* in solidarity with all refugees needing safe human harbor from violence and domination and injustice
and inequality?

Could we arise with characteristic hesitation and restraint and nevertheless
be seen, be heard, be strong enough to change our homes, change our streets,
change our immigration policies, change our total national states into political
and economic asylum for ourselves: the majority of human life?

In this Americanspace disfigured by traditions of hatred and selfishness, we
are all alien and we are, none of us, legitimate.

We are all refugees horribly displaced from a benign and welcoming community.

And the question is: Can we soon enough create the asylum our lives will
certainly wither without?

Well, I behold the miracle of Mandela. And I behold the equally improbable miracle of domestic and international women's groups creating power out
of sorrow and away from pain. I look at the Women's Foundation, and the National Black Women's Health Project, and the National Asian Women's Health
Organization, and the California Abortion and Reproductive Rights Action
League finding out the facts, fighting for our dignified, fearless, and happily
consequential female freedom, and to me the answer is easy, it's obvious. We're
doing it!

Innocent of What?

September 1994

The night of the two "brutal murders" (what do they mean by "brutal"? Is there some other kind?), I drove my Rolls-Royce to McDonald's and, just like that, I got something to eat. I have a witness! He rode with me, this (white) guy who lives in my guest house on my $2 million property in Los Angeles. Driving the Rolls for two Big Macs, a double order of fries, and a large strawberry shake—all for myself—well! The way I see it, I already won my case.

Like I said, many times, I never wanted anybody to see me as a black man. I wanted to be different, to be more than that: a bona-fide mega-rich and famous star.

Didn't I run 2,003 yards on a football field in 1973? Okay, that was a while ago. Okay, I never particularly tried to protect somebody weaker than me. And I never took on people very much bigger or more powerful than me. But, so what? Folks call me a hero because of the way I ran with the ball. They called me a hero and I was having a pretty good time.

Okay, back in 1968, my first wife—she was black—she is black—she told some magazine, I think it was *Look* magazine, that I was "a beast" and "pretty horrible." But that was her slant on things.

I was having a pretty good time. As a matter of fact, she was pregnant with our third child when I saw this eighteen-year-old-fresh-outta-high-school-like-to-blow-me-away. She was so beautiful! So there was my first (black) wife pregnant with our third child and then I meet this girl and she's white and blond and perfect and everything and I went crazy for her and I was this big-time hero and so I started seeing her (the white girl) and ended up making her my second wife. I was having a pretty good time.

And that girl, well, she was my wife for more than fifteen years, you know, and she'd always bring me breakfast in bed—every damn day!—and she never did stop looking good to me. And that's kind of a long marriage as these things go. But, then, you watch those black women out here going off about the white girl was my "problem"—my "downfall," you know, and I'm supposed to be this "Brother" victimized by yellow hair and blue eyes. Can you believe it? I was having a pretty good time.

As a matter of fact, in the two years since my second wife and I got divorced, I've been "victimized," again, by another real beautiful, young white woman I've been dating steadily. I *am* having a pretty good time!

In the newspapers today, they said, "The O.J. of Old Returns: Confident in Court. He smiles and gives thumbs up to his supporters."[31] They said I was "nattily attired." Stuff like that. I'm big! I'm telling you! I already won my case. The papers note that I didn't even "acknowledge" the families of "the victims" (my—white—wife and her friend). But they leave it right there! Nobody's asking how come I wouldn't want to say, "I'm sorry, too," or "I'm grieving, too," or things along that line to the family of my brutally murdered (white) ex-wife—unless I'm not sorry or grieving or whatever. But nobody's bringing that up! No! They concentrate on the fact that I "look like a winner."

Hell, I am a winner! If I was a regular black man, can you imagine the same Los Angeles Police Department that chased down and just about killed Rodney King hanging back, for hours and for miles, while I was riding my Bronco (I left the Rolls-Royce in my garage) with a passport plus $10,000 in cash, trying to figure out what I want to do or where I want to go? Can you imagine that? Hah!

Now Rodney King—he was and is a regular black man. But me? I'm a winner. I had those turkeys talking all kinds of Mr. This and Mr. That. I'm big, I'm telling you! I'm having a pretty good time!

I got three of the baddest, and most expensive (and white) attorneys in the whole United States day and night defending my butt. As a matter of fact, we just decided (Okay, belatedly) to add on a black lawyer for the image thing, plus local L.A. public relations, and so forth. But I'm paying for this! I have that kind of Rolls-Royce bread to burn.

It's like this clown said a couple weeks ago: "Celebrity creates its own color, its own class, and its own laws." I'm here to tell you, that's the truth! I'm so rich and I'm so famous that ABC-TV gave me way more coverage than they gave to Nelson Mandela when he took over South Africa. You ready for that? And more than they ever thought about giving to Ron Dellums, who's been kicking ass in Congress for twenty-some years. And way, way more than they gave to the President's State of the Union. I'm not lying to you. You see what I'm saying? I've already won!

But there are these other women carrying on about "domestic violence." And sometimes that garbage gets on my nerves pretty bad. It's no big deal: Like I've said, many times, it's a family matter.

But these other women march around with these numbers about a domestic violence death every day and a half in L.A. County, where I happen to live, and four million women battered every year, one every five seconds, and 80 per cent of wives and girlfriends needing rescue turned away because there are only 1,500 shelters in the U.S.A. and sixty beds in all of San Francisco and you can choke your wife into unconsciousness and/or beat her bloody and break her arm or her leg or her nose and the law calls that a misdemeanor and I swear! Sometimes this garbage gets on my nerves! Like the nine times in 1989 when my ex-wife (the white one) called the cops because I got pretty damned mad about something and so I beat her up so she'd listen to me better. And that other time in 1993 when she told them I was going to kill her and now she's dead and it's god-damned annoying, sometimes, this "domestic-violence" bullshit!

But I'm having a pretty good time! At first I was kind of depressed. But I got over that. And folks are buying and selling these T-shirts dedicated to me. And I don't have to do anything I don't feel like doing. I don't have to say "Boo!" or "Diddley-Squat" to my (white) ex-wife's family, or anybody. So long as I show up "nattily attired," and "smiling," and "thumbs up," I'm a winner!

And besides, you ever heard of a black man who could pick and choose when he was a black man? You see what I'm saying? I'm different! I made it! I'm not a black man! Just like I always wanted! I'm big! I'm a star! I'm having a pretty good time!

Where I Live Now

January 1995

Less than a month ago, somebody wrote this on a wall at Fairfield University in Connecticut. "Fuck unity, you minorities. The white race is superior. I think we should hang all blacks, chinks, and spics. Let's unite and form a new generation of KKK. To all my white brothers and sisters, let's take over what once was ours. Minorities just cause problems, and we don't need them. All blacks should go to Africa, all chinks should go to hell, and all spics should get on their banana boats and go back to their island. If by 10:30 a.m. all minorities don't leave F.U., me and my fellow brothers will start killing and raping minority bitches."

A few days before this message (signed by "the KKK" and adorned by several swastikas), *The New York Times* committed the unnatural full weight of its Book Review to various popular exercises in behalf of white supremacy.

The next weekend, when I was speaking in Lexington, Kentucky, a white policeman there shot an unarmed eighteen-year-old black teenager in the head, and killed him.

I had arrived in Fairfield, Connecticut, barely twenty-four hours after California, the most populous and the largest and the most heterogeneous state of this Republic, re-elected Pete Wilson.

As Governor, Wilson has accomplished quite a lot. He has established the bizarre notion of an "illegal alien" in the respectable discourse about the issue of immigration to this country, which is a country of Native Americans, African-Americans, and—everybody else, for damned sure—immigrants, or, in the case of Mexican-Americans/Chicanos, forcibly displaced indigenous peoples.

He has further poisoned public debate through the deployment of TV commercials that depict Mexicans as crazed roaches swarming over and through and around defenseless toll booths and paralyzed highway traffic.

He has espoused "three strikes and you're out" and now, with the passage of Proposition 184, that amazing idea has become a law meaning that, within ten years, California will spend 2.5 times more money on prisons than it will spend on education. (Incidentally, at the rate of at least $25,000 a year, the cost of lifetime imprisonment—assuming forty years—is one million bucks.)

And, consistent with his "illegal alien" hysteria, Proposition 187,[32] another new law in California, means that anyone who appears "suspicious" shall be reported to authorities and denied classroom/emergency room entry. Presumably I will be wasting my time if I report anybody who looks like Pete Wilson: White is not "suspect." And, of course, white is smart—very smart. In fact, only those suspicious-looking Asian-Americans tend to defeat white folks at their own game: that same old Stanford-Binet blah-blah that excuses me from my life, really, because, given my genetic deficiency, what can you expect of me, anyhow?

So I arrived in Fairfield, Connecticut, feeling pretty low. My host, a young white senior from Nashua, New Hampshire, Paul Kelley, handed me a copy of the KKK ultimatum to read, once I climbed into his four-by-four. But it was hard to concentrate. Besides the heavy rain outside, Paul was telling me the whole deal of Aryan recruitment on the nearby beaches and anti-Semitism on campus and homophobic attacks, and I was wondering if I had really flown across the entire U.S.A., or was I just turning around and around in one spot: where I live now.

The same experts who think I'm stupid believe that (c.f., *The Handmaid's Tale*) white women of the right genetic composition should be breeding more or that only such women should have babies—regardless of the wishes of these genetic superstars—if "the decline" or "the elevation" of "the intelligence" of "the race" is at stake. And, conversely, one Mississippi politician ran for office by showing a poster of a black woman and her child: A vote for him was a vote against such an affront to eugenic considerations.

I was looking at the students: Asian and African and Hispanic and Native American and white and mostly Catholic and mostly female. It was a small gathering in a small room. But the fact of our common jeopardy was palpable, and as I listened to their modest demands for safety and representation, I felt almost calm: They were working it out. They had to.

None of these facts had changed: The KKK had not been captured or extirpated from their lives. Curricular inclusion of anything resembling multicultural studies was years away. But a fifth of the student population had joined a demonstration against hatred. (Not nothing, but not a majority response, either.)

Back home, it took awhile to get the stats. And when I heard the news, I was dumbfounded: 57 percent of Asian-Americans, and 50 percent of African-Americans, and 30 percent of Latinos had voted for Proposition 187. Talk about critical ignorance and/or horribly successful disinformation!

Where I live now is the same place where, during the 1920s, an involuntary sterilization plan was conceived and implemented. In the 1930s, the Nazis based their forced sterilization policies on the California model.

Where I live now is on the Western side of the Rockies. On the other side, my son was riding his bike from the University of Colorado-Boulder Law School library when a car full of white men tried to run him off the road as they made obscene suggestions about what he should do with himself. Boulder is where there are no Indians around but you do have a mania for 1 percent body fat, no smoking, and, also, threatening phone calls to a young Jewish couple who moved there, recently, and whose car has been vandalized.

Over here, in Berkeley, certain Americans approach other Americans in the supermarket or on the sidewalks asking "the other" Americans if they're in the United States legally, or not, and if they can prove whatever they say.

Where I live now makes me wonder if Nazi Germany's night skies ever beheld a really big moon—a heavenly light that failed to dispel the cold and the bitter winds tormenting the darkness of earth below.

Where I live now there is just such a moon tonight—a useless, huge light above our perishing reasons for hope.

Where I Live Now, Part Two

March 1995

Already, November 1994 feels far away. That was a seriously bad moment. And many of us lost morale because we accepted mass-media reports of a Republican "sweep" or a Republican "revolution." And so we thought we were doomed inside the tightening jaws of racist jeopardy, or worse. We were surrounded by enemies. We were few. We were weak. We had been slammed into the realm of the irrelevant.

It took a little while before we re-examined the arithmetic pertinent to those elections: If only 39 percent of the electorate cast a ballot, and if only 19 percent of the electorate voted Republican, then where was this mythical "landslide," exactly? What was the source for claims of a "monumental mandate"?

To be sure, the majority of the minority of Americans who did vote opted for the ignorant, mean, and self-destructive side of the choices available. And with Newt Gingrich chasing giraffes when he's not racing after more and more personal power, and with Bill Clinton as the redoubtable alternative to leadership of any kind, things in Washington continue to look dangerous and dismal—indeed, like a man-made disaster.

But I have been watching the Japanese response to the natural disaster of a 7.2-point earthquake that has taken the lives of more than 5,000 people, catapulted more than 300,000 into homelessness, and lifted bottom-line attributes into tragic and awe-inspiring relief. Throughout the wrecked cities of Kobe and Osaka, we have witnessed pervasive displays of dignity and communal concern despite ultimate stress. There has been no violence inside that critical context of no water, no blankets, no food. There has been no looting. We have seen a massive loss of life but no loss of civil humanity.

As a matter of fact, citizens of Japan donated $2,450,000 in rescue monies for the California Bay Area, following our 1989 Loma Prieta earthquake, which was horrifying and deadly and, also, a fraction of the fatal force of the Kobe-Osaka ordeal. But are we talking "Japanese" here? Are these the people regularly maligned by the American mass media as "ruthless" and "techno-robots" addicted to "incomprehensible conformity"?

I notice that the elected officials of Japan have not distinguished themselves—through words or deeds—in this hour of devastating and inarguable human need. I notice that this absence of "leadership" has not impaired the resilient and noble spirit of the ordinary men and women who have survived.

Evidently, we belong to a species capable of individual initiative and virtue beyond self-serving ambition and desire.

In the absence of human authority and regulation, for example, we can choose to preserve or to salvage a civil community.

This is pretty big, pretty good, news.

Ten days before the Kobe-Osaka earthquake, I spent a week in Heartland America. God knows I was not eager to go there. Given the American mass media portrayals of the prairie as grounds for extreme provincialism, white/right-wing Christianity, and die-hard zealotry for the never-never-world of "the way things were," I dreaded my trip as a possibly foolish foray into hostile and unfamiliar turf.

Subsequently, I learned that mass-media projections of my people and my culture had induced corresponding dread among some of my would-be hosts at Mankato State University in Minnesota. Furthermore, the anger that drives some of my published writings had predisposed them to perceive me as negative, narrow, and bigoted—and/or "irrational."

Well, Mankato is about seventy-five miles southwest of the Twin Cities. It is certainly white. It's cold. It's a hard place to live. It's mostly Swedish and Lutheran. The average height of a young white man, out there, is six-foot-one. Most everybody eats beef and cheese. And above that town of 42,000 residents, you see an enormous stretch of open sky.

From day one of my arrival, I was met with generosity and kindness plus the intellectual courtesy of my hosts, who had bothered to read and wrestle with my works beforehand. During my stay as a scholar-in-residence, there were several occasions when interested faculty and students shot questions at me or declared their own convictions about, for example, public education, or domestic violence, or problems of diversity, or curtailment of police power, or feminism, or urban planning, or the use of knowledge.

Very quickly, I recognized my environment as welcoming, in the best sense. We did not want to agree or disagree, but we were trying to speak to each other across high barriers of misinformation and visceral response to obvious, and very significant, differences.

In any case, it was not that cold. And it was not that white. The president of the Mankato State Student Association is an extremely persuasive young black man, Kris Hammes. In the highest echelons of the administration, there are two black men, Lewis Jones and Mike Fagin, who enjoy unqualified respect. I twice visited a class in multicultural literature led by a Native American, Gwen Griffin. This is the point: the Heartland is no alien enclave, no haven for mean-spirited and ill-informed activity.

When I met with Mankato State honor students, they told me that so many graduates, male and female, hope to become public-school teachers there is now an astonishing glut: in one instance, 5,000 candidates applied for one opening in a remote school. Mankato inculcates a value system that does not kneel to regular goals of greed and domination.

Above all, I felt safe among these strangers. There is a Minnesota code of honor that reflects their annual battle with sub-zero temperatures and sudden, blinding snow. That code requires everybody to stop and provide assistance to anyone who seems to be stuck or stranded, outdoors, in wintertime. To this golden rule, there are no amendments, no exceptions. And this willing commitment leads to a reliable meaning of civil community that, I believe, makes possible their commonplace kindness and generous poise.

In the absence of social and cultural diversity, it is nevertheless possible to seek and to find bonding information and connections with people unlike yourself.

This is pretty big, pretty good, news.

I am not saying anything like "perfect" or "paradise." But in these times of boastful cruelty, racist scapegoating, and a virulent recrudescence of white-supremacist activity, in these times of the media's malevolent intervention between peoples, it is heartening to know that, on our humble, fumbling-forward, two feet, we can discover or join or rescue human community. We can secure safety and justice and grace for all of our difficult days together without any leadership—besides our own.

In the Land of White Supremacy

June 1995

I used to think I was up against racist belief and behavior. But then, about a year ago, I began to focus on white supremacy. Whatever that might mean, I didn't have Aryan Nation-type in mind. I was watching and listening to an everyday, casual kind of mental disorder: something real homespun and regular, like my (white) doctor saying she'd eaten Chinese food twice last week, but the rest of the time, she'd opted for "American."

Or it might be something ordinary like media references to "The Heartland" as "true" America, even though very few of us live in North Dakota, Minnesota, or, for that matter, Oklahoma, and even though the majority of Americans reside on the East or West Coast. And California, for example, is the most populous as well as the most heterogeneous (non-"Heartland") state in the Union.

These were the kinds of things I began to hook up inside my head. I came to recognize media constructions such as "The Heartland" or "Politically Correct" or "The Welfare Queen" or "Illegal Alien" or "Terrorist" or "The Bell Curve" for what they were: multiplying scattershots intended to defend one unifying desire—to establish and preserve white supremacy as our national bottom line.

Racism means rejecting, avoiding, belittling, or despising whatever and whoever differs from your conscious identity.

White supremacy means that God put you on the planet to rule, to dominate, and to occupy the center of the national and international universe—because you're "white."

Anything or anyone appearing to challenge your center-stage position and its privileges becomes ungodly, or the Devil, or the Devil Incarnate, as in "The Jews," "The Niggers," "The Wetbacks," "The Chinks."

White supremacy moves beyond racist formulations of "superior" or "inferior." White supremacy takes hatred of the unfamiliar to the level of religious war between "good" and "evil." Underlying such a world view is an infantile mentality as obviously infantile as it is "normal" in these United States.

And so the catastrophe of Oklahoma City becomes a possible, and, for some, a reasonable, carefully planned event. Nothing and no one—not a one-year-old baby, not a two-year-old child, not unremarkable American workers going about their boring but useful routines, not mothers or fathers or day-care teachers or any number of the simply living—could interdict or mitigate the murder-crazy determination of white supremacists to declare their hatred of "the government" and their hatred of anyone who fails to mirror their faces set, killer resolute, against us.

It has taken me until the tragedy of Oklahoma City to understand that "The Aryan Nation" is not the name of an organization of some sort. "The Aryan Nation" is the goal of the Christian Coalition and the Patriot Militias and the Contract with America and Governor Pete Wilson. "Come unto me all ye who suffer and who seek asylum and an open road, and I will blow you away! I will efface you from my territory, my Aryan Preserve!"

To impose an Aryan Nation upon these United States would require bodily and juridical and legislative assault upon the constitutional liberties and the constitutional protection that defines basic citizenship here. But Aryan Nation wannabes feel fine about that because only the godly deserve to be free.

To impose an Aryan Nation upon these United States would require overthrow of our government and that's also OK because, as some of us may remember, it's supposed to be a government of and by and for "the people"—and, at last count, "the people" have begun to look less and less like Clint Eastwood playing an unemployed Marine at a Christian Revival meeting.

And, besides, the only democratic justification for centralized, federal government is its provision for the security of the population it presumes to represent. But you cannot provide for the security of a people without justice, without equality, without food, without education, without gainful employment, without housing. And so we pay taxes to "the government" expecting that, in return, we will receive these goods fundamental to our personal security and to the security of our society.

Hence, affirmative action, for example, is a federal government policy. Hence, the viciously orchestrated attack on "affirmative" for the sake of "angry white men" who, statistics inform us, continue to occupy 95 percent of all senior management positions.

I guess that was the picture of one of those angry white men, that photograph of blond, white Timothy McVeigh. Is that the guy who bombed the federal office building and killed 167 human beings because something truly pissed him off? Is he one of those guys "affirmative action" irritated like, so to speak, crazy?

And he wasn't really "Middle Eastern looking," was he? What a shock! He looked "American," one of the sheriffs remarked.

And then there was the President droning on about our task is to cleanse ourselves of this "dark" force.

"Dark," Mr. President?

On the contrary. White. White. American white-supremacist white. The monster is an "American-looking" white man. This violent, paramilitary hatred is absolutely homegrown and growing.

Do not be misled. There is no difference between hating "the government" and hating "the Jews" and "the Niggers" in the mind-mesh of the Christian-white-rights crusade.

And forget about Negro clowns in the tradition of Clarence Thomas—clowns like the University of California regent Ward Connerly, who has risen to national stature by attacking affirmative action, or the Negro head of a right-wing militia group in Alameda, California. There have always been fools who have flared into infamy almost like an awful amusement before the curtain lifts.

Oklahoma City has lifted the curtain.

If we do not see ourselves, at last, stripped of all excuse and scapegoat, if we do not recognize the weakness of our connections to other—all of us different, and different-looking Americans—as the well-spring for white supremacy, then we may as well admit that we are ready to submit to Timothy McVeigh's final agenda for our country: to achieve an Aryan Nation by any means necessary.

Manifesto of the Rubber Gloves

August 1995

So I'm wearing brand new loud blue
Rubber gloves
because
I'm serious about I don't wanna die
from
mainstream contamination
mainstream
poison waters poisonous
like
statistical majorities
that represent
the mainstream
poison waters poisonous
like
neo-Nazi perspectives
that reflect
the mainstream
poison waters poisonous
like
scapegoat policies
that distill
the mainstream
poison waters poisonous
like
the Congress and the Governor and
    the President
and the Supremely Clarence Retrograde
Thomas
Court
of Separated and Unequal
and Proud about That
Last Resort

I'm wearing brand new loud blue
Rubber gloves
because
I'm serious about I don't wanna die
from
mainstream contamination
mainstream
poison waters poisonous
like
the FBI and ATF
and the INS and Secret Service
Security Guards
with or without a cut on anybody's finger
and a pointless
overblown Armed Forces
afraid to fight
unless
it gets a not-a-single-cut-on-a-single-one-
of-your-fingers guarantee
backed by
a would-be
hero's welcome
first for hiding the hell
out of trouble
when the point
might very well
be
"The trouble"
The 600,000 human beings dead
already
anyway

I'm wearing brand new loud blue
Rubber gloves
because I'm serious about I don't wanna
die
from
mainstream contamination
mainstream

poison waters poisonous
like
a serial killer
start anyplace
(next door!)
and slash and dismember
and move on
and on and kill more and more
a serial killer
absolutely
mainstream
tall and good
(looking)
nicely dressed
a dedicated
fast-travelling
serial killer
straight from the heartland oozing
mainstream
poison waters
a Republican
a soft-spoken young man
a believer in Christ Jesus
a serial killer
like
The Pilgrims
like
the early
serial killer
settler
pioneers
beginning with the Indians
and then *xyz*
and then *abc*
and always
hunting down
the poor
and
the niggers
and

the kikes
and
the wetbacks
and
the chinks
and
the faggots
and
the dykes
and
the heathen who
unlike the serial killer
do
not
believe in Christ Jesus

I'm serious about I don't wanna die
from
mainstream contamination
mainstream
poison waters poisonous
at flood-tide heights
and depths
of programmatic and legislative and
        scatter-
shot self-righteous
consecration
to my death!

I'm wearing brand new loud blue
Rubber gloves
because
I'm serious about I don't wanna die
from
mainstream contamination
mainstream
poison waters poisonous
and swollen
all around me
and

as far as I can see

I'm serious
because
I don't wanna die
I don't wanna die
I don't wanna die

—June 18, 1995

My Mess, and Ours

October 1995

Books and papers no longer pretended to pile up. Every surface stunned me with too many questions. My house was a mess.

I decided to withdraw. I carried different sections of my personal chaos into my bed. In the space of ten days, I read: "Extracts from Pelican Bay," a nearby maximum-security prison; two books by Kenzaburo Oe; a *Village Voice* exposé of INS "detention" of 82,000 immigrants; a belated report on the enslavement of seventy-two young women and girls, in Los Angeles; several statistical descriptions of America's binge appetite for locking up more than a million other Americans; and daily newspaper accounts of the current U.S. Congress "at work."

Apparently believing that "affirmative action" is the reason why California schools are no longer always or mainly "white," the governor and his friends voted to abolish affirmative action on our nine University of California campuses as an obvious—if equally deluded, and ignorant, and hateful, and doomed—sequel to their invention of Proposition 187.

President Clinton did nothing to rescue the Muslim peoples of Bosnia from "ethnic cleansing." Photographs documented mass graves barely covering the limbs of Muslim men and women. And "the left" agonized about whether or not verified genocide warrants whatever—*whatever*—will stop it.

Because it was almost the fiftieth "anniversary" of Hiroshima, I began reading, or re-reading, Ronald Takaki, John Hersey, and Howard Zinn.

Dizzy with new information about Allied atrocities committed against the civilian peoples of Hamburg and Dresden, as well as American atrocities committed against Tokyo, Kobe, and Osaka, I felt nauseated by the jingo-lingo of popular "discussions" blossoming around me.

I could barely lift my head. When I did, I found myself watching, by accident, a television special about hundreds of thousands of female babies abandoned in China, where they endure (for as short a time as they may live) orphanage circumstances. The state keeps these babies tied—by their arms and by their legs—to little chairs that double as latrines.

I got out of bed. I walked to the windows overlooking my street. It was sunny. It was quiet. It was early morning. I began to clean. I picked things up.

I threw things out. I alphabetized. I labeled. I put newspaper clippings in green folders. I put business correspondence in a blue folder. Everything connected to my writing went into a red or an orange folder: "poetry," "prison," "race," "family," "women," "children," "violence," "California demographics," "South Africa," "Japan," "Ireland," "Israel," "welfare," "Bosnia," "Los Angeles."

I swept. I mopped. I scrubbed. Now there was the dining room table, after all!

I took books from their shelves and ordered them by type: novels/poetry/current affairs/reference. And then I began to subdivide. To take a break, I Windexed this or that window. I organized the video tapes. I dusted. I brushed my dog.

Exhausted, but very excited, I moved from room to room, sitting down and eying, with expectant pride, the flagrant orderliness of my environment.

Nothing was loose or cluttered. Everything looked clean and settled. There was space to my right and to my left and straight ahead: space. Either things fit unobtrusively into that space or they had become invisible. I had put them away. I had eliminated the mess. I had taken control.

After five minutes of orderly bliss, I realized I was bored, and rather uncomfortable. I had created fake attributes of fake serenity. If I wanted to do anything whatsoever besides sit around—if I wanted to read or write or face-check or even make a phone call—I would have to disturb this still-life-by-a-wannabe-housewife situation.

And so it came to me that I am just a very ordinary 1995 American. Maybe what I thought I was doing with my house is what so many Americans think they're doing with the world and with the U.S.A.—putting away the problems: locking them up, throwing them out, or pasting stupid labels on really complicated varieties of pain and aspiration so that everybody you don't know, and everybody you don't understand, will fit into a blue or an orange folder that will slide into a blue-only or an orange-only filing cabinet that some security guard will slam shut for the sake of tidy appearances.

My domestic maneuvers establish my credentials for the clean-shirt-to-the-fire brigade. In my madness for "neat" and "clean," I may enter that frightening frontier where folks finally say, "Put it away!"/"Clean them out!"/"Tie her to a chair!"/"Hold him in a six-by-three-foot cell!"

And, then, shall we sit down and admire the space around us: all that still-life, all that vanishing connection to our humanity?

The Street Where I live

December 1995

This is one big country. And if people in North Dakota spoke one language, while folks in South Dakota, or New Mexico, spoke another, a different, language, that would seem reasonable to me, even appropriate. And, so, I dispute all the various "nationwide" analyses and projections, each one colder than cold. "Nationwide" is too wide, too broad, to mean anything.

On the block where I live, there are black families, white families, Southeast Asian Americans, Chinese Americans, "interracial" students, elderly folks, newlyweds, Jews, and Christians. This is a short little street of great good calm. And I defy anybody to identify more than two or three things that I may have in common with the household next door. They're black. I'm black. They live on this street. So do I. But what does race or residence in this city mean to them? I have no idea. And beyond that? Personally, I would not assume anything about them or anybody else on my block except that they're likely to be friendly in a California ("If you *ever* need anything ...") way.

So when I started to read and hear about "the great racial divide," a week ago, I thought, "Sure. Is that something like Continental Drift? Or what?" And when I started to read and hear about race as the only and the biggest deal on the table, I thought, "Sure. Is that something like regular black man Rodney King and multimillionaire O.J. Simpson equally symbolize what, exactly? And the fact that, for example, I'm female is, suddenly and forever, beside the point?"

And, so, when some newspaper guy called from L.A. for a comment about the Million Man March, I said, "First of all, I was not invited. Secondly, I have one thing to say to and about anything or anybody wants to sunder me from the black man who is my son: 'You can go to hell!'"

And when a colleague (of sorts) of mine went off about domestic violence "versus" Mark Fuhrman and the L.A.P.D., I said, "How come you can't see that Mark Fuhrman and the L.A.P.D. and racism, per se, suck Mack trucks, absolutely, yes, and, also, anybody busts up his wife is totally reprehensible, and I don't forgive or forget anything or anybody who's just plain ugly and wrong: Mark Fuhrman *and* O.J. Simpson."

And when Minister Farrakhan proclaimed himself "God's Messenger" with not so much as a momentary twinkle of quasi-uneasiness, and when Minister

166

Farrakhan went lyrical about the number nine symbolizing a pregnant woman with "a male child" inside her, and so on and so forth, I thought, "Well, there it is: CNN-TV gives this guy two-and-a-half hours of uninterrupted international television time—way more than the Pope, President Clinton, Nelson Mandela—and then what?" More "nationwide" pseudo-analysis and projection about "the significance" of the importance that CNN-TV, and most of the American mass media, invest Farrakhan with.

And then I read and I heard about who supported and who opposed the Million Man March, for a couple of days, but then, happily, happily, I realized that my local, real life preempts all of these national constructions and destructions.

On Thursday, October 12, 1995, 5,000 Americans of every description rallied at U.C. Berkeley. There were "Queers for Affirmative Action," "Jews for Affirmative Action," "Asians for Affirmative Action," and Native American dances for affirmative action. Everybody was invited to the rally, and everybody showed up. As a matter of fact, the leadership for this fantastic success was a new U.C. Berkeley student organization called Diversity in Action. As the name suggests, the members of this incredibly effective task force include African-American young men with dreads or shaved heads and Irish-American young men with blond ponytails and Chicana young women and Vietnamese-American young men and women, and like that, on and on.

This ecstatic, mighty throng gathered together to demand restoration of affirmative action throughout the University of California system, and to assert our intelligent resistance to demagogic, racialized, un-American manipulations that would deny American history, deplore American diversity, and destroy our manifest, principled unity.

When I spoke, I pointed to the very recent (September 12) finding by the 1995 National Research Council report on the quality of Ph.D. education in the United States: with the most heterogeneous student population in the world, U.C. Berkeley is the leading, the top, university in America, or, as *The New York Times* reported, "No other university even comes close."

Our main speaker for this great day was the Reverend Jesse Jackson, and we greeted him with an endless tumult of genuine cheers and excitement. He came through with a rousing argument in favor of "real world" politics and policies and, therefore, affirmative action. He implored us to "turn to" each other and "not turn on" each other. He inveighed against the list of odious visions out here: racism, sexism, anti-Semitism, homophobia. And he implored us to get angry and vote Gingrich and company out of power in 1996.

On Tuesday, October 17, 1995, our U.C. faculty senate voted 124 to 2 to rescind the U.C. Regents' ruling against affirmative action. This vote does not mean the Regents will have to reverse themselves, but it does mean that the faculty stands with the students who stand with the chancellors, united in opposition to the Regents, and united in passionate support of affirmative action.

The "nationwide" assault on affirmative action began right here, in Northern California. And it looks to me like we may bury that particular outrage right here, where it was born. For sure, the fight is on, and it does seem far from hopeless.

So, yes, this is one big country. I happen to live on the Pacific Rim, which, for better or for worse, harbors the demographic and economic forecast for all of the U.S.A. in the Twenty-First Century.

And I trust what I can see and what I can hear and what I can do on my block, and around the corner, and on the campus where I teach.

And, just now, I am awfully glad to live nowhere else but here: right here.

The following poem by June Jordan appears as an inset in the preceding column, "The Street Where I Live" from the December 1995 issue. The poem is dated October 25, 1995.

On Time Tanka

I refuse to choose
between lynch rope and gang rape
my blues is the blues!
my skin and my sex: Deep dues
I have no wish to escape

I refuse to lose
the flame of my single space
this safety I choose
between your fist and my face
between my gender and race

All black and blue news
withers the heart of my hand
and leads to abuse
no one needs to understand:
suicide wipes out the clues

Big-Time-Juicy-Fruit!
Celebrity-Rich-Hero
Rollin out the Rolls!
Proud cheatin on your (Black) wife
Loud beatin on your (white) wife

Real slime open mouth
police officer-true-creep
evil-and-uncouth
fixin to burn black people
killin the son of our sleep

Neither one of you
gets any play in my day
I know what you do
your money your guns your say

169

so against my pepper spray

Okay! laugh away!
I hear you and I accuse
you both: I refuse
to choose: All black and blue news
means that I hurt and I lose.

Stories of a Visitor

February 1996

Pierce stands about six-three. He looks like a linebacker. He's big. He's smiling at me. He laughs out loud like a happy man.

Most days he works for Budget Rent-A-Car, earning maybe $6 an hour. Before Budget, he worked for a San Francisco tourist attraction restaurant, as the chef. This morning he comes to my house ready to clean the living-room rug, wash the outside windows, fix a sticky door, and tell me stories.

First off is the fact that he may be promoted to supervisor because "my attitude is, like, why not be positive? What have I got to lose?

"Like I was telling my brother—he used to be the skinny one when I was heavyweight into food and not doing much of anything else, but now, he have this stomach out to here, and if I take him to the gym, the other guys ask: "What's that supposed to be?!" pointing to his waistline, which you can't see no more, due to the fact that my brother is very depressed. He stay depressed.

"And his wife? Oh! She the most beautiful, the most generous woman! She put up with him when (I have to admit it, and I'm his brother) I would just walk on out the door! Especially given the fact of the drugs he like to do. But she put up with him.

"And I will drag him aside and try to talk him back to someplace he can deal from but he be saying how he was beat when we was little kids (you know, abused), and how momma didn't do this and didn't do that, or whatever, and there wasn't no money, to tell you the truth, and things was hard and he got hurt pretty bad and me, too, and all of that and I just listen and I listen and I say, 'Yeah, but you know what? You alive! Check that out: alive!'

"And then I change the subject, or keep it going in a new direction or sometimes I go over and I pick him up when I'm taking the neighborhood kids out fishing or down to the basketball courts and little by little I think he gets the point: Be alive! Or, like I say to him, 'Kick in, man! It's your time.'"

And what Pierce likes almost as much as his 1992 Acura Vigor, which he originally leased from his ex-girlfriend who, when he broke up with her, said, "No!" she couldn't afford the payments, so he could keep it, so he did; what Pierce likes almost as much as that Acura Vigor, which, where he lives in East Oakland, looks like must be a set-up for somebody too stupid to know a set-up when you looking at it parked and pretty as can be next to the broke-down sidewalk; what Pierce likes almost as much as that pearly black Acura Vigor is the unbelievably good food his current lady puts on the table day after day, including lemon pies and serious gumbo and sweet sweet potatoes.

And what Pierce likes almost as much as that is what he calls "challenges," by which he means anything all the way from my sticky door to a new model VCR he must take apart and figure out or how to hand-carry and install plate glass without getting glass or blood all over everything.

Pierce is big. He's huge. He works hard. He works fast. And at the end of the day he's running around athletic, or at the end of the week he likes to drive his special lady to this special spot he knows about over in the next county: off the map and kept a secret, this spot, Pierce says, is so beautiful that "it don't matter what you worrying about or what you think you should be worrying about, you just get out the car [the Acura Vigor], and walk maybe a hundred feet and boom! You in another world. Everything so beautiful you don't want to breathe too loud! A couple hours just looking at that beautiful (I mean I can't begin to describe to you how beautiful, except, it's like whoooshhhhh! And all around you the same way, whoooshhhhh!), and you can feel something happen inside you so nice you don't never want to forget about it!"

So, anyway, this new year I'm rooting for Pierce. I hope he gets that promotion. If anybody can convert a Budget Rent-A-Car into a Cadillac experience of sweet sweet potato delight, he can: Pierce is the man!

And, for myself, and for the rest of us, I'm thinking, like he said, "It's our time to kick in."

Justice at Risk

April 1996

Just about every time anybody talks about affirmative action or multicutural education, the presentation seems simple: White Western authorities on beauty and honor and courage and historical accomplishment have denied and denigrated whatever and whoever does not fit into their white Western imagery.

Some people who have been systemically excluded by white Western tradition will never know anything beyond hourly work at a minimum wage. Some people will never know anything besides the pain of physical poverty and psychological self-loathing. Some people will never know anything except dependency upon those who despise them, those who create and impose conditions that enforce despicable dependency.

And so, in order to avoid figurative and literal extinction, and in order to provide for self-respecting knowledge, and social mobility based upon such knowledge, we who have been denied and denigrated now undertake to ascertain our own beauty and honor and courage and historical accomplishment according to our own images of the truth of our distinctive human being.

All of this seems simple.

But public discussion of affirmative action and multicultural studies has been warped by all kinds of media machinations, as political ambitions and lies and panic and your elementary white-supremacy-race-hatred erupt. Politicians like California's Governor Pete Wilson and his devoted appointee, U.C. Regent Ward Connerly, become famous, and infamous. And Wilson tries to run toward the White House propelled by the poisonous uproar against affirmative action that he and his cohorts have conspired to ignite in the first place.

Craziness. But it didn't take much and it didn't take long before "affirmative action" became the so-called pivotal issue, nationwide.

White people everywhere agreed to interviews on the subject. Heavyweight Presidential prospect Colin Powell, a black man, actually got points for his "brave" refusal to condemn "affirmative action" categorically.

National media potentates borrowed from Connerly, and "racial preference" quickly eclipsed "affirmative action."

So now the question put to white Americans changed to, "What do you think about job and college-admission policies that give preference to some racial groups over others? Do you think that's fair?"

This double-whammy, this model of loaded public inquiry, produced great excitement and front-page news: Gosh, no! White Americans didn't think "racial preference" was really "fair." And, as a matter of fact, once you redefined things like that, a whole lot of black and Latino and Asian Americans didn't think "racial preference" was really "fair", either!

Soon our national press exploded with outcries from "angry white men" and a mini-cascade of first-person white student reports from universities overtaken by unqualified barbarians, politically correct thought police, and apologetic, but terrified, would-be employers who had truly wanted to hire the best white man for the job, but could not.

In July of last year, the U.C. Regents voted to end affirmative action throughout the University of California system of public education. And I suppose that everyone opposed to "racial preference" breathed easier as the prospect of preserving a mostly white Western curriculum for mostly white Western students who would later lead or join a mostly white labor force brightened a little bit. Obviously, white Western curricular, educational, economic, and political hegemony does not translate into "racial preference." White Western hegemony is "fair"!

With the U.C. Regents' ruling against affirmative action, I became my own kind of maniac, obsessively trying to fact-check, trying to better understand, this suddenly pivotal, this publicly welcomed "wedge" issue.

Gradually, I acquired a perspective consistent with what I learned.

Affirmative action emerged as a belated national policy some thirty years ago. Given a social predicament that plainly derived from American slavery, and American hatred of men and women of African descent, President Lyndon Baines Johnson resolved in 1965 to "create equality in fact" for a people that "has been hobbled by chains." When President Johnson announced this affirmative resolve, his ambitions seemed minimal, and righteous, to everyone convinced that equality is an undebatable humane value appropriate to a democratic state.

Back then a white majority population in the United States appeared to be assured. Back then, an economy either pursuing new modes of production, capital accumulation and profit, or else an economy expanding upon proven routes to the development of wealth appeared to be infinitely open.

In this context, affirmative action would not and did not seem necessarily threatening to the average white American: As long as you're eating well, you do not mind sharing your food with strangers.

Thirty years later and we live in a country eager to imprison, detain, deport, defund anyone who is neither "white" nor native English-speaking.

Nevertheless, the white population of America is generally in decline while peoples of Spanish-speaking origins and Asian origins double or triple or quadruple their numbers. Any reliable population forecast for California and for the entire United States arrives at the same conclusion: a non-white majority within the lifespan of our children.

Simultaneous to this changing face of our electorate is our changing, our unrecognizable, our apparently running-away, economy. Internationalized and monopolized, our economy has become a game without rules. As would-be productive people, we rise and fall according to the outcome of these twin objectives underlying corporate management: the elimination of labor and the enlargement of profit.

Emerging demographic and economic structures herald the end of white American majority privilege and, also, the end of employment security for all levels of our national labor force.

These are the reasons for our pervasive uncertainty and flux.

These are the dynamics inducing uncontrollable, frightening change today.

Black folks are not responsible.

Women are not responsible.

Gay and lesbian and bisexual Americans are not responsible.

Undocumented immigrants are not responsible.

None of us is responsible for the awesome difficulties of this moment, but we have become the new American majority that will or will not survive these uncertainties and the divisive, scapegoating manipulations of the hateful among us.

Meanwhile and actually:

Although white men, angry or otherwise, constitute 44 percent of the labor force, white men continue to occupy 95 percent of all senior management positions plus 80 percent of the U.S. Congress, four-fifths of the tenured university faculty, nine-tenths of the U.S. Senate, and 92 percent of the Forbes Fabulous 400!

Affirmative action is what's left of our blood-stained aspirations toward universal civil rights. Affirmative action offers a moral alternative to national fratricide.

At U.C.-Berkeley, the most heterogeneous student population in the world attends a public institution of learning that, according to the "1995 National Research Council Report on Quality of Ph.D. Education in the United States," ranks number one. With thirty-five of our thirty-six Berkeley programs placing in the top ten, as *The New York Times* of September 13, 1995, exclaimed, "No other university even comes close!"[33]

An earlier Times article,[34] June 4, 1995, documents the following about U.C.-Berkeley during its ten-year adherence to affirmative action: 1984 entering freshmen, mostly white (61 percent), presented an average S.A.T. score of 1155 and an average GPA (grade point average) of 3.62.

1994 entering freshmen (14 percent Hispanic, 6 percent black, 32 percent white and 39 percent Asian) presented a significantly higher average S.A.T. score of 1225 and a higher average GPA of 3.84.

And an enormously important clarification about "Special Admissions" appeared in a sidebar to that Times report: For the school year 1994-1995, only 3 percent of the entering freshmen came in through "Special Admissions" policy considerations such as economic disadvantages, rural background, musical abilities, physical disabilities, and race. As the director of admissions at U.C.-Berkeley, Bob Laird, explained to me, for the school year 1994-1995, adhering to affirmative-action criteria, 97 percent of all entering freshmen came from the top one-eighth of their class.

On January 19, 1996, the U.C. Board of Regents reconsidered its July 1995 decision against affirmative action. They agreed to this extraordinary second deliberation because their July decree provoked unanimous public denunciation and disclaimers from the then-president of the U.C. system, all nine chancellors, all faculty senates, and all student governments. In contrast to this legitimate educational community, the U.C. Board of Regents is composed of governor-appointees like Ward Connerly, whose professional background can be more than adequately summarized as real-estate development.

On January 19, 1996, the U.C. Board of Regents voted to support its own decision against affirmative action. And so, whether or not our national media experts once more identify affirmative action as the pivotal "wedge" issue nationwide, all the lives, all the values, all the intended justice bespoken by that attempt at more equal, more democratic representation in the curriculum, in the classroom, and at the workplace—all remain at risk.

I look at this craziness and I try to return to a simplicity of perspective again. But I cannot make that return.

The obvious, straightforward case for affirmative action and multicultural studies confronts such reckless ongoing misrepresentation and attack that we who support it find ourselves having to multiply our battle positions in response. In that multiplication, our simplicity of purpose becomes obscure.

And, because we can never get off the battlefield, we may not always acknowledge the complexities we encounter in our reach for new information. And we may feel it is too soon to begin an examination of our own moral conduct. But regardless of the power any of us does or does not possess, we must subject ourselves to just such scrutiny.

Yes, there is the truth of white Western domination.

Yes, there is the truth of our entitlement to self-respecting education about our distinctive human being, whether we derive from a Czechoslovakian, a Filipino, or a Nigerian heritage.

But we need to morally assess the content of our studies of our many selves, even as we affirm our disparate identities. Our studies will have to evolve into revolutionary, interactive confrontation with whatever we may discover.

We will have to embrace what my friend Peter Sellars invokes as "history as creative process," or we will merely become more fluently backwards, more perfectly stuck in what the past can tell us about the past, good and evil, alike.

Where Is the Sisterhood?

June 1996

It eats at my heart. I can't get it out of my head that mothers throw away, or drown, or suffocate, their baby girls. This happens in India, and Africa, and China, which is to say that coming into the world female is extremely hazardous inside the majority cultures of our species.

Seven years ago, twelve-year-old African-American Bracola Coleman was found dead on her kitchen floor. Evidently, she had been fatally wounded by a broomstick jammed into her vagina.

Chinese infant Mei Ming, which means No Name in Mandarin, was recently found decomposing inside a Chinese orphanage, where she had been left to perish without food or any other kind of care.

When my Uncle Teddy called his wife about their newborn baby, and when his wife, my aunt, told him she'd given birth to a baby girl, my Uncle Teddy exclaimed, "There must be some mistake!"

The violation and murder of Bracola Coleman received negligible coverage. We know the tool of her annihilation, but we do not know who she was alive:

On what street and up which stairs and near or far from what refrigerator with cheese or Pepsi or beer inside, did she live?

Where was she heading when she died?

Before, or after, watching what on TV?

What did she ever laugh about?

Why did no one protect her from this last unmitigated desecration of her body?

Her life and her death elicited equal neglect.

On the other hand, the calculated starvation and abandonment of Mei Ming has received international attention as the existence of "dying rooms" for unwanted children, particularly unwanted baby girls, becomes more and more appallingly documented.

But none of this attention will resurrect that child. She died and she lived with No Name.

And nobody knows how she was born or where, or who she might have wanted to become or why.

We know nothing about Mei Ming except the meaning of her name.

My uncle could not kill his daughter by phone, but she killed herself years later, in a tailspin of belief in her own worthlessness. My cousin carried my uncle's name, but without his love his name conferred no safety, no promise of familial esteem; she had no name of her own, no claim to legitimate, beloved standing in the world.

She was just a girl.

When it became clear that my new friend, the African-American head of the local NAACP, intended to rape me, I tried to stop him by asking: "Do you know who I am?" By which I meant that I was his new friend, his political sister: a black woman willing and able to love and admire him. He silenced me with violence.

I could not call myself a name that would compel his nonviolent recognition and respect.

I could not call myself a name that he would have to answer with his own.

I was just a girl.

India, China, Africa are not white, Western countries. Bracola Coleman and my cousin Lynnsely Rutledge did not yield to white, Western assault.

In the newsprint photo of Mei Ming, suffering has consumed her. She is emaciated, diseased. The violence of the affiction of No Name could not be more clearly conveyed. Her executioners were neither Western nor white.

We cannot say of twelve-year-old Bracola Coleman, "She's dead." We cannot even say of Mei Ming, "She's dead." "She" never existed for us. Denied and despised, these children died from No Name. And the lethal brutality that befalls those of us carrying No Name into the world is no longer, anywhere, theoretical.

I am saying America is not colorblind, but evil is. Hatred opens up an inhumane temptation for every kind of people on Earth.

These dead children should summon us to a further commitment, building upon affirmative action and its original, limited aims.

These dead children died nameless, belonging nowhere in particular. We did not know them and, therefore, could not save them from their ignominious existence.

Building upon affirmative action as we have first conceived of it, we should now move against our own legacies of acquiescence, complicity, hatefulness, and cowardice. Whoever we are, we need to interact actively with all of our cultures of origin. In this sense, self-criticism is way overdue. And we need to exorcise inertia from our notions of acceptable behavior, or even belated self-criticism will lapse into mere embroidery upon comfortable habits of self-absorption.

Every single one of us is No Name in the universe of somebody else who is No Name to you and me.

And the problem is this: Between Nobody Real and Nobody Real, every imaginable violation, every imaginable violence, seems distant, or abstract, and, therefore, possibly unreal, and, therefore, unimportant, or impossible to interdict.

I am calling for a righteous redefinition of affirmative action so that we will attend to emergency issues specific to female life, as well as issues adhering to bedeviled constructs of racial identity. I believe that righteous affirmative action means that we extirpate all historical hatred attached to our names—whether that brutal negativity points to a slavemaster, the manager of a brothel or young children for sale, an uncle, Snoop Doggy Dog, Patrick Buchanan, Timothy McVeigh, or yet another movie showing black women in BMW convertibles and expensive clothes, with zero political consciousness, zero community usefulness.

Where is the movie about Ms. Fannie Lou Hamer? (Who?)

Why are there voluminous surveys and findings pertinent to young black men but no comparable intelligence available about black women and young black girls?

Where is the sisterhood?

Why is it that all black women do not declare ourselves The Welfare Queens United?

Is there any doubt about the sadistic and boastful scapegoating of black women who raise children by ourselves and then ask for recognition, respect, and sometimes assistance?

Is there any amazingly difficult research still to be accomplished before we discover that AFDC adds up to 1 percent of the national budget, and that there are more white women on welfare than black women, and that there is no statistical proof that children raised by their single mothers do more poorly than children of Patrick Buchanan's parents?

Where is the sisterhood?

Why do we keep silent when the so-called Welfare Queen comes up?

Or when we hear about the genital mutilation of girls?

Or when we read about a young black mother terrified and bullied into jumping off a bridge?

Where is the sisterhood?

If we do not join together for the sake of the neediest among us, then what is the purpose of our unity?

The United Nations 1995 Report on the World's Women, Trends and Statistics begins with this stunning announcement: "There are fewer women in the world than men." In an ancillary but earlier 1992 U.N. report, *The Sexual Age Distribution of the World's Population,* we learn that men have outnumbered women, worldwide, since 1965.

In a 1990 *New York Review of Books* article entitled, "More Than 100 Million Women Are Missing," the writer, Amartya Sen, reports that gainful employment is decisive in the determination of female longevity and that unequal nutrition and unequal health care correlate with the declining ratio of women to men.

Sen calculates the shocking, awesome, number of deaths implied by inequality and neglect, and arrives at her estimate of "more than 100 million women missing"—more than 100 million female lives extinguished by contempt.

When you interlink this contempt with female infanticide and the increasing popularity of interrupting pregnancy if, otherwise, a baby girl will be born, you guarantee the mute evaporation of hundreds of millions of female lives ahead of us.

This documented, but utterly disregarded, vanishing of female life has taken place all around us, and recently.

Where is the sisterhood?

Would your or my multicultural studies include or omit this information?

Why is this years-ago-documented loss of female life nevertheless "news" in 1996?

Any affirmative action deserving our faith and our hard work must militate against the perishing of the female of our species. That perishing, that endangerment, remains, shamelessly, hidden. And that endangerment flourishes inside the majority cultures of the world—African, Indian, and Chinese.

Systematic, careless, and traditional hatred of female life leads, inexorably, to gender genocide, and nothing less than that.

And, in the context of genocide, what will affirmative action require?

And where is the sisterhood?

As a female member of our endangered species, I am searching for relevant proof of sisterhood: I am searching for relevant proof of brotherhood hinged to that sisterhood.

I want to pursue the collective, and the creative, securement of all of our legitimate names for all of our, finally, legitimate lives.

I need to establish my legitimate name inside the consciousness of strangers. I need to learn the legitimate names of the strangers surrounding me. Then, perhaps. I can hope, at last, to find something possibly useful, possibly affirmative to say.

In the name of Bracola Coleman and Mei Ming, who perished unknown among us, I commit my heart and my mind to this further, lifelong, student undertaking.

Eyewitness in Lebanon

August 1996

When American pundits talk about "The Middle East," they mean Israel: what favors or what threatens Israeli interests.

And so, for example, the country and the people of Lebanon no longer exist because Israeli leaders have decided to focus upon Syria, Jordan, and Turkey "to the North."

Hence, when you come upon a listing of Middle Eastern states in our own media, you rarely will find Lebanon anywhere on the page.

If I had not recently traveled to Lebanon, I would probably note this currently commonplace omission as "disquieting" or "odd."

But I went there, to Lebanon. And I'm back. And I'm real. And Lebanon is real. And this poisonous pretense to the contrary seems to me insolent and ominous, at best.

What's the brainstorm here: that if Israel and the United States agree to "disappear" Lebanon, then whenever Israel follows up its various invasions of that tiny place with outright annexation, nobody will notice because Lebanon will have become nowhere, anyway?

This is my eyewitness reaction to the country and the people of Lebanon. This is my eyewitness reaction to the Israeli sixteen-day war against Lebanon. It is not well-tempered.

My life requires perpetual revolt against a double standard that puts me on the Easily Invisible side of the ledger, the Don't Matter and No Count side of things, the Be Good/Keep Quiet/ Say "Thank You" side of the equation.

And Lebanon is on the wrong side, just like me. Lebanon is not white. Lebanon is not overwhelmingly Christian or Jewish or European. It's an Arab nation.

It's very small. It's half the size of Israel, which is the size of Massachusets. And even including what's left of the 300,000-plus refugees who sought shelter there after their expulsion from Palestine in 1948, the total population of Lebanon is half that of Israel.

When Israel forced more than 400,000 Lebanese citizens to flee from their homes and villages three months ago, that amounted to 14 percent of the entire population.

A truly huge number of women and children were suddenly rendered homeless.

Lebanon maintains the only democratic Arab government. Arab peoples regard Lebanon as the heart of Arab culture, and for a long time almost every political and artistic movement in the world found its way into the cafés and secret meeting places of Beirut.

Today there is scarcely a structure in all of Beirut that does not bear the markings of shrapnel. The downtown area resembles the ruins of Pompeii. Everywhere you see soldiers and gigantic construction cranes revising the scenery before your eyes.

I went to Lebanon because I believe that Arab peoples and Arab Americans occupy the lowest, the most reviled spot in the racist mind of America.

I went because I believe that to be Muslim and to be Arab is to be a people subject to the most uninhibited, lethal bullying possible.

Why isn't it general knowledge that the United States successfully introduced U.N. Resolution 425 in 1978, calling for the immediate and unconditional Israeli withdrawal from Lebanon? That resolution has never been revoked—or enforced.

Why isn't it general knowledge that Israel "occupies" Southern Lebanon in absolute violation of international law, U.N. Resolution 425, and the sovereign rights of the people of Lebanon?

How does it happen that Hezbollah becomes synonymous with "terrorist" when members and followers of Hezbollah are, actually, Lebanese men who live in Lebanon and who have won substantial representation in the Lebanese parliament and who are fighting the illegal Israeli occupation of Lebanese land?

What will it take before "terrorist" becomes the adjective attached to Israeli depredations that include massacres of civilians and the calculated destruction of water reservoirs and electrical power plants?

When will we establish and abide by a No Exceptions policy: the same one standard for valuation of human life and the moral measurement of our deeds?

On Monday, May 6, 1996, the top headline of England's *The Independent* declared: MASSACRE FILM PUTS ISRAEL IN DOCK. In an exclusive report by Robert Fisk, the facts of Israeli knowledge of the massacre at the U.N. refugee camp at Qana appeared, accompanied by still photos from a video film of the entire assault. The Israelis murdered 200 women and children. These were refugees taking shelter inside the U.N. compound, and the Israelis knew their exact location.

When the story came out, I thought: Here was the Rodney King video of the Middle East. At last, here was incontrovertible evidence of Israeli lies and Israeli savagery that no one could now refute.

Surely even Bill Clinton would be forced to become less unconditional in his support of Israel. Perhaps even the multibillion-dollar habit of aid to Israel would finally be reexamined and curtailed.

But my relief was naive. That video is the Rodney King video of the Middle East, but Arab life is less than and lower than African-American life, and so nothing happened. This incontrovertible evidence of Israel's planned massacre received nominal notice on the news and then, like Lebanon, it disappeared.

What did I see in Lebanon? I saw a poor, dusty stretch of difficult earth between the sea and the mountains.

I saw the darkness and I felt the chill and I beheld the squalor of what we like to call "refugee camps."

I saw a six-year-old girl with no family left, and a parking lot full of orphan boys and girls.

I saw a man bereft of his wife and nine children.

I saw the mangled materials of a house bombed into nothing usable.

I saw death and I heard death and death is not beautiful, and sometimes the lamentations for the dead clouded the air.

I heard Prime Minister Rafik Hariri saying, "We have the feeling of proud" because not everyone had died.

I savored sweet coffee reasons for solidarity with Lebanese resistance to anti-Arab and anti-Muslim hatred and assault.

I saw overwhelming variations on grief beyond all language.

I watched a woman setting out a jasmine plant that would probably manage the atmosphere and, possibly, flourish.

Not a Good Girl

October 1996

She's not thirteen. She learned a long time ago that you improve a messed-up situation by inventing your own rules. She runs on champion stamina and the well-directed energies of an infuriated fighter.

She is not a good girl.

She sets things up so she can win. She forgives nothing. She forgets nothing.

She puts her body on the line whenever her mouth says "No!"

She has rescued many thousands of women and children from starvation, abuse, penury, and the brutality of no medical care.

Her name is Vivian Stromberg.

And, on the International Olympic Scoreboard for a do-right, free-style, heavy-hitting, marathon leader, she'd find herself with very little competition, anywhere.

We—she and I—go back to Fidel Castro throwing fried chicken bones off the terrace of his Hotel Theresa suite in Harlem. Hell, we go back before that.

When I first met Vivian, she was a young mother with a long braid of dark hair down her back, and two little girls she brought to just about all the protest demonstrations that sustained her own idealistic excitement.

From the beginning, she was full of conviction, and obdurate, and completely impatient with apathetic anything.

She knew Castro was way better than Batista.

She wanted to stop the war against Vietnam.

She hated racist or hypocritical Americans.

She loved Joan Baez, Bob Dylan, Richie Havens, and crowds of people singing songs.

She complained all the time, and she worked against the reasons for her aggravation.

She wore out the grunt routines of fliers and phone calls and fliers and phone calls. She got tired but she never quit.

She became a formidable adversary and an invaluable advocate.

She became a compelling, regular speaker at the rallies she helped to organize.

She became pivotal to New York City politics, and she earned various designations, such as "touchstone," "spark," "whip," and "spine."

She would find out about police violence or foreign-policy deceit before most of the rest of us made our morning cup of coffee.

And when Vivian found out about something corrupt and revolting, she always went into ferocious first gear: organizing the willing and the lazy into some decent show of concern and public condemnation.

In 1983, the poet Kathy Engel founded MADRE,[35] whose motto is: "Joining hands and hearts with women and children for peace and for justice." Kathy's founding board of twelve included Vivian Stromberg and me. MADRE's first delegation delivered one ton of baby cereal and powdered milk to Nicaragua. Since that characteristically useful first mission, MADRE has become a 20,000-member, multiracial, national women's organization that has raised more than $6 million for medical and education services for women and children in Central America, the Caribbean, the Middle East, the former Yugoslavia, and the U.S.A.

In 1990, when she retired from teaching public school in the South Bronx, Vivian Stromberg became full-time executive director of MADRE. Since then, she has conceived and conducted three "Mother Courage Peace Tours."

The first of these ventures combined women from Egypt, Israel, the Occupied Territories of Palestine, Jordan, Iraq, Kuwait, Turkey, Western Europe, and the United States in a coast-to-coast speakout against the Gulf war: "Bring Our Sons and Daughters Home Now!"

Emboldened by the passionate success of this tour, MADRE purchased ten tons of milk and medicine for Iraqi civilians who were suffering from our sanctions against their country. Vivian arranged for these emergency supplies to travel via a giant truck caravan, from Amman to Baghdad. This extraordinary convoy managed to arrive in Baghdad exactly one year to the day after the onslaught of our allied bombardment.

The second tour responded to the crisis for women in the former Yugoslavia, and called for:

- the U.N. War Crimes Tribunal to try all war crimes against women, including rape and forced pregnancy;
- the enforcement of women's rights by international bodies;
- the U.N. World Conference on Human Rights in Vienna, held in June of 1993, to include the rights of women as human rights;
- the United Nations to ratify the Convention on the Elimination of All Forms of Discrimination Against Women, which would secure equal

rights for women in all fields: political, economic, social, cultural, and civil.

In addition, MADRE donated $97,000 worth of milk for Bosnia-Herzegovina, which was distributed by UNICEF to all in need, be they Muslim or Serb or Croat.

Then, in 1995, there was the inauguration of "Klinik FANM," the first women's clinic in Port-au-Prince, a resource made possible by MADRE donors.

And, in 1996, the third Mother Courage tour flew a U.S. human-rights delegation to Lebanon. This group witnessed the effect of the Israeli bombing throughout southern Lebanon and, in particular, the devastation of the U.N. peacekeeping camp at Qana. MADRE was able to arrange for the delivery of $143,500 of emergency medical aid.

You get the idea. If it's humanly possible, MADRE and Vivian Stromberg will mitigate desperate need with a shipment of shoes, a new ambulance, industrial looms, antibiotics, textbooks, or rice, beans, corn, and flour. They deserve our national thanks and our very personal support. MADRE's political, life-sustaining work is an amazing achievement. And it is galvanized and guided by an amazing peace warrior, Vivian Stromberg.

For Clinton, With Disgust

November 1996

Bill Clinton is not a pretty man.
He's a liar.
He's a coward.
He's a killer bully clown.
He drivels.
He swivels.
He's the man I'm voting for.
It's disgusting.
It's beneath the bottom of the barrel.
It's disgusting.
It's a fact.
He's the man I'm voting for.
I figure maybe five or six people's lives depend on the difference between Clinton and Dole.
I'm voting for that differential.
Five or six beats zero.
And, so far, he hasn't attacked (the concept of) public education.
And, so far, he hasn't bailed on abortion rights.
So far, he hasn't trashed (the concept of) universal health care.
So far, he appears certain that the L.A. Dodgers do not belong in Brooklyn.
So far, he doesn't play ping-pong with Patrick Buchanan.
And that's about it. At the moment, that's the sum total to his credit. "Not nothing" is the best that anyone can say.
And I'm voting for him. And I do not appreciate this set-up.
Clinton versus certifiable crazies?
Spineless as against insensible?
Hypocritical rather than "Just Don't Do It!"?
Reliably turncoat versus reliably mean?
All of this insults the lowest-common-denominator intelligence of the lowest level of low-life out here.
And that's the choice.
And I hate it.

I detest Bill Clinton: what he's not done and what he's done.

Not stupid, ignorant, or senile, and he signs that legal assault upon the welfare of the poor, and then he goes to war against the country of Iraq? And if there's no money to feed and house and day-care and job-train needy children and their mothers, how come there's no problem paying for a war against Iraq—or any other convenient straw-man target in the Third World?

Not stupid, ignorant, or senile, and he did what to stop "ethnic cleansing" in Bosnia?

And when did official/photo-op visits to burned church rubble become acceptable alternatives to anti-discrimination affirmative policies?

And who in the world cares about what Bill Clinton thinks about marriage, let alone same-sex marriages?

And how does he get his mouth around rhetorical garbage blaming legal and illegal immigrants for our collapsing post-industrial economy of, for, and by the fewer and fewer of the few?

Not stupid, ignorant, or senile, and he's just about indistinguishable from Pat Robertson on prisoner rights?

And, excuse me: What's up about black women?

He humiliated Lani Guinier!

He "disappeared" Jonetta Cole!

He fired Joycelyn Elders!

And he has made me feel worse than a fool.

I celebrated his election.

In 1992, I voted for Bill Clinton because I guess I believed that to know the good is to choose the good.

And I was wrong.

Because Clinton knows whatever he knows, but he doesn't give a damn about anything besides percentage points.

I was wrong.

Because Clinton in 1992 described a democratic state as somewhere with "no life to waste," and I thought he was serious.

And I was wrong.

And here we go again!

I will vote for him, again. But not because I believe anything he says is true, or principled, or trustworthy, or deep, or merciful. Or serious.

I will vote for Clinton because I still believe there is "no life to waste."

And, for the sake of the five or six people's lives potentially protected by the evanescent difference between Clinton and Dole, I will vote Democratic on the Presidential line.

A Gathering Purpose

January 1998

So there was something called A Million Black Women's March, and any-where from 300,000 to one and a half million black women converged on Phil-adelphia ("We are standing, we are unified"). Yet as far as I can tell, not a single solitary piece of paper circulated for signatures to demand a single solitary any-thing.

Not one.

Women standing, unified, 300,000 plus, in one place and no political pur-pose to that gathering,

No proposal for A Government Responsibility Act to thwart the cruelty and the shamelessness of the ongoing, and intensifying, war against the poor.

No specific outcry for rescue funds for public education, and rescue funds for public or subsidized housing, and rescue funds for job training and retrain-ing, and rescue funds to establish acceptable, attainable, child care.

No specific petitions to stiffen state and federal penalties for violence against women even though poor black women are, by far, those women most victim-ized by violence in our homes and on our streets.

Not one petition?!

So what was the idea, really?

To look bigger than ordinary and to gain an uplift of spirit that looks "good" in photographs of that one-day event?

I think that was a shocking waste of women's power: a shocking grassroots defusion of the undeniable, justified feelings of fury and terror that result from unmet basic needs.

Black women traveled long distances hoping to find other black women and to call out loud a purpose that would transform both the personal and the political future of their lives.

But there was no utterance of such a purpose.

And the future doesn't bode well for a second summoning of black women who will have to puzzle though the apolitical weirdness of the first.

In the same papers full of the news of black women standing together under the rather odd motto of "Repentance, Resurrection, Restoration"—I mean odd, given the verifiable victimized history of black women to date—was the story of sixteen-year-old Lo Eshé Lacy, a popular black teenager who was killed by a drive-by bullet as she sat in the back of a parked van, hanging out with friends.

Six hundred people attended the funeral services for Lo Eshé. One of them remarked that she thought it would help "if we could let them know we love them while they are alive." By "them" she meant black kids, and black girls, especially.

I couldn't agree more. But I don't see how the Million Black Women's March said anything about love for black girls because nobody prominent at the march spoke on black violence in black communities—whether that violence is so-called domestic, or whether it's omnipresent, or whether it's a matter of a lousy crapshoot with your apparently incidental life at stake.

We, women, we know about coming together in grief.

We, women, we know about coming together against loneliness.

We, women, we know about coming together in love, and in acts of committed, reliable, kindness.

But we, women, we still do not know about and crave and insist upon coming together in power for power: coming together for a specific, collective, political purpose, each and every time we convene a meeting of as many of us as we can persuade to stand or sit together, united.

In a forthcoming essay entitled "Welfare and Work," the redoubtable political scientist Frances Fox Piven spells out the real-deal economics behind the poor—who are disproportionately female and disproportionately women and children of color. Piven shreds the popular rhetoric about both welfare and work. Behind the pieties, the catch-phrase castigations of these poorest of poor American women, Piven illuminates the economic interests served by such shameless cruelty and abuse. She writes, "Women, barred from welfare aid, will compete in a segment of the labor market which is already saturated with job seekers, with the result that wages for those who are already earning little will be driven down."

Citing another paper, "Cutting Wages by Cutting Welfare," written by Lawrence Mishel and John Schmitt, Piven indicates that "wages for the bottom 30 percent of workers will fall by 11.9 percent. In California the drop will be 17.8 percent and in New York, 17.1 percent."

Overall, Piven argues that "a politically mobilized business community is raising profits by squeezing wages, and using its formidable influence to change public policies so as to bolster its efforts. From this point of view, welfare cutbacks are associated with seismic shifts in the power relations between employers and employees. Of course, they are only a component of a much larger class strategy, a business war against labor."

Notice how these "seismic" shifts affect women, who confront the meanest set of alternatives: life-destroying penury on "welfare," or life-destroying penury on lower and lower wages for increasingly humiliating and futile "work." And if Republicans succeed in denying people on workfare the basic labor rights that other Americans enjoy, then anti-welfare vigilantes will have created an ancillary social disgrace.

As Piven explains, "In the absence of these protections, workfare means the creation of a virtually indentured labor force of welfare recipients."

And so I ask the question: How come?

When Clinton's welfare-reform atrocity rose into public view, where was the mobilized, national, women's community?

Where was the mobilized African American community, and the national community of Latinos? And where were the elderly Americans, and the children's-rights activists?

And how come we are now only a few weeks away from national implementation of the Personal Responsibility Act that will no longer allow education and job training to count as "work" and that will lock poor people into poverty—especially women and especially the nine million children dependent upon hopelessly impoverished American women?

How come?

There is a god-awful crisis on the way: Regardless of federal budget percentages, poor women will soon become less able to resist the burdens of impoverishment. They will be less able to overcome the multiple challenges of illness, incomplete and irrelevant education, the dearth of trustworthy and affordable child-care options, unemployment, and the calculated evaporation of public housing to shelter them and their children.

We women desperately need to come together in power, right now, for the power to recreate the world as a universal safe house for our highest aspirations and our universally neglected, or forsaken, human rights.

The Stoning of Bill Clinton

November 1998

I do not entirely admire Bill Clinton, the President. I deplore his eviscera-
tion of programs to help the poor. I recoil from his preference for punishment
rather than prevention of crime. I resent his retreat on health care, our natural
environment, and sexual freedom. I no longer believe he will ever move his support for affirmative action, and public education, beyond rhetorical niceties and
staged conversations. I despise his treatment of Lani Guinier and Dr. Joycelyn
Elders.

That's domestically speaking.

I disagree with Clinton's African, Middle Eastern, and European policies
across the board: As regards a principled willingness to interdict genocidal conflict, he has failed. As regards an even-handed respect for U.N. resolutions and
international law, he has failed. As regards unambiguous action and resolve to
value human life above all other concerns, he has failed.

That's Bill Clinton, the President, beyond our national boundaries.

But I do not hate Bill Clinton.

And I'm black. And I'm part of the imperturbable black majority who feel
horror and dread as we witness the merciless prosecution of the man, Bill Clinton, who is our President.

As a people, we have been hunted down, held below the law, and subjected
to all manner of intrusive violations of our personal days and nights.

As a people, we have never known justice. We forever contend with a fath-
omless hatred of our existence, official lies about that hatred, and a criminal
justice system that too often discriminates against us.

And so, we worry about the shunting aside of regular precepts and practices
of law—such as the secured confidentiality of grand jury proceedings, or the
privileged lawyer-client communication, or the right to a jury insulated against
extraneous details—sexual or other.

As a people, we have suffered under the staggering hypocrisies about "fair-
ness," "family values," and "Christian" morality.

And so, we resist and reject self-righteous displays of hatred for the President. When we read and we hear allegedly "Christian" denunciations that disregard New Testament tenets of embrace rather than judgment, and humility

rather than vengeance, we recognize familiar rock-bottom perversions of America's highest ideals.

When we watch the intended, prurient destruction of the most powerful white man in the world, we step back, aghast for our safety.

If the number one white man can be set upon and attacked and gnawed at and reduced to a quivering disaster of ridicule and revulsion, then what protections should we now assume for our infinitely less powerful identity and status?

But there is more to our sadness and alarm.

We who have achieved the right to family, we who have wrested recognition as a man or a woman or a child only in spite of incredible suffering, unspeakable humiliation, and systematic assault upon our entitlements to declare our lives our own unfinished business, we look at Bill Clinton, the President, and we see a man.

We do not see a monster, an alien, a disease, or nobody's brother, nobody's son.

We see a man.

And we do not cast stones. And we do not rejoice at the stoning of this man. And we tremble, and we grieve for him, and for ourselves.

O, California!

January 1999

Along with just about two times as many eligible voters as any other state, I live in California. Crystals, gurus, and tofu burgers aside, California is home to the nonwhite, non-native-speaker-of-English population emerging as the new American majority, nationwide. And California is where Democratic candidates defeated Republicans, all the way to the governor's house, November 3, 1998.

That was the pivotal night when women, Hispanics, and blacks left the "liability" and/or "special-interest" categories of public discussion and became, instead, the "indispensable-to-victory" vote.

It's as though the California electorate finally yielded to eyeball levels of common sense and saw through hate-mongering propaganda.

It's as though this most important national gathering of citizens decided to rebel against East Coast punditry, East Coast politicians, and East Coast witch-hunting, Puritan-wannabes.

Of course, this completely surprised the East Coast experts—because they had overlooked one big clue: Most of us living in California are neither stupid nor slow. In fact, most of us used our best powers of concentration and ingenuity in order to get out, and away, from the East Coast, as soon as we could!

And now that we're here, now that we constitute the undeniably happening, prophetic, righteously heterogeneous polyglot of California—the forecast multitudes for twenty-first century America—we do seem to be generally cheerful, obsessively fit, and very, very busy.

We do not have time to drift into official invasions of an individual's sex life, for example. We respect privacy rights. We honor consensual sexual relationships. And so the city of San Francisco continues to take on national corporations and demand same-sex partnership health benefits.

While Washington, D.C., pushes a sanctimonious, no-carrot foreign policy that refuses to consider anyone's interests other than its own and threatens to drop more bombs on innocent Iraqis, we talk with and walk with and teach and listen to and dispute and coalesce with the diversity our California residence insists upon, dawn to dusk.

Oh, we have a few problems!

California is where anti-immigrant, anti-affirmative action, and anti-bilingual education managed to pass under hugely well-funded blizzards of disinformation.

It's right here, on the Pacific Rim, that you will find more prisons than schools constructed during the past ten years.

But it's also right here that 6,000 high school students took the day off to demonstrate against the nearest police headquarters, less than a month ago.

It's also right here where you'll run into an amazing, high incidence of activist poets of every age, race, and ethnicity.

This is where public-defender law and environmental-protection law consistently attract a staggering surplus of first-rank graduates riveted to values of justice and beauty and the preservation of human life.

This is where underpaid junior high school teachers refuse to obey any law that will jeopardize the equality of education they mean to realize, and protect, in their classrooms.

And this is where the most remote street crossing is wheelchair accessible, and supermarkets and the post office and theaters compete to welcome the disabled in most thoughtful ways.

This California is where I stockpile water and canned tuna fish because I expect the worst earthquake any day now.

And this is where I store these disaster provisions among night-blooming jasmine flowers, wild thriving mint, and the miniature Japanese maple tree that's grown as high as the roof of my house.

Two nights ago, my students and I went to an Arab American restaurant that calls itself Café Europa. We went to feast on lamb and figs and hummus and couscous and iced rose water.

We went, all twenty-three of us, to honor our visitor, the brilliant Lebanese American poet Haas Mroue.

And, once the drinks arrived, I asked everyone to send up a toast in his or her home language.

So we heard Gaelic and Scarsdale ("I, like, totally, totally toast to my B.F.F.: Best Friends Forever") and Hebrew and (Suchow Dialect) Chinese and Arabic and Igbo and Spanish and Black English and French and Georgia Southern Belle and so on, as tall glasses of iced rose water traveled from one mouth to the next. And then we passed the pita bread and laughed about our California version of communion, of community.

It was just one dinner. But we knew it was more than enough to take us through the night.

Breast Cancer: Still Here

February 1999

Activism is not issue-specific.
It's a moral posture that, steady state,
    propels you forward, from one hard
hour to the next.
Believing that you can do something
    to make things better, you do
something, rather than nothing.
You assume responsibility for the
    privilege of your abilities.
You do whatever you can.
You reach beyond yourself in your
    imagination, and in your wish for
understanding, and for change.
You admit the limitations of individual
    perspectives.
You trust somebody else.
You do not turn away.

Because I was born small, female, black, and working-class, I found myself challenged by several interlocking implications of powerlessness. I could either yield to my apparently predetermined, powerless destiny or I could try to defy that forecast.

I have chosen active revolt as my response to destructive meanings of my identity.

Long ago, I ran across Bertolt Brecht's assertion that evil comes with a name and a home address attached to it.

Evil is not abstract.

Evil extrinsic to one's self is usually as obvious and as undeniable as Jeremy Strohmeyer stuffing seven-year-old Sherrice Iverson's head into a toilet.

But when the evil—when a wanna-be killer disease—waits within your personal flesh and skin and bones, then what?

Whose name and whose address should you pursue—besides your own?

Surely, you must be at fault! You host the enemy!

At the very least, you must have collaborated with, or encouraged, the hateful residence of that enemy inside the first and last territory of your existence.

All of a sudden you confront the challenge of none other than yourself.

No longer is it only the case that something is wrong in Rwanda, or Washington, D.C., or East Oakland, or U.C.-Berkeley. Something is wrong in you!

This is what happens when cancer seizes the cells of your life.

I can testify about one kind of cancer. I know about breast cancer. I know about it because I am a survivor. I am a five-and-a-half year survivor of that interior, deadly assault.

So I know how the activist question changes to how shall I actively oppose, and try to eliminate, an ultimate, inside enemy: an ultimate cellular threat to everything good that belongs, specifically, to me.

I know how you become your own enemy because you blame yourself for an alien invasion of your corporeal turf.

You suppose that you consumed too much high-fat food, or that you abbreviated some ideal commitment to breast-feeding your son, or that you neglected regular exercise, or that you forgot to try to side-step heavy stress whenever it exploded in your face.

It was something you did, or something you didn't do.

So, it was—it is—your fault, for sure: your deficiency, your fate.

And how do you fight that?

I didn't fight, for quite a while. But I saw the beloved members of my personal universe fighting for me.

I saw Adrienne Torf go ballistic when Alta Bates Hospital returned a biopsy report on the wrong breast.

I saw Angela Davis exhaust the literature on breast cancer therapies.

I saw my son deciphering annotated directories to the allegedly best oncologists in the country.

And then I visited the Women's Cancer Center in Oakland and, while I listened to their kind offerings of advice, it began to occur to me that I was part of a god-awful epidemic: My personal travail was part of a huge cataclysm—an extreme affliction that kills women.

I hadn't realized that "a woman will die from breast cancer every twelve minutes," or that "one out of eight women in the United States will develop breast cancer in her lifetime."

I'd simply gone for a routine mammogram. I'd done no homework. But, soon enough, I began to suspect the staggering magnitude of this disease.

And here I am, today, trying to assume responsibility, and trying not to turn away from an enemy that never seems to sleep or opt for permanent relocation.

Here I am, hoping to take heart from those who gather themselves against individual impotence.

Here I am, hoping to hearten those who still hesitate to publicly address this most private ordeal that, nevertheless, depends upon public visibility for its vanquishment.

Here I am.

But I did not easily arrive at this activist posture: not as relates to breast cancer. It's been an uncertain journey, for me.

I've had to acknowledge the privileges I possess and enjoy:

The privilege of a childhood that forced
    me to fight back
or die.
The privilege of a West Indian temper
    that does not forgive
or forget medical mistakes that have
    meant physical agony
and unwarranted mutilation, both.
The privilege of an elite education that
    enables me to sort, and
assess, and synthesize, all kinds of
    information.
The privilege of poetry that compels me
    to the task of
making rather than breaking connections.

And then there are those privileges that follow from survival, or, as Holocaust survivor Elly Gross recently declared, "I guess it was my destiny to live."

As a survivor, I owe something big to those who didn't make it.

It is absolutely amoral good luck that I did not die.

As Dr. Susan Love told me when I met with her, face to face, "The truth is, we just don't know: We don't know what causes breast cancer. And we don't know why some women survive and others don't. We do not know."

That conversation took place five years ago. Since then, national rates of invasive cancer have continued to rise, not fall. In 1998, "178,000 new cases of

invasive breast cancer will be diagnosed among women in the United States,"
according to *Cancer Facts and Figures* by the American Cancer Society.

I see this as an intolerable status quo!

These facts justify hysteria and disruptive running through the streets.

These facts should inspire unstinting, relentless research, as well as daily and
nightly organizing, house by house.

And then there is survival itself: the humiliation, the complications, the
exasperations of good will and faith!

Because you live beyond the diagnosis of breast cancer and beyond the mutilation of mastectomies, and beyond the unlikely and exhausting requirements
of rehabilitation, and beyond the incredible assault of chemotherapy, and beyond the truly problematic fall-out of almighty Tamoxifen, people say you have
survived.

And you believe it. You believe them.

But then the doctors examine you every three to six months. They send you
for blood tests, and they poke at you, and they order X-rays and mammograms
and, gradually, you realize that they're looking for something you thought you
could forget about. They're looking for cancer—in your breasts, or lymph nodes,
or lungs, or wherever! They're looking for cancer because they expect it to reap-
pear: It's not gone! It's quiet, or not yet traceable. But it's probably coming back.

If you catch a cold, or if your back aches, or if you're feeling tired, or if
you gain weight, or if you lose weight, the doctors crunch into emergency gear,
demanding CAT-scans and biopsies and further blood tests and, gradually, you
realize that the doctors do not believe that you're OK. The doctors do not trust
your description of a cold as "just a bad cold and a cough." The doctors think
they know something you don't: They think that they know that you're mor-
bidly always at risk.

And maybe you are, and maybe you're not.

But, meanwhile, an onslaught of side effects assails and capsizes your efforts
at reasonable morale.

Is there a whole lot of blood on the sheets the morning after a night of
wondrous romance?

Did no one ever tell you that Tamoxifen thins the walls of your uterus so
that passionate sex may, indeed, produce significant bleeding?

Do your primary physician and your gynecologist insist that you enter the
hospital for a surgical D&C?

And did no one ever tell you that Tamoxifen increases your chances for
uterine cancer?

And do you notice a lessening of your sexual ardor?

Did no one ever tell you that Tamoxifen suppresses your sexual patterns of, and capacities for, sexual desire and response?

No?

And if and when you stop taking Tamoxifen—if and when you finally arrive at the magical five years afterward moment and the oncologist says, "Congratulations!" and you throw away what's left of that magical Tamoxifen medicine—does your hair suddenly just fall out?!

And did no one warn you that abrupt, but temporary, hair loss commonly occurs, post-Tamoxifen?

No?

Then you're just like me, and I'm just like you: stumbling into difficult episodes of terror that result from terrible, and very expensive, medical care.

But whether you're newly diagnosed, or a possible survivor, or one of the millions of folks related to somebody battling breast cancer, I hope that we can agree that I am, very much, still here, and you are still here, and we are still here, together. I hope we can agree on that much because that's the only way we can win this one: consciously and faithfully together—on purpose!

From the Kosovo Series: First Three Poems

June 1999

April 7, 1999

Nothing is more cruel
than the soldiers who command
the widow
to be grateful
that she's still alive

April 9, 1999
(for Ethelbert)

In Brooklyn when the flowering
forsythia escaped the concrete patterns
of tight winter days
I didn't think about long
distances
or F-117's in contrast
to a lover or an army
on the ground
up close
and personal as washing out a shirt
by hand
the soapsuds and the fingers and the cloth
an ordinary ritual
to interdict the devils of 2,000 lb. bombs
dropped from more than 25,000 feet above
the children
scrambling from the schoolyard
suddenly aflame

until you called from Washington

D.C.
to say
"Oh, let me be
that shirt!"

April 10, 1999

The enemies proliferate
by air
by land
they bomb the cities
they burn the earth
they force the families into miles and miles of violent exile

30 or 40 or 80,000 refugees
just before this
check-point
or who knows where
they disappear

the woman cannot find her brother
the man cannot recall the point of all
    the papers somebody took
        away from him
the rains fail to purify the river
the darkness does not slow the trembling
        message of the tanks

Hundreds of houses on fire and still
    the enemies do not seek and find
        the enemies

only the ones without water
only the ones without bread
only the ones without guns

There is no international TV
There is no news

The enemies proliferate

The homeless multiply
And I
I watch I wait

I am already far
and away
too late

too late

From the Kosovo Series: Next Three Poems

July 1999

Kosovo Exchange, April 11, 1999

Through nights of bleeding
feet and babies lost to one
mis-step on ice or
stony mountain trail

my peaceful friend relinquishes
his pencil
and begins to inch his way
towards a gun
as I release the rifle
nestling in my head
and then attempt
to hold him
close
    (for m.r.)

April 12, 1999

Sex, food, and war
cyberspace addicts
insist the buttons and the on-line
icons indicating universal on and off and stop
and go
deliver just about everything you know
and more
everything (just about)
as good as actual
anesthesia actual
caress

And like the (e-mail) lover
claiming
"Love! Love!"
who will not alter all the virtual
terms
of the engagement
that obliterate the (anyway invisible)
beloved

so do computer-driven warriors
claim "Rescue!" "Mercy!" "Moral
Imperative!" but
meanwhile blast and kill
the living
who need real time face
to face
and mouth to mouth

recovery

April 29, 1999
Dedicated to The Third World Liberation Front
Students at U.C. Berkeley

You can't help but worship
with this raggedy last
vigil
against ethnic cleansing
under a full moon
close to the campanile
where all the bells hold still

And not the President
And not the Chancellor
And not the C. E. O.
And not the Army Chief of Staff
And not his Holiness Himself

can influence the candles

lit
intermittent and among the young
believers
breaking bread at midnight
as their oath
to stay together
aching for another light
to bless the weather and the outcome
of this whispering
this unruly
witness

From Kosovo to Berkeley

No more starve and freeze
no more touch or shoot or seize
no more purging of all the people!

(so they talk and sign their names
in chalk)

They give up food and bed and roof
as proof
they will not sleep
before the morning wakes the world
on just
such sweet demand
and hungering
and few
they stand
the darkness down

Good News of Our Own

August 1999

This spring, beyond Kosovo, beyond Littleton, Colorado, something else was happening: something neither European nor violent nor white, but huge and verifiable, nonetheless.

And this something else was good news.

In fact, this good news was so good and so new the national media kept it a secret so that "copycat" could remain a noun of negative implications, only.

I am referring to the huge good news of nonviolent students, here at U.C. Berkeley, who put their lives at risk in order to secure Ethnic Studies. I am referring to the huge good news of nonviolent students, here, who won every single one of their completely idealistic demands.

Organizing themselves into the Third World Liberation Front, they resolved that the violence of the concept and the execution of all forms of ethnic cleansing would stop right here.

Many of these new heroes had opposed California Propositions 187 (against immigrants), 209 (against affirmative action), and 227 (against bilingual education). They had struggled hard. And they had lost each of these battles. These seventeen to twenty-two year olds had never known victory. They didn't fight expecting to win. They fought on because, as participant Maria Poblet explained, then you could hope to say, "At least we came down on the right side of history. At least our kids won't be ashamed of us."

Word got around that U.C. Berkeley's Ethnic Studies department was staggering from a $300,000 budget cut. By September, seven courses of Asian American, Native American, and Chicano focus would be gone. I called the chair, Professor Ling-chi Wang, who confirmed these fast-traveling rumors and added that, by the end of '99, he'd be forced to eliminate as many as twenty additional courses. Almost 60 percent of the department's regular offerings would disappear!

This crisis continued a pattern of benign neglect: no replacement of retiring faculty allowed, and no new hiring to strengthen the curriculum.

As I listened to Professor Ling-chi Wang, I could hear little besides extreme fatigue except when he spoke of "The Students." A week earlier, they had occupied the building that housed his department, and they had continued that nonviolent occupation until police came and "cleared the premises."

After choke-holds and other police abuse, that occupation had ended, yes. But it would begin anew within twenty-four hours: a revitalized student uprising that would stun the entire Bay Area.

These students vowed to oppose the deletion of any people, anywhere. They dedicated their minds and their bodies against "ethnic cleansing" and for Ethnic Studies.

On April 29, key leaders of the Third World Liberation Front helped to raise more than $1,300 for Kosovar refugee relief at a major student poetry reading.

Then they, and the other poets, and hundreds of enthusiastic supporters, walked through the campus darkness to the headquarters of the Chancellor.

It was close to midnight and cold. Two large soft loaves of bread circulated, and each of us broke off a morsel and consumed it. Some folks held candles not even flickering in that still air.

And then the hunger strike became official. It was on. Five U.C. Berkeley students and one San Francisco State University student would accept nothing more than water and juice. The rest of the Third World Liberation Front—about 125 students—would stay with the strikers day and night, camping outside the Chancellor's office.

As midnight and the hunger strike merged, there was much hugging and many whispered admonitions of "Take care" and "I love you."

I saw Professor Ling-chi Wang near the center of this impromptu ritual and three or four other faculty from his department. I could tell he was crying, and when he drew near, we hugged each other as well. Above us, a full moon sidled near the sword tip of the campus campanile, and at this moment all the bells held still.

Of the six hunger strikers, two were students I know really well. I was unable to think of anything useful to say. I just did not want them to die.

That was the first of seven nights. The students insisted they would negotiate with the Chancellor. The Chancellor refused to negotiate with the students.

Student resolve deepened. Hunger strikers weakened. General support began to abound.

I worried more and more because I knew for a fact that the students conceived of things in noble ways and on noble levels that would astound, if not utterly mystify, the Chancellor. He might actually believe the strike to be nothing more than a tactical bluff. But, actually, there was no bluff at the heart of the strike.

At first, press was hard to come by. Saturation stories and printed speculations about Columbine High School vied with extremely managed "news" accounts of NATO's bombings along with mass Serbian expulsion of "ethnic Albanians."

But on Day Five, in the middle of the night, the Chancellor ordered campus police to arrest and remove the students. Five of the six hunger strikers, plus more than seventy members of the Third World Liberation Front, were handcuffed and driven to Santa Rita jail in Dublin— about an hour and a half away from Berkeley.

Several hours later, local TV network crews, newspaper reporters, and columnists showed up for an on-campus press conference convened by the Front. At a parallel outdoor rally, an enormous outpouring of high-spirited people materialized.

From the arrests forward, local TV and print media swarmed all over the hunger strike. KMEL, the number one hip-hop radio station, not only endorsed the strike, but broadcast ongoing bulletins.

Outraged by the arrests of nonviolent students, and incensed by police seizure of students on their fifth day of nothing but water and juice, activists and ordinary folks, alike, became galvanized.

An amazing diversity of people—race, age, class—showed up. At one demonstration, more than 1,000 listened to in-person labor union endorsements representing more than 100,000 workers in California, including: the Service Employees International Union; the Hotel Employees and Restaurant Employees Union; the San Francisco State Professors' Union; the United Farmworkers; the Associated Graduate Student Employees (which has not yet been recognized as a union by the University); the San Francisco Labor Council; and the Alameda County Labor Council.

Now one might suppose that such massive labor union solidarity with the students might have captured at least a paragraph on the international wires. But that news never made it even to New York.

Nor did the passionate, live presentations coming from Pastors for Peace, and the Mexican American Legal Defense and Education Fund, and the South Asian Community Center, and the ACLU, and the NAACP, and the National Lawyers' Guild, and elected members of Berkeley's City Council, and 100 percent of the Asian and Asian American faculty within the Department of Ethnic Studies.

Nor did the live solidarity presence of dozens of students from other schools—San Francisco State University, Stanford University, Santa Clara, Vista, Laney Community Colleges, and four high schools from as far away as Fremont.

Nor did the dramatic reappearance of leaders from the first Third World Liberation Front of 1969 who, with their agitation, inaugurated Ethnic Studies.

Nor did the medical staff, who devoted themselves to monitoring the health of the strikers, and who volunteered daily, onsite ministrations: Dr. Floyd Huen, Dr. Peter Diekter, and Pam Cameron, Director of Clinical Services for the Tang Student Medical Center.

On Day Seven of the strike, professors Ron Takaki, Carlos Muñoz, and Norma Alacon publicly pledged to be arrested with the students should any further police harassment occur.

Off campus, Lee Halterman, who served as general counsel for former Congressman Ron Dellums, contacted our current Congresswoman, Barbara Lee, and Halterman and Lee phoned the Chancellor's office, urging him to negotiate with the students.

Carole Migden, Chair of Appropriations for the State of California, called the university's lobbyist and let him understand that she, too, believed the Chancellor should negotiate with the students, and that he should move on it before any of the students suffered serious harm.

And, also, on Day Seven of the Hunger Strike, Alison Harrington had to be hospitalized, late afternoon. She was that weak, that disoriented.

An ambulance drove right up to the Chancellor's door, and carried Alison away for emergency care.

In the hospital, Alison continued to refuse food and, instead, sent back a poem with these lines:

I WANTED TO GIVE YOU A POEM
I GIVE YOU MY BODY INSTEAD

It was 3:10 P.M., Day Seven. In my school office, I was on the phone alternating between a difficult conversation with the Chancellor's chief of staff and an update to State Assemblywoman Migden when a student handed me a penciled note: "Alison's about to be hospitalized right now!"

I don't remember what exactly I said next but I know I used the most forceful language I could muster. This was precisely what must not happen: Not one of the students should become a sacrifice to non-negotiations!

Apparently, Migden got back to the university's lobbyist and underscored the ultimate state of things: She had more than $60 million worth of requests from the Chancellor on her desk, at that very moment. And if he maintained his intransigence, he would not likely remain a happy man.

Meanwhile, several hundred students had witnessed the ambulance rescue of Alison Harrington, and that news fired across campus. That night of Day Seven, an awesome rally just kept going and going in front of the Chancellor's locked door.

On the morning of Day Eight, the Chancellor met and negotiated with the students and the Ethnic Studies department chair and faculty. This is what the students and their allies secured, after several hours: eight full-time faculty; the Administration's commitment to seed an institute for race and gender studies; the Administration's commitment to rebuild a multicultural center; and student participation in the all-important decisions related to Ethnic Studies.

I got the victory call at 8:20 P.M., Day Eight. I asked if Alison was OK. And she was.

I have taken pains to describe the motivation of these heroes and the humility of their posturing and the pivotal varieties of their off-campus comrades who pitched in because this was, this is, a historic, nonviolent victory.

I wish we could change the Clinton and Company channel and watch TV specials about How Did This Come About? Where did these young American freedom fighters acquire their ideals and their savvy? What was the source of their fortitude?

The New York Times and *People* magazine could, just for once, abandon the usual pantheon of their ill-chosen few and, just for once, run profiles of these nonviolent heroes: You know, interview their parents and, just generally, let Littleton, Colorado, go.

Littleton was predictable: entirely mainstream, entirely predictable.

But this news, over here, is waiting for no one to catch up. The alliance between students and labor, and students and elected politicians, and students and faculty, and students and students—Latino, Latina, Asian American, white, black—this complex alliance is news mobilizing more and more good news on the way.

Nonviolence up against the concept and the execution of "ethnic cleansing" is major, major news.

And I am proud to pass it on.

The Hunters and the Hunted

October 1999

"You're looking for me."

With those four, casual words, Aryan Nation member Buford O. Furrow Jr. presented himself to the FBI in Las Vegas, August 11, 1999.

One day earlier, Furrow was hunting for Jews. He wanted to kill Jews. He wanted America to wake up. He thought that killing Jews would help to interrupt a dangerous national sleep during which "the spawn of the devil"—Jews, blacks, homosexuals—have gained something or other powerful and good at the expense of Christian white people.

On August 10, Furrow attacked a Jewish community center in Los Angeles. Firing a made-in-China Norinco 9-millimeter semi-automatic rifle, Furrow wounded five Jews, including three small children. One of these victims, five-year-old Benjamin Kadish, remains in critical condition as I write.

On August 10, just after this furious assault, Furrow spotted somebody he presumed to be "Asian or Hispanic"—or, in short, not white. Furrow shot and killed this man, Joseph Santos Ileto, with nine bullets fired from a Glock 9-millimeter semiautomatic gun. (Originally, this gun was used by police in Cosmopolis, Washington.)

The night of the shootings, and that murder, I'd been reading my mail, rather carelessly, until I came across a large Xerox of a photograph. It showed many people crowded together, and a blue ballpoint circle was drawn around two of their heads. In the margin—scrawled in ink—there appeared this explanation: "My mother and my brother."

I looked more closely at the Xerox and wondered who might have sent that picture to me, and why.

Riffling through the papers on my table, I found the cover letter: It came from seventy-year-old Elly Gross ("born Berkovits"), who was thanking my students for poems written to her almost a year ago.

I'd heard Elly Gross in an interview with Laura Flanders on Pacifica Radio and, stunned by her matter-of-fact tenacity, I'd rushed to my class to tell about this amazing woman, this Auschwitz survivor, who was now a plaintiff against Volkswagen.

Elly Gross is part of a class action suit seeking compensation for the slave labor forced upon her, and thousands of other Jews, in 1944.

What struck me to my soul was her spontaneous, on-air declaration. She said: "I guess it was my destiny to live."

She meant that her life hopes to honor the memory of her mother and her five-year-old brother who were waved to the left—to their death—by a white-gloved Nazi officer, June 2, 1944, while she was waved to the right, first to Auschwitz, and then to slave labor at Fallersleben.

She meant that to live is not just a given: To live means you owe something big to those whose lives are taken away from them.

She was alive. And she was hoping "to make things right" by testifying to the heinous wrongs committed against her and her family and her people.

I did not know about Furrow and the L.A. shootings until the morning afterwards when the *Times* arrived and I saw a still photograph of cops leading strands of Jewish children by the hand across what looked like ghastly, uninhabited space.

#

Fifty-five years since 1944, and here comes this heavily armed, self-righteous, white supremacist hunting Jews in Los Angeles, California. On that Wednesday morning after Furrow opened fire, I confronted an up-to-date newspaper photograph of Jewish children struggling for safety. Next to that I placed the old photograph taken moments before the Nazis sent Elly Gross's mother and brother "to the left"—to be gassed at Birkenau.

It was more than half a century later, and here we were, again.

And here we are.

#

Finally, there's a picture of Joseph Santos Ileto printed in the papers. He could have been my father or my son.

#

Buford O. Furrow Jr. is a member of the Aryan Nation and, leveling his murderous aim at Jews and one "Asian or Hispanic" Filipino-American, he has earned his entry into "The Phineas Priesthood," which grants membership to those who kill Jews, homosexuals, and people who are not white.

In the Bible (Numbers 25), a man named Phineas murdered an Israeli who "brought unto his brethren a Midianitish woman in the sight of Moses."

Phineas, when he saw "it" (an interracial/intertribal coupling), "he rose up ... and took a javelin in his hand:

"And he went after the man of Israel into the tent, and thrust both of them through, the man of Israel, and the woman through her belly. So the plague was stayed from the children of Israel....

"And the Lord spake unto Moses, saying, Phineas ... hath turned my wrath away from the children of Israel, while he was zealous for my sake among them....

"Wherefore say, Behold, I give unto him my covenant of peace...."

Today it is Christian Identity followers who aspire to such zealotry and divine acclaim.

Through literal elimination of those perceived to be apart from God's wish and those who do not qualify as God's people, the Phineas Priesthood publicly confirms its own violent notions of religious and racial virtue.

#

In June, a gay couple was murdered near Redding, California, and three Sacramento synagogues were set afire.[36] Two brothers, Matthew and Tyler Williams, have been arrested and charged with all of these crimes.

In connection with this violence, police have been investigating organized white supremacist activity.

In the June 24 *Sacramento Bee*, William Pierce, leader of the National Alliance, said: "We have a number of people in the Sacramento area, but they don't get involved in the burning of synagogues. *That's strictly against our policy.*" (My italics.)

On the other hand, Matt Hale, head of The World Church of the Creator, responded in this way: "Certainly there is nothing immoral about torching the den of the serpent."

In July, Benjamin Nathaniel Smith murdered a black man and a Korean American man.[37] He also wounded six Orthodox Jews and one Taiwanese American, before killing himself. That rampage took place in Indiana and Illinois.

On August 11, Buford O. Furrow Jr. told FBI officers, "You're looking for me."

#

The impending millennium is a completely Christian construction. As we approach what would be the two-thousandth birthday of Jesus Christ, the American media blithely ignore the remarkable, restrictively religious meaning that underlies millennial hoopla and hysteria. Hate groups do not.

From the Aryan Nation through the Phineas Priesthood, these organizations/ideologues/soldiers of the Lord/maniacs/loners/racists/anti-Semites/homophobes are running hard and fast to imminent glory.

They mean to purify the world or, at least, these United States. They perceive themselves as persecuted heroes—American Kamikazes bound to destroy or be destroyed.

By definition, a supremacist cannot coexist with anyone different. Coexistence with "the spawn of the devil" belies intolerable cowardice and promises only eventual suicide.

Seized by an ideological need to kill or be killed, these supremacists choose homicide, arson, and any other wildly terrorist tactic they deem necessary to their ultimate self-defense.

They believe they have lost their place: their standing, their purity, their power. They strike because they have been stricken from their rightful, righteous ruling of the land. God, Himself, has been eclipsed by those who do not worship and obey His commandments.

#

Several elements unite these recent terrorist outbreaks:

1. Jewish places of worship and community centers are being attacked, but Jews have not been murdered, so far. Clearly, the last two murderous ravings have sought to change that fact.

2. Black men, gay men, Asian men are murdered, but no places of worship or community centers specific to the race or religions of these men are attacked.

3. Apparently, these killers cannot be satisfied until their irreversible wrath condemns a social variety of victims to terror, or death, or both: These multiple targets bespeak a fiendishly fused hatred that is religious and racial and heterosexist, all at once.

4. So far, there is a pattern to the attacks. The terrorists want to wake up America for a religious war against Jews, and while they're at it, exterminate what is not human—men of color and/or homosexuals. The first is a crusade; the second is almost an afterthought.

5. Every single so-called Christian component of this terrorism relies, exclusively, on the Old Testament of the Bible for its validation.

But in Christianity there is no way around the teaching of the Gospel according to Matthew, Chapter 7, Verses 1-3: "Judge not, that ye be not judged. For with what judgment ye judge, ye shall be judged, and with what measure ye mete, it shall be measured to you again. And why beholdest thou the mote that is in thy brother's eye, but considerest not the beam that is in thine own eye?"

6. We, the spawn of the devil, have become prey to the spawn of the "godly": those who arrogate to themselves the judgment of good and evil; those who reject the humility required of all religious believers; those who, instead, assert themselves as "good" enough to condemn and destroy anyone else who challenges their moral and racial supremacy.

7. It is a commitment to purity, to absolutism, and to certitude that motivates this violence inevitably.

#

On Friday the thirteenth, three days after the L.A. shootings, I went to Berkeley's Congregation Beth Israel.

I went to the 7:30 P.M. service at sundown.

I went there in solidarity and in grief.

I went there to honor the hope of the survival of Elly Gross.

I did not, and I do not, believe that Buford O. Furrow Jr. acted alone. I did, and I do, believe that there are thousands of other men hunting for Jews, and for me.

As I understand the mentality of these killers, I am a walking ground zero because I am, obviously, not white. The synagogue is ground zero because the killers assume that everyone inside is Jewish.

I wanted to confront murderous, insane concepts of Jews and of myself, my people, and begin the conversion of "targets of opportunity" for death into opportunities for unified resistance to hatred.

#

I almost drove past the synagogue. It's a small corner building surrounded by small homes of comparable size.

There was no security posted anywhere.

Inside, a clean white room was simply divided in half by a waist-high fence. Men would sit to the right and women to the left.

The space felt humble to me, and bare. Fewer than twenty people were milling about or reading from the prayer book, aloud.

Towards the front, four or five women busied themselves with preparations for dinner. A couple of little children sat on their fathers' laps or ran across the scarred wood floor.

Several people smiled at me, and I smiled back.

It began to feel really familiar, this gathering to worship with no pomp, no pretense, and yet a pervading air of purpose, pride, and joy.

It reminded me of a shanty one-room church on John's Island, South Carolina, where only five people came for evening service.

It reminded me of a glass of hot tea in Belfast where it was dark inside a haphazard shop, and cold, and dangerous, and nobody cared about that danger.

The rabbi, Eli Finkelman, welcomed me, and when I asked if the scheduled guest speaker was really coming, he said, "Yes, but he's late!" and we laughed.

(It was 8 o'clock and the service had yet to begin.)

Eventually, perhaps sixty men and women prayed and sang and swayed and bowed their heads and sat and stood and prayed, together, in that congregation.

And I watched the children, peaceful in that space, and I marveled at the bravery of their parents who had brought them there, depending only on the strength of their good faith for their security.

And then there was communal dinner and the washing of hands with cold water from a large, plain basin.

The rabbi invited me to sit at his table, "so you'll know somebody!"

He blessed the bread and offered prayers and I was allowed to break that holy bread with them. I was allowed to sip the sweet wine passed around.

#

The scripture was Leviticus 24, verses 10-22.

The topic was "The Dynamics of Rage."

The speaker (visiting from Baltimore) was late.

He began his interactive lecture sometime after 10 P.M. I found myself riveted to his utterly respectful and creative deconstruction of the text. He asked the congregation, "Does it make sense?! What's wrong with this story?!"

It was the companion piece to Numbers 25. This scripture centered on the son of an interracial marriage between an Israelite woman and an Egyptian father. He "went out" and fought with a (100 percent) Israeli and blasphemed God. And so, Moses asked God what should be done. And God said that the Israelites should stone that man because he had blasphemed God. And so the Israelites stoned him to death.

I was thinking that, as with Numbers 25, this was an example of scripture and verse inveighing against The Other/the outsider/the impure.

But the speaker was encouraging fanciful conjectures and logical criticisms: What did it mean, he "went out"? And why would he blaspheme the God of the Israelites?

In order that we be able to disperse before midnight, the speaker would only raise more and more questions and contribute more and more illustrious interpretations that did not agree with each other.

He would not give us the answers.

We would have to leave that small white room and return to the darkness beyond its doors, without the answers.

He did suggest that the son of that interracial marriage had "gone out," and fought, and blasphemed God because he'd been set up—doomed: "He had no place to be." And perhaps he had found that unendurable. And perhaps he had raged against this radical displacement imposed upon him.

But, then, what was the meaning of God's response to that understandable rage? The speaker said he would continue the next morning, at 10:30 A.M.

It was time to go somewhere, home.

And I felt at a loss as I was about to leave this orthodox community that had welcomed me into its own light.

And I thanked Rabbi Finkelman for the privilege of sitting among them. And he thanked me for my willing solidarity. And we embraced. And both of us said, "Take good care."

And I headed into the night beyond the synagogue, by myself.

#

And maybe the unity of resistance to hatred that will stop that hatred seems improbable.

Maybe an orthodox Jewish congregation will never stand in protective vigil outside a gay and lesbian community center, or the clinic of an abortion provider.

Maybe a black student organization will never rally for Asian American rights.

And maybe gay and lesbian activists will not bodily interpose themselves between a synagogue and a Phineas Priest.

Maybe none of us will ever recognize that all of us are wrongfully, equally, condemned: "the spawn of the devil."

Maybe.

But, meanwhile, I am moving on an irrepressible wish that all of us will: all of us will build that circle of our common safety that all of us deserve.

I'm saying, "Are you hunting for Jews? You're looking for me!"

A Letter to Maria

October 2000

Dear Maria!

You'd like to talk with me about the Civil Rights Revolution. That's what you say, at the end of an evening when you come by my house almost delirious with radiant pride and excitement:

"It was fucking fabulous!" you exclaim. "I wish I was there, right now!"

In three years of trial and triumph as a star young activist and as a politically committed intellectual and poet, you have never seemed so exhilarated, so obviously tripping on good work well done. Not even when you proved pivotal to the filling up of eighteen buses with U.C.-Berkeley students bound for the strawberry fields of Watsonville: Not even then!

So, looking at your face, and listening to your report on L.A., I know a couple of things, for sure:

1. L.A. was huge news for progressive, and radical, fifteen- to twenty-four-year-olds.

2. Except for independent media people and their soaring appearances on cable-access TV channels across the country, and their deepening impact upon radio airwaves, and their Internet ingenuities, your huge news exploded entirely off camera and microphone.

Instead, PBS, for example, and CNN, for another example, drearily competed in irrelevant, boring, and inane coverage of the largely irrelevant, boring, and inane Democratic Convention. (Did I say it was irrelevant, and inane?)

And then you showed me color photographs: The Spanish-speaking black workfare mother you translated for, at a rally, the small group of black and Latino and white and Asian teenagers intent upon a moment of tactical reevaluation, the multiracial mass gatherings of this truly new youth movement (40 percent under eighteen) that regards a nineteen-year-old as "an adult organizer," and all the publicly lifted words about money for school, not prisons, and housing for the poor, as well as the homeless, and no more criminalization of "youths," and no more police lies, no more police violence, and Yes! to every kind of human right, including the right Not To Be Ignored and/or Misrepresented!

It was thrilling to watch and listen to your great, bursting pride about your part in the young leadership that figured out how to keep the violence-baiting

LAPD at the periphery of thousands of other young, and determined, Americans who just wanted to exercise their constitutional right to demonstrate against state brutalities, and elected official hypocrisies, and nauseating pieties.

You managed to outwit police power deployed against the people our Constitution was designed, in fact, to protect!

You and your comrades never swerved from your political agenda even though the safety of your and my Constitutional freedoms does not appear in the Republican or the Democratic platform!

You completely ignored the commonplace of no candidate for the Presidency of the United States convening a press conference in order to declare all-of-the-above unconstitutional, and, you know, wrong.

Undeterred, you stayed on your predetermined, and idealistic, mission!

As close to L.A. as I am—an hour's flight would have put me on those streets—I could not escape newspaper and TV characterizations of you and your many thousands of comrades as "anarchists" or "hopelessly diffuse" or "mostly white" or "far far left" or "beside the point, because they do not vote," and so forth.

Nevertheless, before that week shut down, I did piece together some bare-bones information: 2,000 delegates, 10,000 to 15,000 super-LAPD-police, plus perpetual helicopter harassment versus several hundred to 6,000 of you and your kin—mostly young, mostly multi-everything, and, always, overwhelmingly, and self-consciously, and ecstatically, nonviolent.

And then you showed up, shining! And when you exclaimed, "I wish I was there right now!" you made me remember a black fifteen-year-old girl, about thirty-five years ago, who told reporters, "We are all so very happy!"

That interview took place in Birmingham, Alabama, just days after the heinous murder of other black girls in the Sixteenth Street Baptist Church. And I heard what she had to say and, for the first time, I understood the spirit of resistance:

1. It feels terrific.
2. It knows it will prevail.
3. It's immune to enemy assessment.
4. It agitates for one's life, one's soul.
5. It's basically, and ultimately, collective.
6. and 7. IT FEELS TERRIFIC!

Back in her day, the movement relied upon press coverage that was neutral, if not sympathetic.

Just as Gandhi realized the futility of his gigantic political ambitions unless the (sympathetic) world press covered the tactics of India's nonviolent surging toward independence, so did Dr. Martin Luther King Jr. make sure to secure international press attention for our second American Revolution.

Now you and the rest of America's progressive, and radical, peoples confront a hostile or inaccessible or perverse press community, in general.

And, therefore, your morale relies much more upon nonvirtual, in-your-face, on-the-ground, at-the-meetings live interchange and support.

And, further, the fantastic eruption of independent TV and radio and Internet heroes and heroines becomes daily more crucial to your national, and international, outcome.

In 1965, that fifteen-year-old black girl spoke as an exception to the rules about "important people" and newsworthy folks.

Now, as you yourself testify, fifteen-year-old male and female teenagers compose the core of their own new movement. Without them, there is nothing "there."

And also, at last, there's a brilliant, female equality of presence at every level of your insurgency!

But one thing has not changed:

In 1965, most of the participants in the Civil Rights Revolution could not vote.

In 1965, throughout the South, it was deadly dangerous to be black and even try to register to vote.

So voting, or the right to vote, was a goal, yes, but not an overriding objective, nor was it a strategy, nor was it a tactic.

The overriding objective was freedom from American apartheid: its violence, its short-circuiting of our dreams whenever and wherever we lifted our eyes to the hills, hoping to behold the full light of the opening skies. And others of us—black Americans living up North—didn't worry about voting or not voting: We were forced, instead, to worry about where could we, and how could we, raise a family and what kind of school, and what kind of work, and what kind of housing could we get, finally, if we did this, and we did that, and that, and that on the streets and on the roads of this broken-off country founded by religious fanatics and by the smiling buyers and sellers of African slaves.

So voting was not exactly the point, or the way.

Just as, now, you burst into hilarious laughter when I ask you if you will vote, in November.

Voting is not the point.

And, meanwhile, the activist, political consciousness and energies of teenagers in deliberate, or haphazard, racial and ethnic array—leading themselves, and delighted by the collective entity they have become—Maria, that's altogether as new as this second millennium!

So, let's have that conversation about the Civil Rights Revolution.

But there's no worry and no hurry! You're already studying that literature, those films, and the manifestos; you're already studying how history repeats, or evolves.

The big deal is today and tomorrow morning: Just this minute and then the next determines whether you or I do whatever we can to stop the injustice, and the tyrannies, surrounding us, and inside our hearts.

Right now is the only time we own!

—*Dedicated to Maria Poblet.*

New Year Poem

February 2001

Dedicated to Sara Glickstein
(which means "luck stone," in German)

Say Vashahva!
That's Warshawa
or
(to you and me)
just WARSAW

But to Sara/
Sarenka/Saruch
that's where Nazis murdered
her relatives unable
fast enough
to alter into refugees
who fled
East to Soviet prisons thrusting
them
into Serbia
where mosquitoes and
starvation killed
one uncle
and then almost
stole herself
a baby girl
away

Now sixty-one
she tells me, "Stalin, we survived. And we escaped
from Hitler. But today my landlord's
trying to evict us!"

So small
Sarenka stands inside a bookstore
with a lightly woven shawl
around her narrow shoulders

as she blinks
excited
wistful
just to recommend
another something beautiful
a thought
an English sentence
she will whisper to her friends
delighted
not to lose
another lovely word
beyond the Russian
and the Polish
lost already
lost

"And how are you?" she
always asks.

It may be
I am thinking of tomorrow's
chemotherapy
or the hatred of white
people
for my people

the erasure of my face
the structured eclipse
of every wish
to count

to amount to more than 3/5ths
of some/anyone's
imagination

but I listen to her inquiry
I note the nascent trembling
of her aerial composure

and I answer her,
"I'm fine."
—*December 21, 2000, Berkeley*

The Invisible People:
An Unsolicited Report on Black Rage

March 2001

We do not play.

Ninety percent, or more, of us voted for Gore, nationwide. "I would have been amazed if we'd voted any differently!" the distinguished political scientist Charles Henry exclaims. He's chair of African American Studies at U.C.-Berkeley, and he speaks without hesitation: "As an electorate, we are very sophisticated." And, rapid-fire, he cites several instances when black folks shifted our votes to whatever column held the most for us, on a programmatic level. "Besides," he amplifies, "per income grouping, we weigh in more active than white Americans: more aware of the differences among candidates, more attuned to the content of the choice, and more likely, through daily conversations, and, even, literal organizing efforts, to keep political matters front and center."

He's talking with me as readily as, just an hour before, Nobel Laureate Toni Morrison answered my call.

I'd rung her up and asked. "What do you think of this mess? This stolen election?"

The questions, themselves, evidently relieved her from a punishing sense of isolation and disregard. Until I asked, nobody from the national media had bothered to make such an inquiry! "It's more than sinister," she said. "It's really really frightening, on every level I can think of.... You know there's always been a fascist strain, here: It's not even political in the sense of this party or that. It's like a virus that can attach itself to Democrats or Republicans or whatever. And we know it's around. We can tell because black people are the nexus. United States politics have always been determined by the South. Look at the 'New South' or, under Nixon, 'The Southern Strategy.' It's finally about how Presidential candidates make accommodations with the South: It's about race! Because, what doesn't change is the dispossessing and the disenfranchising of black folks. That's precisely what the Electoral College was invented to guarantee: To give power to smaller states that allowed no woman and nobody black to vote."

As eagerly, and with comparable passion, Robert Allen, editor of *The Black Scholar*, tells me: "Of course, it was, first and last, about race: this stolen election. And then Gore didn't want to touch it because Gore didn't want to break with white supremacy—even though that meant he'd lose the election! That's how much white supremacy means to him. Can you imagine? He'd rather lose the Presidency than stand with black folks!"

And then I was standing with Sweet Honey in the Rock's Bernice Johnson Reagon, who was preaching, clear as clear: "Oh, we really do vote against people! We were voting against Bush, against Ashcroft, and all the rest of it. And we knew, because we know: You have to play the game that's on the board. We didn't have time for Ralph Nader or anybody like that. This was too serious! And now look: If I wasn't living in it I wouldn't believe it." Observing that 54 percent of eligible black voters made it our business to vote, Reagon says, "Now we have to push for 84 percent! Let's expose the system: It's a system set up for low turnout. So let's push it, let's make it collapse! Let's see how many of these elections they can try and overthrow. Everywhere there should be voting inspection teams to create a lot of heat. Every university should be examining the electoral process closely right where it is. Make it The Number One ongoing research. Get the students to do the investigations. We have to be inventive. And make this one fired-up little country!

"You know, we need to keep the culture of rage, keep it spiked! You have to dig deep to get back to as bad as this is. You have to go back to Rutherford B. Hayes and *Plessy v. Ferguson*. I'm saying, let's make it 84 percent turnout in two years, and then see what happens!"

Toni Morrison still mourns for the many black people who died just trying to secure, or exercise, the right to vote, and she says, "Oh, yes! Vote! Dress yourself up, and vote! Even if you only go into the voting booth and pray. Do that! It's a ritual of respect for the blood shed so we could do this thing, so we could, so we would, count." When I tell her I've spoken with Bernice, and what she's said, Toni is audibly happy, audibly relieved. In fact, she says, just having our long distance phone conversation is a big help—out of the isolation and the disregard. Bernice gives me a big hug and a big smile when I convey Toni's thoughts, and the love that Toni sends to her.

All four of these African Americans share a raging and a sorrow at the discount of our people. We have moved from The Invisible Man to The Invisible People. It's a raging and a sorrow at the terrible meaning of that discount—for us, and for democracy itself.

All four of these faithful Americans have devised, per force, a survival of The Greater Evil, more than once in their lives. And so they view this most recent triumph of The Greater Evil with profound shock, anger, and alarm.

As Toni Morrison sees it, "This is NOT just the Republicans! This is the crowd in control of the Republicans—which is really terrifying. So, if they do what they used to do—like encouraging recession and starving our public schools—the future is very, very bleak."

And, while these four faithful Americans have struggled through the absolute bleak before, there's an absolute difference, now: In contrast to the days and weeks and years of the civil rights revolution, "We don't have any outlets, any newspapers, any media! It's like *Pravda*," Toni declares. "Or, worse! Because there's no news! For example, you wouldn't know there were truly massive protests in D.C. Or who knows about the speeches and the demonstrations in Tallahassee? It's a capitalist consolidation of the press—with consequences the same as *Pravda*: Horrifying distortion and sabotage!"

To which I must add, "Whites Only," in the public consciousness, and on the public forums. Where is there record of any major national newspaper or TV channel attempting—before, during, and after The Stolen Election of 2000—to find out what black people were thinking, and why? How is it acceptable to what's termed the American Left, that, until January 25, 2001, nobody asked our Nobel Laureate, Toni Morrison, for instance, for her thoughts, and her feeling, about our national crisis? And, certainly, nobody asked me to write this report!

What does such disregard, and such indifference to our black presence, our black rage, connote?

Well, we're pushing on toward an 84 percent black turnout in 2002. We'll expose the system. We're going to push and push and make it collapse.

Whether y'all ready or not!

The following poem by June Jordan appears as an inset in the preceding column, "The Invisible People: An Unsolicited Report on Black Rage" from the March 2001 issue.

Democracy Poem Number One

Tell them that I took
a number
and I waited
and I waited
like everybody
else
and I never got
called
but I keep that scrap
of paper
in my pocket

just in case

Scenario Revision #1

September 2001

Or
suppose that gorgeous
wings spread
speckled
hawk
begins to glide
above my body lying
down
like dead meat
maybe start to rot
a little bit
not moving
see
just flat
just limp
but hot
not moving
see
him circle closer
closing closer
for the kill
until
he makes that dive
to savage
me
and inches
from the blood flood lusty
beak
I roll away
I speak
I laugh out loud

Not yet
big bird of prey
not

7/23/01

Do You Do Well to Be Angry

November 2001

(The Book of Jonah, 4:4)
Dedicated to Stephanie Yan

Into that infamous Tuesday inferno of fire and structural collapse, a humbling number of men and women fell to a horrifying death. And now the rest of us remain, stricken by fear, stricken by grief.

We have become a wilderness of jeopardized love ones, and terrifying strangers.

I am an American.

I listen to our leaders calling for "the eradication of evil," and I am wondering, who among us is without evil?

What nation, what people, what stretch of my own personal history is good without blemish, without blame, without crimes of inertia, at least?

Was our firebombing of Dresden a terrorist attack?

Or Hiroshima?

Or the bombing of Beirut?

Or our bombing of Baghdad?

Is there anything for which we, as a nation, need to atone?

Is there anyone I have not recognized as equal to myself?

What will help?

I am an American.

What will comfort so many other Americans, so suddenly bereaved?

And how shall we arrange for safety, anywhere?

I am an American.

And my leaders reach for an unparalleled, international, military mobilization towards an extremely dangerous, an extremely ambiguous goal: "the eradication of evil."

For one thing, it appears that some religious multitudes may truly believe that we are, that I am, in fact, that "evil."

In the sixty-seventh surah of the Qur'an, it is written:

And We have,
(from of old),

234

Adorned the lowest heaven
With Lamps, and We
Have made such (Lamps)
(As) missiles to drive
Away the Evil Ones
And have prepared for them
The Penalty
Of the Blazing Fire. (verse 5)

They will say: "Yes indeed;
A Warner did come to us,
But we rejected him
And said, 'Allah never
sent down any (Message):
Ye are in nothing but
An egregious delusion!" (verse 9)

They will further say:
"Had we but listened
Or used our intelligence,
We should not (now)
Be Among the Companions
of the Blazing Fire!" (verse 10)

I am an American.

And I believe we are all "Companions of the Blazing Fire."

There can never be any exemptions from any absolutist view of "good" and "evil."

More than 5,000 have perished here. And, in turn, tens of thousands will perish elsewhere. And, in turn, there will be more and more thousands perishing from the universal arrogance of our universal propensities to judge, and to identify, other human beings as the ones to be "eradicated."

I am an American.

I am the daughter of peasants who begged and borrowed their way to these United States.

They wanted an escape from no-shoes-no-drinkable-water poverty.

They wanted the freedom and the justice that a nation separating church from state could offer, realistically.

They wanted to belong to the always possible undertaking of equality.

They wanted to seek and find refuge in a country ruled by law. They thought themselves equal to the challenge of equality: not better than anybody, not good, but equal to that.

And I am proud to strive with such sweet hope for such fundamental need.

I do not believe I am good. Or that we share a national legacy of innocence to protect and perpetuate.

Who is more violent than we?

We now confront huge questions, in extremis, questions exploding from the tattered soul of our imperfect, interconnected destinies.

Where in the world did those suicide pilots come from?

Why are we cozying up to the self-appointed military rulers of Pakistan?

Why are we relying upon close collaboration with the only government that deems the Taliban legitimate?

Why do our crisis managers persist in bypassing and/or second-rating India, the world's largest democracy—which happens to exist less than 800 miles from Afghanistan?

What's going on?

Or, why, exactly, did George W. Bush give the Taliban $43 million, only four months ago?

Who is eradicating what?

Nineteen years ago, Ariel Sharon, today Israel's prime minister, invaded Lebanon, and that invasion murdered more than 17,000 human beings, and that invasion culminated in the massacre at the Palestinian refugee camps of Sabra and Shatila.

Who is not a terrorist?

At the beginning of September, the United States of America walked out of the World Conference on Racism. It seems that an apology for the "barbarities" of slavery was one especially contentious issue. And so there was no apology, no acknowledgement of responsibility: The subject came up. The USA walked out.

And who is "the Companion of the Fire"?

What is the "Message"? What was the "Warning"?

The atrocity of September 11, 2001, is a crime against humanity. No atrocity is less than that. And such a heinous crime should be prosecuted, and duly punished, with all possible speed.

This summer, when Israeli Prime Minister Ariel Sharon was reported (*Christian Science Monitor*, July 30, 2001[38]) to be facing "the prospect of setting an international legal precedent by becoming the first serving prime minister to stand for crimes against humanity," he was not, thereupon, hunted down, or victimized by efforts at assassination.

I am an American.

I believe we can do no less than cling to the rule of national and international law.

In response to the atrocity of September 11, 2001, I hold to our American principles of due process.

Let us move to identify, and apprehend, whoever has done this terrible deed. Bring him, bring them to an international court of justice—there to be tried, and, if the evidence warrants, there to be convicted and punished, accordingly.

We, Americans, must not allow ourselves to become what we abhor: a terrorist force, furiously striking out at the known and the unknown poor peoples of Central Asia and the Middle East.

We must not permit ourselves to act as a terrorist people!

We must love and promulgate equality of human rights with everything we've got.

No one hates America because America is free, America is just. Those who hate Americans, those who hate you and me, hate us whenever we have failed to respect the self-determination and the reaching toward the equality those other human beings desire, and deserve. Double standards deriving from avarice and/ or racial or religious supremacist "ideals"—of whatever race, of whatever religion, theirs or ours—these are the origins of rage and self-immolating violence that will destroy an unpredictable, vast number of human lives.

As of September 11, 2001, the world we thought we knew went down.

And how shall we rebuild?

And should we reconstruct, or should we dare ourselves into an unforeseen millennial recovery, a millennial upholding of our best ambitions, a millennial declaration of a slow kiss dedication to equality and justice?

I am an American.

And I want to join a multi-national and a multi-religious and a multi-racial, *secular* coalition to stop all the violence!

It is not bin Laden's jihad but the greater jihad that we should embrace: the interior struggle against egotism and supremacist notions of every kind.

Ours is a struggle to fathom and to assume responsibility—for justice, and for the rapid demise of double standards of all degrees, all forms.

I am an American.

And I respond to the alleged summoning by Osama bin Laden with another idea, another story some millions of people may truly believe: It's the Old Testament story of Jonah.

The Lord wanted Jonah to travel to Ninevah—a wicked city—and to warn the inhabitants that they must change their ways. But Jonah was afraid, and he tried to flee the Lord. So the Lord caused Jonah to end up in the belly of a whale. And there Jonah stayed for three days and three nights.

And then the whale delivered Jonah out of the sea and back to the land because Jonah called to the Lord out of his distress.

And then, a second time, the Lord asked Jonah to travel to that wicked city, and make known the Lord's displeasure with their ways.

And Jonah went. And the king of that city "removed his robe, and covered himself with sackcloth, and sat in ashes." And then the king decreed: "Let everyone turn from his evil ways and from the violence which is in his hand. Who knows, God may yet repent and turn from his fierce anger, so that we perish not."

And God repented. And Jonah was annoyed, "exceedingly": Why would God redeem them? And the Lord asked, "Do you do well to be angry?"

And the Lord asked Jonah, "Should I not pity Ninevah, that great city, in which there are more than 120,000 persons who do not know their right hand from their left, and also much cattle?"

Who among us knows his right hand from his left?

I am an American.

And I hope we will learn, soon enough, that sometimes there is no difference.

Sometimes I am the terrorist I must disarm.

Sometimes I am the Penalty, and sometimes I am the Companion of the Fire.

Berkeley, 11:04 p.m., September 25, 2001

Bibliography

Personal Papers

June Jordan's personal papers are held at the Schlesinger Library at Harvard University's Radcliffe Institute for Advanced Study. Most of the papers are open for research. For a detailed finding aid of the papers, go to http://oasis.lib.harvard.edu/oasis/deliver/~sch00345

Books by June Jordan in Chronological Order

Jordan, J. (1969). *Who look at me*. New York, NY: Crowell.

Jordan, J. (1971). *His own where*. New York, NY: Crowell. [Young Adult Literature; A Feminist Press 2010 edition is now available]

Jordan, J. (1971). *Some changes*. New York, NY: Dutton. [Poetry]

Jordan, J. (1972). *Dry victories*. New York, NY: Avon. [Young Adult Literature]

Jordan, J. (1972). *Fannie Lou Hamer*. New York, NY: Crowell. [Children's Literature]

Jordan, J. (1974). *New days: Poems of exile and return*. New York, NY: Emerson Hall.

Jordan, J. (1977). *Things that I do in the dark: Selected poetry*. New York, NY: Random House.

Jordan, J. (1980). *Passion: New poems, 1977-1980*. Boston, MA: Beacon Press.

Jordan, J. (1981). *Civil wars*. Boston, MA: Beacon Press. [Essays]

Jordan, J. (1985). *Living room: New poems*. New York, NY: Thunder's Mouth Press.

Jordan, J. (1985). *On call: Political essays*. Boston, MA: South End Press.

Jordan, J. (1989). *Lyrical campaigns: Selected poems*. London: Virago.

Jordan, J. (1989). *Moving towards home: Political essays*. London: Virago.

Jordan, J. (1989). *Naming our destiny: New and selected poems*. New York, NY: Thunder's Mouth Press.

Jordan, J. (1992). *Technical difficulties: African-American notes on the state of the union*. New York, NY: Pantheon Books. [Essays]

Jordan, J. (1994). *Haruko: Love poems*. New York, NY: High Risk Books.

Jordan, J., & Adams, J. (1995) *I was looking at the ceiling and then I saw the sky: Earthquake/romance.* New York, NY: Scribner. [Libretto]

Jordan, J. (1997). *Kissing God goodbye: Poems, 1991-1997.* New York, NY: Anchor Books.

Jordan, J. (1998). *Affirmative acts: Political essays.* New York, NY: Anchor Books.

Jordan, J. (2000). *Soldier: A poet's childhood.* New York, NY: Basic Civitas Books. [Memoir]

Jordan, J. (2002). *Some of us did not die: New and selected essays.* New York, NY: Basic Civitas Books.

Jordan, J. (2005). *Directed by desire: The collected poems of June Jordan.* Port Townsend, WA: Copper Canyon Press.

Articles by June Jordan in Chronological Order

Jordan, J. (1973, May 15). Black English: The politics of Translation. *School Library Journal,* 21-24.

Jordan, J. (1974, May 18). Whose burden? *New Republic, 170*(20), 8-9.

Jordan, J. (1981, Sept. 26). South Africa: Bringing it all back home. *New York Times,* 1.23.

Jordan, J. (1982, June 28). Black in a changing America: A case for the real majority. *Boston Globe* [Special Section], 1.

Jordan, J. (1986, June 29). Thank you, America! A nostalgic snapshot of a black immigrant family who found the American dream in the rich life of the ghetto. *Newsday,* 58.

Jordan, J. (1986). The difficult miracle of black poetry in America or something like a sonnet for Phillis Wheatley. *Massachusetts Review, 27*(2), 252-262.

Jordan, J. (1988). Nobody mean more to me than you and the future life of Willie Jordan. *Harvard Educational Review, 58*(3), 363-374.

Jordan, J. (1988, Nov. 20). Park Slope: American amalgam; Walt Whitman ideal. *New York Times Magazine,* 51.

Jordan, J. (1988, Nov. 29). The rainbow next time. *The Village Voice, 33*(48), 23.

Jordan, J. (1989, Jan. 6). Next time the rainbow. *New Statesman & Society, 2*(31), 31-35.

Jordan, J. (1989, March 10). A break in the clouds. *New Statesman & Society, 2*(40), 26-30.

Jordan, J. (1994, March/April). Who's rocking the boat. *Ms, 4*(5), 70+

Jordan, J. (1995, May). Steady on my way. *Essence, 26*(1), 74.

Jordan, J. (1997, April 28). Affirming action. *Nation, 264*(16), 29-31.

Jordan, J. (1999). Still writing, still fighting. *Black Issues Book Review, 1*(6), 45+

Recordings of June Jordan

Hacker, M., & Jordan, J. (1992, March 31). *The Academy of American Poets Poetry Audio Archive.* [CD/Poetry Recording]

Jordan, J. (n.d.) *The June Jordan collection.* Pacifica Radio Archives. [CD/ Recordings of selected speeches and interviews by June Jordan between 1968-1991]

Jordan, J., & Torf, A. (2003). *Collaboration.* ABongo Music. [CD/Poetry and Music Recording]

Books, Articles, and Dissertations about June Jordan

Alston, V. R. (2005). Moving towards home: The politics and poetics of environmental justice in the work of *June Jordan. Interdisciplinary Literary Studies: A Journal of Criticism and Theory, 7*(1), 36-48.

Ards, A. (2002). The faithful, fighting, writing life of poet-activist June Jordan 1936-2002. *Black Issues Book Review, 4*(5), 63-64.

Brogan, J. V. (1997). From warrior to womanist: The development of June Jordan's poetry. In Reesman, J. C. (Ed.) *Speaking the Other Self: American Women Writers.* pp. 198-209. Athens, GA: University of Georgia Press.

Davenport, D. (1985). *Four contemporary black women poets: Lucille Clifton, June Jordan, Audre Lorde, & Sherley Anne Williams (A feminist study of a culturally derived poetics.)* University of Southern California. [Dissertation]

Erickson, P. (1994). After identity: A conversation with June Jordan. *Transition, 63,* 132-49.

Erickson, P. (1990). Putting her life on the line: The poetry of June Jordan. *Hurricane Alice: A Feminist Quarterly 7*(1-2): 4-5.

Finn, P. (2003). June Jordan's legacy. *New Labor Forum, 12*(1), 123-127.

Fish, C. J. (2007). Place, emotion, and environmental justice in Harlem: June Jordan and Buckminster Fuller's 1965 'architextual' collaboration. *Discourse, 29*(2-3), 330-345.

Gumbs, A. P. (2010). *We can learn to mother ourselves: The queer survival of Black feminism.* 1968-1996. Duke University. [Dissertation]

Houtchens, B. C. (2003). A great loss, a treasured legacy. *English Journal, 92*(3), 114.

Jocson, K. (2009). Steering legacies: Pedagogy, literacy, and social justice in schools. *Urban Review, 41*(3), 269-285.

Jocson, K., Burnside, S., & Collins, M. (2006). Pens on the prize: Linking school and community through contest-inspired literacy. *Multicultural Education, 14*(2), 28-33.

Jocson, K. M. (2005). Taking it to the mic: Pedagogy of June Jordan's Poetry for the People and partnership with an urban high school. *English Education, 37*(2), 132-48.

Jocson, K. M. (2004). *Writing as right/rite: Promoting literacy, social and academic development through poetry in the lives of urban youth.* University of California, Berkeley. [Dissertation]

Kinloch, V. 2006. *June Jordan: Her life and letters.* Westport, CT: Praeger Publishers.

Kinloch, V., & Grebowicz, M. (Eds.). (2004). Still seeking an attitude: Critical reflections on the work of June Jordan. Lanham, MD: Lexington Books.

Metres, P. (2003). June Jordan's war against war. *Peace Review, 15*(2), 171+.

Monaghan, P. (1996, February 23). Poetry for the People: Finding a voice through verse. *Chronicle of Higher Education, 42*(24), B7.

Muller, L., & The Poetry for the People Collective. (1995). *June Jordan's Poetry for the People: A revolutionary blueprint.* New York, NY: Routledge.

Remembering June Jordan. (2002). *Women's Review of Books, 20*(1).

Semitsu, J. P. (2002). Defining June Jordan. *New Crisis, 109*(5),

Splawn, J. P. (1996). New world consciousness in the poetry of Ntozke Shange and June Jordan. *CLA Journal, 39*(4), 417+.

Stanton, B. (2009). *On location: Race and family in the poetry of Sonia Sanchez, June Jordan, and Cathy Song. Indiana University.* [Dissertation]

Sutton, S. S., & Menezes, S. (2002). In remembrance of June Jordan, 1963 to 2002. *Social Justice, 29*(4).

White, W. R. (2001). *Dissonant hu(e)-manity: Another way to be differently in the work of Audre Lorde and June Jordan.* University of California, Santa Cruz. [Dissertation]

For assistance locating any of the above resources, contact Stacy Russo at russo_stacy@sac.edu

Endnotes

1. Erickson, P. (1994). "After identity: A conversation with June Jordan and Peter Erickson." *Transition, 63*, 132-149.
2. "Where Is the Rage?" (*The Progressive*, Oct. 1989)
3. "Mandela and the Kingdom Come" (*The Progressive*, Apr. 1990)
4. "Finding the Way Home" (*The Progressive*, Feb. 1989)
5. "Where I Live Now" (*The Progressive*, Jan. 1995)
6. Lehrman, K. (1993, Sept/Oct). Off course. *Mother Jones, 18*(5), 45+
7. In 1964, Jordan collaborated with the architect Richard Buckminster "Bucky" Fuller on a re-design of Harlem. (For more information on this collaboration, see Cheryl J. Fish's article "Place, Emotion, and Environmental Justice in Harlem: June Jordan and Buckminster Fuller's 1965 'Architextual' Collaboration" in the Spring & Fall 2007 issue of *Discourse*.) According to the finding aid for Jordan's personal papers at the Schlesinger Library, "With Fuller's support, Jordan received an award for creative writing from the Rockefeller Foundation (1969), as well as a Prix de Rome in Environmental Design (1970)." While conducting research with Jordan's personal papers at the Schlesinger Library, I discovered Fuller's book *Operating Manual for Spaceship Earth* was included as required reading on several of Jordan's course syllabi.
8. Lisa Steinberg was a six-year-old victim of child abuse in New York City. She died from trauma she sustained from Joel Steinberg, a man who helped to raise her. See "Steinberg given maximum term of 8Y to 25 years in child's death." (1989, Mar. 25). *The New York Times*, p. 1.1.
9. Daniels, L. (1989, Feb. 5). Experts foresee a social gap between sexes among blacks. *The New York Times*, pp. 1+.
10. See Toner, R. (1989, Apr. 10). Right to abortion draws thousands to capital rally: Protest aimed at court marchers opposed to efforts to narrow or to overturn Roe v. Wade decision. *The New York Times*, p. A1.
11. This is a reference to the Exxon Valdez Oil Spill, which was the largest tanker oil spill in United States history. The environmental disaster occurred when the ship ran aground and ruptured. See "Largest U.S. tanker spill spews 270,000 barrels of oil off Alaska." (1989, Mar. 25). *The New York Times*, p. 1.1. Jordan also mentions this disaster in the preceeding column.
12. This is Jordan's experience of the Loma Prieta Earthquake of October 17, 1989, which registered a magnitude of 6.9 on the Richter scale. The epicenter was near the Loma Prieta peak in the Santa Cruz Mountains, approximately 60 miles south of San Francisco. Initial reporting on deaths was higher than the actual number of individuals who lost their lives; sixty-three people died. See Wills, J. (2003). In *Dictionary of American history*, Ed. S. I. Kutler, volume 3, 3rd edition, p. 240, New York: Charles Scribner's and Loma Prieta Earthquake information on the U. S. Geological Survey website at http://earthquake.usgs.gov/regional/nca/1989
13. During the Loma Prieta Earthquake of October 17, 1989, a portion of the Bay Bridge collapsed. The bridge spans the San Francisco Bay and connects Oakland to San Francisco.
14. A section of Interstate 880 in Oakland, a two-tiered freeway, collapsed during the October 17, 1989, Loma Prieta Earthquake. The highest number of fatalities from the earthquake occurred at the site of the freeway collapse, although the total number of fatalities from the earthquake (63) was much less than originally predicted and reported.
15. See "Gunman kills 14 women at Montreal University: Killer targets feminists, commits suicide." (1989, Dec. 7). *The Washington Post*, p. a41.
16. See 1) "2 in an 'earth' group hurt as car explodes." (1990, May 25). *The New York Times*, p. A19.; 2) Bishop, K. (1990, May 26). Environmentalists hurt, then held, in blast. *The New York Times*, p. 1.1.; and 3) Swartz, S. (1990, Sept. 3). The assault was the bombing that shattered

Earth First! Member Judi Bari's life the latest attack in a war against women? *Sun Sentinel*, p. 1D.

17. According to the finding aid for Jordan's personal papers at the Schlesinger Library, she accepted a joint appointment at the University of California, Berkeley in 1988 as Professor of African American Studies and Women's Studies. Prior to her move to Berkeley, she taught at numerous institutions, including Sarah Lawrence College; Yale University; University of Madison at Wisconsin; and SUNY Stony Brook.

18. Cody's Books was a famous bookstore in Berkeley, California, that was founded in 1956. For many years it was located a few blocks from the University of California, Berkeley campus on Telegraph Avenue. The bookstore expanded to a second Berkeley location in 1998 and a San Francisco store in 2005. The Telegraph store closed in 2006. Cody's ultimately went out of business in 2008. See Howerton, M. (2008, June 20). "Cody's Books closes after 52 years in Berkeley." *The Berkeley Daily Planet*. Retrieved November 19, 2013, from http://berkeleydailyplanet.com/issue/2008-06-19/article/30362

19. For additional information on the Oakland Firestorm of 1991, see Gross, J. (1991, Oct. 26). Oakland struggles to restore hills, and faith. *The New York Times*, p. 1.1.

20. See Muller, L., & The Poetry for the People Collective. (1995). *June Jordan's Poetry for the People: A revolutionary blueprint*. New York, NY: Routledge.

21. The ad "African American Women in Defense of Ourselves" appears on p. 53 of *The New York Times* on November 17, 1991.

22. Four Los Angeles police officers were acquitted of the charge of assault with a deadly weapon in the beating of African American motorist Rodney King. See Serrano, R. A., & Wilkinson, T. (1992, Apr. 30). All 4 in King beating acquitted, violence follows verdicts. *Los Angeles Times*, p.1.

23. Several days of violence erupted in Miami, Florida, in 1980 when four white police officers were acquitted in the death of Arthur McDuffie, an African American man. See Crewdson, J. M. (1980, May 20). Guard reinforced to curb Miami riot; 15 dead over 3 days. *The New York Times*, p. A1.

24. See Martinis, C. (1992, Oct. 2). Vigil mourns loss of 2 killed in fire at Salem House. *The Oregonian*, p. A01. and Martinis, C. (1992, Sept. 30). Police see skinhead-arson link. *The Oregonian*, p. C01.

25. This is likely a reference to the following column: Quindlen, A. (1993, Mar. 10). Gynocide. *The New York Times*, p. A19.

26. This is a reference to the murder of Hattie Mae Cohens. See note #24 above.

27. Dr. David Gunn was shot outside of the Pensacola Women's Medical Services Clinic where he worked. See "Doctor shot to death at anti-abortion protest." (1993, Mar. 10). *Chicago Sun-Times*, p. 3.

28. See note #6 above.

29. Dr. Baruch Goldstein, a U.S. born Israeli physician, committed a mass murder of twenty-nine Palestinians at a mosque in Hebron. Initial reports of fatalities were higher. See Haberman, C. (1994, Mar. 1). West Bank massacre: The overview. *The New York Times*, p. A1.

30. This is likely a reference to the following article: Wilkerson, I. (1994, May 16). 2 boys, a debt, a gun, a victim: The face of violence. *The New York Times*, p. A1.

31. For a sample article, see Deutsch, L. (1994, July 23). "100 percent not guilty, says O.J." *The Oregonian*, p. A01.

32. For a chronology of Proposition 187, See "CA's Anti-Immigrant Proposition 187 is Voided, Ending State's Five Year Battle with ACLU, Rights Groups" available on the ACLU website at: https://www.aclu.org/immigrants-rights/cas-anti-immigrant-proposition-187-voided-ending-states-five-year-battle-aclu-righ

33. The exact quote Jordan cites could not be confirmed, but she is referring to the following article: Honan, W. H. (1995, Sept. 13). New ranking of doctoral programs serves up familiar names and a few surprises. *The New York Times*, p. B7.

34. See Applebome, P. (1995, June 4). The debate on diversity in California shifts. *The New York Times*, p. 1.1.

35. See http://www.madre.org

36. See Vanderbeken, J., & Finz, S. (1999, July 12). Link sought between arson, slaying cases: Redding brothers may be tied to 3rd death. *San Francisco Chronicle*, p. A1.

37. See Salter, S. (1999, July 8). Mr. Smith goes on a rampage. *San Francisco Examiner*, p. A-23.

38. Blanford, N. (2001, July 30). Sharon begins to take war-crimes lawsuit seriously last week, Ariel Sharon hired a lawyer and warned army leaders to travel with caution in Europe. *The Christian Science Monitor*, p. 7.

Index

www.ingramcontent.com/pod-product-compliance
Lightning Source LLC
Chambersburg PA
CBHW021420110726
47901CB00008B/2239